THE GOLD COAST REGIMENT IN
THE EAST AFRICAN CAMPAIGN

BY THE SAME AUTHOR

IN COURT AND KAMPONG.
STUDIES IN BROWN HUMANITY.
"SINCE THE BEGINNING."
IN A CORNER OF ASIA.
"BUSH-WHACKING."
A FREE-LANCE OF TO-DAY.
FURTHER INDIA.
"SALLY"—A STUDY.
SALEH—A SEQUEL.
HEROES OF EXILE.
MALAYAN MONOCHROMES.
THE FURTHER SIDE OF SILENCE.
GERMAN COLONIES: A Plea for the Native Races.

H. Walker Barnett & Co.

LIEUT.-COL. R. A. DE B. ROSE, C.M.G., D.S.O.
Commanding the Gold Coast Regiment.

Frontispiece.

THE GOLD COAST REGIMENT IN THE EAST AFRICAN CAMPAIGN

BY SIR HUGH CLIFFORD, K.C.M.G.

The Naval & Military Press Ltd

Published by
The Naval & Military Press Ltd
5 Riverside, Brambleside, Bellbrook
Industrial Estate, Uckfield, East Sussex,
TN22 1QQ England
Tel: +44 (0) 1825 749494
Fax: +44 (0) 1825 765701

www.naval-military-press.com
www.military-genealogy.com

In reprinting in facsimile from the original, any imperfections are inevitably reproduced and the quality may fall short of modern type and cartographic standards.

TO

LIEUTENANT-COLONEL R. A. DE B. ROSE,

C.M.G., D.S.O.,

AND TO THE

OFFICERS, NON-COMMISSIONED OFFICERS
AND MEN

OF THE

GOLD COAST REGIMENT OF THE WEST
AFRICAN FRONTIER FORCE

THIS BOOK IS DEDICATED

IN ADMIRATION OF THEIR COURAGE, THEIR STEADFASTNESS AND THEIR
ACHIEVEMENTS, IN SYMPATHY WITH THEIR HEAVY LOSSES, AND IN
GRATITUDE FOR THE LUSTRE WHICH THEY SHED UPON THE
COLONY WHOSE NAME THEY BEAR

BY

THEIR SOMETIME GOVERNOR AND TITULAR
COMMANDER-IN-CHIEF

HUGH CLIFFORD.

CONTENTS

CHAPTER		PAGE
I.	THE VOYAGE TO AND ARRIVAL IN EAST AFRICA	1
II.	THE ADVANCE ON THE DAR-ES-SALAAM—LAKE TANGANYIKA RAILWAY	10
III.	THE PASSAGE INTO THE ULUGURU MOUNTAINS — THE BATTLES AT KIKIRUNGA HILL AND AT NKESSA	25
IV.	IN THE KILWA AREA—GOLD COAST HILL	43
V.	IN THE KILWA AREA—IN THE SOUTHERN VALLEY OF THE LOWER RUFIJI	61
VI.	IN THE KILWA AREA—MNASI AND RUMBO	78
VII.	IN THE KILWA AREA—NARUNGOMBE	93
VIII.	THE HALT AT NARUNGOMBE	107
IX.	THE ADVANCES TO MBOMBOMYA AND BEKA	119
X.	NAHUNGU AND MITONENO	134
XI.	RUANGWA CHINI TO MNERO MISSION STATION	148
XII.	LUKULEDI	161
XIII.	EXPULSION OF VON LETTOW-VORBECK FROM GERMAN EAST AFRICA	180
XIV.	TRANSFER OF THE GOLD COAST REGIMENT TO PORTUGUESE EAST AFRICA	197
XV.	THE ADVANCE FROM PORT AMELIA TO MEZA	211
XVI.	THE ENGAGEMENT AT MEDO	232
XVII.	THE ADVANCE FROM MEDO TO KORONJE AND MSALU	250
XVIII.	THE EXPULSION OF VON LETTOW-VORBECK FROM THE NYASSA COMPANY'S TERRITORY AND THE RETURN OF THE GOLD COAST REGIMENT TO WEST AFRICA	268

CONTENTS

APPENDICES

		PAGE
I.	THE MOUNTED INFANTRY OF THE GOLD COAST REGIMENT	279
II.	HONOURS AND DECORATIONS EARNED IN EAST AFRICA	286
III.	STRENGTH OF THE REGIMENT AND EXPEDITIONARY FORCE AT VARIOUS PERIODS, AND DRAFTS DISPATCHED TO IT FROM THE GOLD COAST	290
IV.	LETTERS OF APPRECIATION FROM THE GENERAL OFFICER COMMANDING PAMFORCE, AND FROM THE GOLD COAST GOVERNMENT. RESOLUTION PASSED BY THE LEGISLATIVE COUNCIL	292
	INDEX	295

LIST OF ILLUSTRATIONS

	FACING PAGE
LIEUT.-COL. R. A. DE B. ROSE, C.M.G., D.S.O.	*Frontispiece*
CAPT. J. F. P. BUTLER, V.C., D.S.O.	28
MAJOR G. SHAW, M.C., CAPT. E. G. WHEELER, M.C., MAJOR H. READ	92
GROUP OF OFFICERS	140
MEN IN MARCHING ORDER	160
THREE NATIVE N.C.O.'s	230
2·95 BATTERY	196
SERGT. SANDOGO MOSHI, D.C.M.	288

MAPS

	PAGE
KIKIRUNGA HILL	27
GOLD COAST HILL	52
KIBATA AND NGARAMBI AREA	62
OPERATIONS AGAINST MEDO	*facing* 238
GENERAL MAP OF THE EAST AFRICAN CAMPAIGN	*end of volume*

THE GOLD COAST REGIMENT
IN THE
EAST AFRICAN CAMPAIGN

CHAPTER I

THE VOYAGE TO AND ARRIVAL IN EAST AFRICA

WHEN during the latter days of July, 1914, the prospect of war with the German Empire became imminent, the Gold Coast Regiment was rapidly mobilized, and detachments took up pre-arranged strategical positions on the borders of Togoland. On the declaration of war on the 4th August, the invasion of this German colony was promptly undertaken; and the Regiment, which had been joined at Lome, the capital of Togoland, by a small party of Tirailleurs from Dahomey, pursued the retreating enemy up the main line of railway to Kamina—the site of a very large and important German wireless installation—where, on the 28th August, he was forced to an unconditional surrender.

On the 18th September Major-General Dobell, who had been appointed to command the British and French troops which were about to undertake the invasion of the German Kameruns, arrived off Lome; and the bulk of the Gold Coast Regiment,

ARRIVAL IN EAST AFRICA

leaving two companies to occupy the conquered territory in Togoland, and a small garrison in the Gold Coast and Ashanti, joined this Expeditionary Force.

In the Kameruns stiff fighting was experienced, and it was not until the 11th April, 1916, that the Gold Coast Regiment returned to its cantonments at Kumasi, after having been continuously upon active service for a period of twenty months.

In Togoland and in the Kameruns alike the Regiment had won for itself a high reputation for courage and endurance; and the fine spirit animating all ranks was strikingly displayed by the enthusiasm with which the news that the force was again required for active service overseas was received, though at that time the men had enjoyed only a very few weeks' rest in their cantonments at Kumasi. Nor was this due to the courage born of ignorance, for the Regiment had learned from bitter experience the dangers and difficulties of the type of fighting in which it was about once more to take a part. The pursuit through bush and scrub, or through wide expanses of high grass, of a stubborn and crafty enemy is a task which, as many British regiments have learned in places spattered all up and down the tropics, imposes a peculiar strain upon the nerves and upon the endurance of the forces which engage in it. The enemy, who alone knows his plans and his objectives, and whose movements are designed to avoid rather than to seek contact with his pursuers, unless he can attack or sustain attack in circumstances specially favourable to himself, possesses throughout the immense advantage of the initiative.

ADVANTAGES OF THE PURSUED

If he elect to retreat, the pursuer must plod after him, whither he knows not, through country which is not of his choice, and with the character of which he has had no opportunity of rendering himself familiar. If the enemy resolves to make a stand, it is almost invariably in a position which he has selected on account of the advantages which it affords to him; and when in due course he has been ejected from it, the pursuit through the Unknown of an elusive and usually invisible enemy begins *ab novo*, in circumstances which the apparent success has done nothing material to improve. These facts combine to render a campaign in the bush a heart-breaking and nerve-racking experience, even when the enemy is an undisciplined native levy armed with more or less primitive weapons. In the Kameruns, however, and to a much greater degree in East Africa, the enemy was composed of well-trained native soldiers, with a good stiffening of Europeans; he was armed with machine-guns and magazine-rifles; he was supplied with native guides intimately acquainted with every yard of the country; and he was led with extraordinary skill and energy by German officers. It was bush-fighting on a scale never hitherto experienced, with all the advantages which such fighting confers upon the pursued, and the corresponding disadvantages inherent to the pursuit, exaggerated to an unprecedented degree. Yet the men of the Gold Coast Regiment, who in the Kameruns had already had more than a taste of its quality, celebrated the fact that they were once more to engage in such a campaign with war dances and clamorous rejoicings.

ARRIVAL IN EAST AFRICA

By the evening of the 5th July, 1916, the Gold Coast Expeditionary Force had assembled at the port of Sekondi. It consisted of four Double Companies—A, B, G, and I—with a Pioneer Company, and a Battery of two 2·95 guns, and 12 machine guns, and a number of carriers. Its strength was 36 British officers, 15 British non-commissioned officers, 11 native clerks, 980 native rank and file, 177 specially trained carriers attached to the battery and to the machine guns, 1 storeman, 204 other carriers, and 4 officers of the Royal Army Medical Corps—in all 1428 men—under the Commanding Officer of the Gold Coast Regiment, Lieutenant-Colonel R. A. de B. Rose, D.S.O.

The present writer, who at that time was Governor of the Gold Coast Colony and its Dependencies—Ashanti and the Northern Territories—had come round by sea from Accra to wish the Regiment God-speed. On the evening of 5th July, Colonel Rose and all the officers who could be spared from duty, were entertained by me at a banquet, given in the Court House, at which all the leading officials and the most prominent members of the European and African unofficial community of Sekondi were present.

Officers and men, who at that time had been fighting almost continuously since the 4th August, 1914, save for the brief rest which they had recently enjoyed at Kumasi, presented on this occasion a very smart and workmanlike appearance. They were thoroughly well-equipped and thoroughly seasoned troops, with achievements already to their credit of a kind that had filled the Colony to which they belonged with pride.

DEPARTURE FROM SEKONDI

By midday on the 6th July the embarkation of this force with all its stores and equipment, on board the transport Æneas, was completed. The men were transported in lighters to the ship's side, and thence were slung inboard in batches of half-a-dozen or more in the sag of a canvas sail—a rough and ready, but very effective, expedient, which delighted the struggling groups of men as the sling bore them aloft and deposited them, screaming with laughter, in inextricable knots upon the deck. At about 2 p.m. the transport got under way, taking a southerly course at right angles to the coast, which here runs east and west. The phenomenon was witnessed by excited groups of natives from the beach at Sekondi, for never within living memory had any ship bearing their countrymen steered a course that was not parallel to the shore; and when the vessel at last disappeared below the skyline something like consternation prevailed. It was as though she, and all aboard her, had dropped suddenly into the depths of some unknown abyss. Superstitious fears were further stimulated by the fact that an eclipse of the sun occurred on that day, and much discussion arose among the men as to whether the omen should be regarded as of favourable or of evil portent.

The voyage round the southern extremity of the African continent, and up the east coast to the neighbourhood of Mombassa, was uneventful. The Æneas called at the Cape and at Durban. At the latter place the whole of the Regiment was allowed ashore, and was taken *en masse* to see the "movies," a new experience which astonished and delighted them. They were also paraded, inspected, and addressed by the Mayor—a stimulating ordeal which, however, in the popular estimation took a second place when compared with the miracles beheld at the cinematograph. Cold weather was met with when rounding the Cape, but the men appeared to feel it very little; and the force was in fine fettle when, on the 26th July, the *Æneas* arrived at Kilindini, the port of Mombassa, after a journey that had occupied exactly three weeks.

Kilindini is a land-locked harbour, and the town, which is a somewhat incongruous modern adjunct to ancient and picturesque Mombassa, consists mainly of sheds, warehouses, and wharfs.

Disembarkation was effected by lighters, which were towed alongside a jetty, and here a stroke of ill-luck greeted the Regiment at the outset of its career in East Africa. For weeks not a drop of rain had fallen at Kilindini, but now, when the disembarkation was in full swing, a sudden tornado blew up from the sea, bringing a downpour by which officers and men were speedily soaked to the skin. There was no alternative, however, but to carry on, and drenched and rather woe-begone, the force was presently landed. Two trains were awaiting the Regiment at a point distant about a couple of hundred yards from the jetty; but the day being a Sunday, the Sabbatarian principles of the local porters, which may have owed their inspiration either to indolence or to piety, forbade the natives of Kilindini to engage in servile work. In pouring rain, therefore, the men set to, and in a creditably short time all the baggage, stores, and equipment had been transferred from the lighters to the railway waggons; and at

THROUGH THE MOUNTAINS

4 p.m. the first train started upon its journey up-country. This train consisted of passenger carriages, but that which followed it some six hours later was mainly made up of covered trucks. The men, with the steam rising in clouds from their brown knitted jerseys, were packed in batches of ten into the carriages and trucks; and in this fashion the journey up the main line toward Nairobi was begun.

While daylight lasted the way led mostly through open grass country apparently very sparsely inhabited, which was succeeded later by what looked like dense thorn-jungle, and the junction at Voi was reached by the first train at about midnight. From this point the military authorities had constructed a loop-line, which runs in a south-westerly direction through the mountain range, of which on the north-west Kilima-Njaro is the studendous culmination, until it effects a junction with the German railway from Tanga to Moschi at a point some twenty miles south of the last-named place. At dawn, therefore, the men of the Regiment, shivering for their skins, looked out upon wide expanses of mountain scenery—a vast sweep of hillsides, rounded summits and undulations, covered with short grass, and strewn with gigantic boulders of rock. In the distance Kilima-Njaro was frequently visible, with its crest covered by perpetual snow. The line ran from Voi to the junction with the Tanga-Moschi railway at heights varying from 6000 to 9000 feet; and the men of the Gold Coast Regiment, who are accustomed to regard 60° F. as registering a temperature which is almost unbearably cold, and who were still damp from the drenching they had received at Kilindini, suffered seriously from the low temperature. The fact that nearly half of them were accommodated in trucks, which though roofed had only half walls, rendered the exposure all the more severe. A few halts were allowed in order to enable the men to stretch their legs; but time did not admit of much cooking being done, and for the most part the, to them, unnatural foods of bully beef and biscuit, and draughts of ice-cold water, were all that they had to restore the natural heat of their bodies. It was an extremely trying experience for troops recruited in the Tropics, and many cases of pneumonia subsequently resulted, not a few of which proved fatal.

From the junction the trains bearing the Regiment proceeded eastward down the captured German railway, in the direction of the sea and Tanga, to Ngombezi, which is distant some forty miles from that terminus. Here they arrived on the 29th July, having been joined on the preceding day by Captain H. C. C. de la Poer, as special service officer. Captain de la Poer had long been resident in East Africa, possessed much local knowledge, and spoke Swahili fluently. Ngombezi is situated at a height of some 2000 feet above sea-level; and on detraining, the Regiment went into temporary camp, the officers and men bivouacking under shelters fashioned from blankets and waterproof sheets.

On the 30th July the Regiment was inspected by General Edwards, the Inspector-General of Communications. The service kit of the Force consists of a green knitted forage cap, a khaki blouse, shorts and putties of the same material, with the leather sandals which are known in West Africa as *chuplies*. The men of the Regiment, all of whom at this period were recruited from the people of the far interior which lies to the northward of Ashanti, are for the most part sturdy, thick-set fellows, with rather blunt but not pronouncedly negroid features, which show traces in some instances of a slight admixture of Arab blood. They are at once strong and active. They possess great pluck and endurance and are very amenable to discipline; and their fidelity to, and confidence in, their officers have become a by-word. For the rest they are as tough and business-like looking a body of men as any judge of good fighting material need desire to see.

General Edwards, at the end of his inspection, expressed himself very much struck by the physique of the men, and by their smart and soldierlike appearance. He emphasized the fact that no other unit which he had inspected had arrived in the country so well and efficiently equipped—a fact which caused great satisfaction on the "Home Front" in the Gold Coast when his opinion was duly repeated to the Colonial Government; and he forthwith wired to the Commander-in-Chief reporting that the Regiment was fit to take the field immediately.

This was the first sprig of laurel won by the Corps after its arrival in East Africa. It was destined in the course of the long campaign upon which it was about to embark to garner others wherefrom to fashion the substantial crown which it eventually brought back in triumph to the Gold Coast.

CHAPTER II

THE ADVANCE ON THE DAR-ES-SALAAM—LAKE TANGANYIKA RAILWAY

THE military situation, at the moment when the Gold Coast Regiment received its orders to take the field, was approximately as follows. Tanga, the coast terminus of the more northerly of the two German railways, had fallen some time before, and the whole line from Moschi to the sea was now in the hands of the British. A column of Indian troops was moving down the coast with Sandani at the mouth of the Wami river, Bagamoyo at the mouth of the Kingani, and Dar-es-Salaam, the terminus of the principal railway, as its successive objectives. The enemy had been driven, not only away from the Tanga-Moschi railway, but to the south of the Pangani-Handeni-Kondoa-Irangi road; and General Smuts had established General Headquarters on the left bank of the Lukigura River, which falls into the Wami on its left bank at a point distant some sixty miles from its mouth.

The Commander-in-Chief had with him here the First Division under Major-General Hoskyns, consisting of the 1st and 2nd East African Brigades under the command respectively of Brigadier-General Sheppard and Brigadier-General Hannyngton. With the exception of a machine-gun detachment of the Loyal North Lancashire

MILITARY SITUATION 11

Regiment, which was attached to the 2nd East African Infantry Brigade, both these brigades were composed of Indian troops. The Gold Coast Regiment was about to join up with the 25th Royal Fusiliers, and with it to form the Divisional Reserve.

On the right, the Second Division, which was composed of South African Infantry and mounted troops, under Major-General Van der Venter, had its advanced base at Kondoa-Irangi and for its objective Dadoma, on the main railway which runs from Dar-es-Salaam to Kigome, near Ujiji, on Lake Tanganyika.

Between the Second Division and General Smuts' troops, a force composed of South African mounted men, under the command of Brigadier-General Brits, was operating independently, with Kilossa on the railway as its objective. It was General Smuts' intention to attack the railway with the First Division at Morogoro, a mission station, which lies not quite fifty miles due east of Kilossa.

It had not yet been found possible to establish a main base at Tanga; and at the moment all supplies were being landed at Kilindini, and were conveyed thence, by the railway route which the Regiment had followed, to Korogwe on the Tanga-Moschi line. An advanced base had been formed at Handeni, five-and-thirty miles to the south-east of Korogwe; and for six weeks General Smuts had been compelled to remain inactive in his camp on the Lukigura River, while sufficient stores, etc., were being accumulated to render a further and continuous advance possible.

His plan, as will be seen by the disposition of

his forces, was to attack the main German railway line, as nearly as possible simultaneously, at Dar-es-Salaam on the coast, at Morogoro, at Kilossa and at Dadoma. This would have the effect of depriving the enemy of the use of the line and of driving him to the south of it; after which an attempt would be made to expel him from the country north of the Rufiji River.

The Regiment had been inspected by General Edwards on the 30th July, and on the 4th August, leaving the Depôt Company to establish itself at Korogwe, they left their temporary camp at Ngombezi and began their march to Msiha, the headquarters of the First Division on the banks of the Lukigura. It was now that their troubles began, and the nine days of that march live in the memory of officers and men as perhaps the most trying period of the whole campaign.

Though the altitude was not great, the climate was cool even at midday; but while the Europeans belonging to the force found it wonderfully bracing, the men missed the genial warmth of their native land, and at night suffered greatly from the cold.

The line of march led along an unmetalled track, over which motor-lorries had been ploughing their way for weeks, and the surface had been reduced to a fine powder some six to eight inches in depth. The constant passage of lorries, and now the first-line transport of the Regiment—which consisted of mule-carts and of the carriers who had accompanied the force from the Gold Coast—and the plodding feet of the men on the

TRIALS OF THE MARCH

march stirred up this loose deposit into a dense fog of a dull-red hue. As the day advanced, each man became plastered with particles of this fine red dust, which seemed to possess peculiarly penetrating properties, till one and all resembled so many figures fashioned from *terra cotta*. Eyes, nostrils and mouths became filled with this stuff, occasioning acute thirst; but the way was waterless, save for a few foul holes half filled with brackish water.

The lot of the rear-guard was the hardest, for the second-line transport, locally supplied to the Regiment, consisted of South African ox-wagons, each of which was drawn by a team of sixteen oxen driven by Cape boys. The imported cattle had many of them become infected by *trypanosomæ*, and not a few were literally on their last legs. The exigencies of the situation, however, rendered it necessary for these luckless brutes to be driven as long as they could stand; but progress was incredibly slow, and frequent halts were occasioned to unyoke some miserable ox, which had fallen never to rise again, and thereafter to rearrange his yoke-fellows. At the best, as they crept forward, the floundering wagons with their straining teams churned the dust into impenetrable, ruddy clouds, which, mingling with the fog already caused by the passage of the infantry, well-nigh smothered the men who formed the rear-guard. Though the actual length of each day's march was fairly short, the last man rarely reached the camping-place until long after dark.

The physical trials to which the rank and file were exposed—the choking dust, the raging thirst which it occasioned, the inadequate supply of brackish water, met with at long intervals, which seemed powerless to appease even when it did not aggravate their sufferings, the nauseating stench arising from the putrifying carcases of dead horses, mules and oxen, with which the line of march was thickly strewn, the bitterly cold nights, and the ominous way in which man after man succumbed to pneumonia—were rendered almost unbearable by reason of the superstitious fears by which the men were haunted. The memory of that long railway journey, which half of them had made in open trucks, through the freezing cold of the nights and early mornings high up in the mountains, was still fresh in their minds. They had seen many of their comrades suddenly stricken by pneumonia—to them a by no means familiar disease—and killed thereby after a few days or hours of painful struggle for life. Now they found themselves in an unknown land, separated from their homes by immeasurable distances, with wide expanses of sour scrub spreading around them, and holding for them no promise of finality; while day after day, they plodded, parched and choking, along that interminable road, saw their fellows succumb at every halting-place, and learned presently to believe that the water with its salt-taste, which was alone available to allay their thirst, and of which they could never obtain enough, was a poisoned draught that was killing them. This was a devil's country to which their officers had brought them—a land of evil spirits out of which they could never hope again to win their way. The Europeans—officers and non-commissioned officers alike—sought ceaselessly to cheer and hearten-up their men; but for the first time in the memory of any of them, their efforts met with no response. The men had become unrecognizable. Usually the most cheerful and light-hearted of mankind, they wore now a sullen, hang-dog air. They were sulky, suspicious and resentful. For the first time in the history of the Regiment their confidence in their officers—which to these men has become a religion—had been strained almost to the breaking-point. And their officers knew it. " You could not get a grin out of them at any price," said one who had seen his men in many a tight place, and had never known them to show even a passing sign of discouragement or depression; and when you cannot conjure a grin out of the gnarled features of a man of the Gold Coast Regiment, something very like the Trump of Doom has sounded for him.

The Regiment, after resting on the 8th August at Handeni, and drawing a fresh supply of rations, pushed on for another four days to Mahazi, where it duly reported its arrival to the headquarters of the First Division.

The front had now been reached, the enemy was close at hand, and there was a river of running water to delight the hearts of the parched and dust-coated men. The reaction was immediate. There was no lack of grins now; and these found their reflections in the faces of a band of anxious officers, as they listened to the cheerful babble resounding from their new encampment. It is a music that is discordant enough at times, but now it was more than welcome after the sullen silence of suspicion and distrust that had brooded over the camp and the line of march for more than a week.

On the 13th August the Regiment moved forward on the road to Turiani. The country in which they found themselves was no longer grey or powdered red with dust, but actually green, though it was still, for the most part, covered by waist-high scrub and grass, and the folds of the undulating plain rendered any extended view impossible. The proximity of the enemy, as is usual in warfare of this type, was more certain than his whereabouts, and all military precautions were henceforth taken during the day's march to Turiani, and during the subsequent advance.

On the 15th August the Regiment moved to Chasi, and on the 16th August, after working all day at the construction of two bridges, the camp was advanced to Kwevi Lombo, near the Makindu River, and established at about 11 p.m.

On the 17th August the Regiment received orders to move forward in the early afternoon to Dakawa, where fighting had been in progress all day. The men, resting in camp after their hard day and late night, had listened all the morning, like a pack of terriers quivering with excitement, to the familiar sounds of machine-gun and rifle-fire; and after a march of four and a half hours they reached Dakawa at 7 p.m. Here General Smuts had established his headquarters, and Colonel Rose personally reported to him the arrival of the Regiment. General Smuts ordered the Regiment to sit down and rest until the rising of the moon, and then to proceed to a ford two

MARCH TO THE NGERE-NGERE 17

and a half miles west of the main road. At dawn, if the enemy was still in position, they were to cross the river and join General Enslin's Brigade, which belonged to the force operating independently under Major-General Brits.

These orders were duly carried out, the Regiment being guided to the ford by the celebrated scout, Lieutenant Pretorius, a way for the infantry having been beaten down through the tough high grass by a body of South African mounted men. This movement was carried out by the Regiment with the least avoidable noise. The enemy, however, becoming aware that the ford was occupied, drew off during the night; and next morning, therefore, the Regiment returned to its own division, and camped near a broken bridge over the Mkundi River, a left affluent of the Wami. Here it remained until the 23rd August, when it moved forward eight and a half miles to Kimamba, and thence, on the 24th August, to a camp on the banks of the Ngere-Ngere, a small stream which falls into the Ruwu on its left bank a few miles above Mafisa.

This latter day's march calls for a word of description. The Regiment, which was now acting as part of the reserve to the 2nd East African Brigade, marched last of the fighting troops, with the heavy transport and the actual rear-guard still further behind it. The country traversed was a flat plain broken by frequent undulations, and grown upon by shortish grass, brittle and wilted by the sun. Mean-looking trees were spattered all over the plain, but were usually wide enough apart to permit of the easy passage of armoured motor-cars. Of these a number, under the charge of naval officers, accompanied the marching men, scudding up and down the column and searching the country in the immediate neighbourhood of the line of march, much as a dog hunts on all sides of a path along which its owner is walking. Occasionally, a deep donga would be met with, which could not be negotiated by a motor-car; and then the marching men would turn to with their picks and shovels, fill in a section of the dried-up watercourse, and so fashion a temporary road across it which enabled the cars to pass. This was accomplished over and over again with great ease and rapidity; and for the rest, the country presented no serious obstacle to the use of these armoured vehicles.

August, in East Africa, is of course the height of the dry season, and in all tropical regions of this continent the dry season means a fierce heat, beating down during all the hours of daylight upon a parched and thirsty earth, and refracted from the wilted vegetation with an almost equal intensity. It means that every stream has run dry, and that even many of the larger rivers have shrunken into mere runnels. It means that sun-dried grass and scrub and the very leaves upon the trees have become brittle and inflammable as tinder; and that the bush fires, for the most part self-generated,—such as those which of old so greatly affrighted Hanno and his Carthaginian mariners on the West Coast of Africa—are ubiquitous,—are columns of smoke by day and pillars of fire by night. Any sudden change of wind at this season of the year may cause the traveller to be unexpectedly con-

A BUSH-FIRE

fronted by a wall of flame, raging almost colourless in the fierce sunlight, advancing on a wide front with innumerable explosions like the rattle of musketry, and with a rapidity which is apt to prove highly embarrassing.

During this day's march the natural heat was intensified by these constant conflagrations, above which the agitated air danced in a visible haze, and from which there came a breath like that from a furnace, bearing in all directions innumerable charred and blackened fragments of vegetation. Through this heated atmosphere the marching troops plodded doggedly onward, parched with thirst, and playing an eternal game of hide and seek with the attacking bush-fires. Many narrow escapes occurred, and the first-line transport of the Gold Coast Regiment was once fairly caught, the casualties including 6 oxen, an army transport cart, 2 wagons, 10,800 rounds of small arm ammunition, 20 picks, 42 shovels, one rifle, some private kit, and a quantity of rations, all of which were burned to a cinder. Eighteen other oxen were so badly burned that they had to be slaughtered, their meat being issued as rations to the Divisional Reserve.

Another element besides fire, however, seemed to conspire this day against the advancing force; for the exact position of the Ngere-Ngere could not be located, and when the Regiment arrived at the place where it was to bivouac for the night, there was no water to be found in its vicinity. Water had, however, been discovered some miles further on, and carts were dispatched to fetch it. Darkness had already fallen, and the outlook was sufficiently depressing; but an officer of the Gold Coast Regiment, who happened to push his way into a patch of thick bush adjoining the camping-place, quite accidentally discovered the river by the simple process of pitching headlong into it. The Ngere-Ngere is a very winding stream, and though its neighbourhood was indicated by a belt of thick bush, the greenness of which could only be due to the proximity of water, the leading troops had missed this point on the road, to which the river happened to approach to within a distance of a few yards, and owing to an abrupt bend, which the bed of the stream takes at this place, the nearest point at which its banks were again struck was about a mile distant.

At once the glad tidings were given, and the men speedily obtained all the water they required. The Gold Coast Regiment had bivouacked for the night near the scene of its discovery; but though a start had been made that morning at 5.30 a.m., it was a late hour before the last troops struggled into camp.

Shortly after the Dar-es-Salaam railway had been crossed at Massambassi by the main force, B Company was placed at the disposal of Colonel O'Grady—an officer of the Indian Army, who had won for himself in the Himalayas a great reputation as an Alpine climber—and proceeded with him and a remnant of the East African Mounted Rifles into a clump of fertile, well-watered and hilly country, which was comparatively thickly populated, and where a number of German foraging-parties were believed to be at work. The tracks leading through these hills were wide enough for

ROADS OF BARE-FOOTED FOLK 21

two to march abreast, but after the manner of native paths all the tropics over, they took no account of gradients, but led straight up each precipitous ascent till the summit was reached, and thence plunged down the opposite slope to encounter a fresh rise when the valley level was reached. It is inevitable that all paths in hilly country, which are made by folk who habitually go bare-footed, should deal with ascents and declivities in this switchback fashion; for roads scarped out of the hill's face, unless they are constructed on scientific engineering principles, are speedily worn away by the annual torrential rains. This renders them agonising to men who do not use boots, for though the act of walking on the side of the foot is uncomfortable enough even for men who are well shod, it is excruciating to those who go bare-footed; and in their estimation any strain on the lungs and on the back-sinews, which the constant climbing and descent of hills entail, is preferable to this much more painful means of progression.

Through these hills went Colonel O'Grady, the handful of white men composing the detachment of the East African Mounted Rifles—some dozen survivors of that gallant corps which had seen such hard times and had done such splendid work during the earlier phases of the campaign—and B Company of the Gold Coast Regiment. The valleys were thickly planted with native food-stuffs of all descriptions, including such luxuries as sugar-cane bananas, etc.; and eggs and fowls were also obtainable in moderate quantities. Patrols were sent out in all directions at once, to forage for the little force and thoroughly to search the surrounding country for German forage-parties. One of these—a body of eleven Germans, genially intoxicated to a man on native beer, and quite incapable of resistance—was brought in by the East African Mounted Rifles, and a few Askari,[1] who were also engaged in foraging, were captured by B Company. When this group of hills had been thoroughly searched, Colonel O'Grady released B Company, which at once rejoined the Regiment. The latter, meanwhile, had been following in the track of B Company, and at daybreak on the 3rd September, the whole corps entered the mission station at Matombo.

These mission stations are a feature of erstwhile German East Africa. They are, for the most part, charmingly situated, generally upon the crest of a hill, whence a magnificent view of the surrounding country can be obtained. They consist, as a rule, of one or more substantially built two-storeyed buildings constructed of mud, or of locally made bricks, lime-washed, and roofed with red tiles, which are also manufactured on the spot. The church, which usually flanks them, is built of rough blocks of stone, as is that at Matombo, or of bricks or mud, as the case may be; and it is often surmounted by a tapering, red-tiled spire. The eminences upon which these stations have been established, and the land around their feet, are set with gardens, groves of fruit trees, and patches of cultivation, all of which obviously owe their existence to European initiative and supervision.

The native congregations ordinarily occupy a number of scattered hovels—built much further

---

[1] Askari = Native soldier.

A HUN PHYSICIAN

apart from one another than is the native habit in West Africa—thatched with grass, and placed at a respectful distance from the buildings occupied by the missionaries. The latter in German East Africa, unlike their prototypes on the West Coast, apparently did not welcome the too close proximity of their proselytes.

The mission buildings at Matombo were found to contain a number of Germans, who were supposed to be too old for active service, and a good many of their women and children. The church, which had been converted into a hospital, was full of German sick and wounded, who had been left in charge of a medical man of their own nationality. This interesting individual was allowed to continue his ministrations, and it was always believed—whether rightly or wrongly it is impossible to say—that he subsequently made use of the liberty thus accorded to him to signal the movements of the Regiment to his compatriots posted in the Uluguru mountains, the entrances to which the British were now engaged in forcing.

The whole of this hilly area was thickly populated by people clothed only in a kind of kilt made of grass, who, though many of them had been impressed by the Germans to serve as carriers, appeared to take no very close interest in the movements of either of the opposed forces. The Uluguru mountains were their home—the only world they knew; and these hapless folk had no alternative, therefore, but to remain where they were, watching with the philosophical resignation so characteristic of a tropical population this strife of gods or devils which had temporarily transformed the quiet countryside into an inferno. It was only occasionally that their equanimity was ruffled for a space by the chance explosion of a shell in close proximity to their dwellings.

General Smuts' drive had so far proved successful, and the Germans, fighting a more or less continuous rear-guard action, but offering no very stubborn or prolonged resistance at any given point, had been forced back, first on to the line of the Dar-es-Salaam-Lake Tanganyika railway, and then across it into the mountainous country which lies between the railway and the low-lying valley of the Rufiji River.

The Gold Coast Regiment had itself crossed the railway line at a point some miles to the east of Morogoro, and had thence penetrated into the hilly country to the south for a distance of some fifteen miles, camping on Sunday, the 3rd September, in the neighbourhood of the mission station at Matomba. This place is situated on the northern edge of the Uluguru Mountains—highlands which occupy an area measuring approximately a hundred miles square—out of which it was now the task of the First Division to endeavour to drive the enemy, who had sought refuge in them.

It was on the 4th September, 1916—the day on which the mission station at Matomba was quitted—that the Gold Coast Regiment was fated, for the first time, to take a more active part in the East African campaign.

CHAPTER III

THE PASSAGE INTO THE ULUGURU MOUNTAINS—
THE BATTLES AT KIKIRUNGA HILL AND AT
NKESSA

THE task which the First Division had before it was to force a passage into the Uluguru Mountains, the main entrances to which the enemy was preparing stoutly to defend. The principal highway lay some distance to the east of the Matomba mission-station, and here the main battle was in progress; but commanding the road, along which the Gold Coast Regiment marched when it moved out of its camp at Matomba, the enemy had occupied a very strong position, and was using Kikirunga Hill—a sugar-loaf-shaped mountain crowned with a clump of trees and underwood, rising clear above its fellows to a height of perhaps 3000 feet—as an observation point. The Regiment was ordered to expel him, if possible, from this hill,

At 7 a.m. on the 4th September the Regiment moved out of camp, and about two hours later the enemy opened fire with a couple of howitzers, upon the road a little ahead of the marching troops. No casualties were inflicted, but the Regiment was halted, moved off the road, and took up a sheltered position on the right side of it, in a gut between two hills.

Captain Jack Butler, V.C., D.S.O.—who had won both these distinctions while serving with the Gold Coast Regiment in the Kameruns—was then sent forward with the Pioneer Company to reconnoitre the enemy's position.

Captain Butler and his men advanced up the road, which climbed steeply, with many windings and sinuosities, towards the head of the pass— leading into the Uluguru Mountains—which was situated near the foot of the hills of which, on the left side of the road, Kikirunga is the culminating point. This road ran, from the spot where the Regiment was halted, up a sharp ascent and along a narrow valley, on either side of which kopjes of gradually increasing height rose at frequent intervals. The first of these, situated about a mile and a half from his starting-point, and lying to the left of the road, was occupied by Captain Butler and the Pioneer Company, and a picket was sent out to take up a position at a spot where, a little further on, the road took a deep U-shaped bend toward the left.

From the kopje occupied by the Pioneers a general view of the enemy's position could be obtained. On the left front, about a mile away as the crow flies, Kikirunga arose skyward from the huddle of lower hills in which it has its base, and from one of the slopes of these, somewhat to the right of the peak, an enemy machine-gun opened fire upon the position which Butler had occupied. The beginning of the U-shaped bend which the road took to the left lay beneath and slightly to the right of Butler's kopje; and on the far side of this loop, where the road, which

KIKIRUNGA HILL

throughout ran between an avenue of mango trees, wound back towards the right, another kopje, about a hundred feet higher than that upon which the Pioneers were posted, ran steeply upward to a crest which was held by the enemy, and from which presently another machine-gun also opened fire.

The road, still climbing steeply, wound round the foot of this kopje, and between a succession of similar hills; and from the right of it a big clump of mountains, some 2500 feet above valley-level, rose in a great mass of grassy and boulder-strewn slopes. All these hillsides were covered with shaggy, sun-dried grass about two feet in height, broken by many outcrops of rock, a few trees and patches of scrub, with little copses and spinneys in the valley-hollows between hill and hill. In the middle distance a great dome-shaped peak, some miles further away than Kikirunga, rose majestically, dominating the landscape and presenting a wide facet of precipitous grey cliff to the eye of the observer. The view obtained from the kopje which Butler had occupied was a splendid example of tropical mountain scenery; but from the standpoint of the leader of an attacking force its strength was even more impressive than its beauty. The enemy had had ample time in which to choose his ground, and he had availed himself to the full of his opportunity.

It was not till nearly five o'clock in the afternoon, however, that the Pioneer Company became heavily engaged; and Captain Butler presently went forward to the picket which he had placed near the bend of the road to see how things fared

CAPT. J. F. P. BUTLER, V.C., D.S.O.
60th Rifles.

DEATH OF CAPT. BUTLER

with them. It was while he was lying here on the road beside his men that he and several of the picket were wounded by a sudden burst of machine-gun fire from the kopje immediately in front of him. In all, twelve men of the Pioneers were wounded during the afternoon, but the Company held firm, and maintained its hold upon the kopje which Butler had occupied. Late in the afternoon B Company, under the command of Captain Shaw, was sent forward to reinforce the Pioneers, and to make good the ground which had been won. This was successfully accomplished, the wounded were evacuated to the rear, and the men dug themselves in, and dossed down for the night in the excavations they had made.

Captain Butler died that evening of the wounds which he had sustained during the afternoon. A young officer possessed of at once a charming and forceful personality, of an absolutely fearless disposition and of more than ordinary ability, Captain Butler, V.C., D.S.O., had won for himself a conspicuous place in the Gold Coast Regiment, and had earned the devotion and affection of the men in a very special degree. His death, in this the first action in which the Regiment had been engaged since its arrival in East Africa, was felt to be a specially malignant stroke of ill-fortune, and was mourned as a personal loss by his comrades of all ranks.

During the night, orders were sent to Captain Shaw, who was now commanding the advanced companies, to push forward at the earliest opportunity. This he did at dawn, creeping in the darkness to the point of the road where Captain

Butler had been wounded, and thence up the grassy hill to the road above it. Here the charge was sounded, and the men with fixed bayonets rushed up the kopje, which was captured after a few shots had been fired. In this charge Acting-Sergeant Bukari of B Company displayed conspicuous bravery, which was subsequently rewarded by a second Distinguished Conduct Medal. This fine soldier was promoted to non-commissioned rank on the field, and awarded a D.C.M. for conspicuous gallantry when fighting in the Kameruns. Now, in this his first fight in East Africa, he again won that coveted distinction; but his subsequent history was a sad one. Evacuated to the rear suffering from only a slight wound which, during the long journey to the base at Korogwe, on the Tanga-Moschi railway, was allowed to become septic, he died in hospital before ever he had learned of the second reward which his dash and courage had earned for him.

During the rest of the day the force under Captain Shaw's command continued to fight its way from kopje to kopje up the road, the Pioneers under Lieutenant Bray and B Company under Captain Shaw alternately advancing under the protection of the other's fire. In this manner, by evening, a point distant about 400 yards from the head of the pass was reached and secured.

Meanwhile, the 1st Battalion of the 3rd Regiment of the King's African Rifles was advancing up the northern slope of the big clump of mountains, which have been described as rising on the right side of the pass. As soon as this was observed, a gun of the Gold Coast Regiment was brought

MAKING PROGRESS

into action to assist the advance of the newcomers. The enemy was heavily shelled, but owing to the commanding positions which he occupied, it was not found possible to push home the infantry attack, the King's African Rifles not having yet won possession of the crest of the mountains. None the less, considerable progress was made during the day, and B Company succeeded in capturing the highest point of the spur round which the road ran.

At dusk on the 5th September Captain Wheeler with A Company relieved B Company, and took over from it the ground which it had won, B Company forthwith going into reserve. During the day, moreover, Major Goodwin made a reconnaissance with half of I and half of G Company for the purpose of finding out whether a flanking party could be sent over the hills to join up with the King's African Rifles. He was able to report that this could be accomplished.

During the night of the 5th–6th September, the enemy received reinforcements, and shortly after dawn he opened a violent machine-gun fire upon the advanced positions occupied by the Gold Coast Regiment. Two guns of the Battery were brought up, and all the commanding heights held by the enemy were heavily shelled by them, assisted by two guns belonging to the 5th South African Battery. By noon the enemy's fire slackened, and the King's African Rifles began to make their presence felt on the summit of the mountains to the right of the pass, which they had now succeeded in occupying. G Company, under the command of Captain Poyntz, had been sent early in the morning to join up with the King's African Rifles by the path discovered the day before by Major Goodwin, and this junction was effected by about 2 p.m. An hour later the enemy's fire ceased, and by 4 p.m. Kikirunga Hill, the capture of which was the task that had been set to the Gold Coast Regiment, was duly occupied.

The casualties during this two and a half days of fighting numbered 42 in all, including Captain Butler and 6 rank and file killed, 3 men dangerously, 13 severely, and 19 slightly wounded. Among the latter was Colour-Sergeant Beattie. The doctors and their staff of stretcher bearers, etc., had a heavy time during these few days, as they not only attended to the wounded and evacuated them to the rear under fire, but also conveyed all the more serious cases back to the mission station at Matombo.

On the side of the enemy the casualties suffered were difficult to ascertain, but he lost three Germans and three native soldiers killed, and there were numerous signs of considerable damage having been inflicted upon him, while a number of rifles and some ammunition were picked up in the positions from which he had retired. In the type of warfare in which the Regiment was now engaged, however, it almost invariably happens that the fugitive force is able to inflict more casualties upon its pursuers than it is likely itself to sustain. As has already been observed, it enjoys the advantage which the selection of the ground confers, and can always occupy positions from which it can do the greatest damage to an advancing enemy with a *minimum* of risk to itself. It is also able to break

GOOD WORK BY THE REGIMENT

off an engagement at the precise moment that best suits its convenience and advantage; and the possession of machine-guns further enables it to fight a delaying rear-guard action, and to mask the fact of its retirement, to the very last moment. It rarely happens in fighting of this class that the holding of a given position is a matter of any special importance to a fugitive force. The latter therefore hold it as long as it pays to do so, and thereafter can abandon it without danger or embarrassment, as soon as its defence threatens to become inconvenient. The pursuing force, on the other hand, has only one course open to it—to attack the enemy whenever and wherever he can be found, to inflict upon him as much injury as circumstances permit, but above all, to keep him on the move and to allow him as little rest and peace as possible. It is an expensive business, and it becomes increasingly difficult as lines of supply and communication progressively extend. It is, however, the only method whereby bush-fighting can be efficiently prosecuted; and expense and difficulty are qualities inseparable from this kind of warfare.

The following telegram was received by Colonel Rose from Brigadier-General Hannyngton, commanding the 2nd East African Brigade, on the evening of the 6th September :—

"Please tell your Regiment that I think they all worked splendidly to-day, and I wish to thank them for their good work."

On the 7th September, while the King's African Rifles advanced, the Gold Coast Regiment rested and reorganized. On the 8th September, however, it pushed forward along the road which it had opened for itself under the lee of Kikirunga Hill, and made its way *via* Kassanga into the heart of the Uluguru mountains. These are a clump of high hills, covered with grass and patches of scrub, and strewn with boulders, and the road was scarped out of the hillsides, with a steep slope running skyward on the one hand, and a *khudd*—over the edge of which, from time to time, a transport mule toppled—falling away no less steeply on the other. The view of the marching men was for the most part confined to the grassy slope on one side of them, to the valley tilted steeply downward on the other, and across it to the rolling, boulder-strewn hills, smothered in long shaggy grass, green or sun-dried, with the blue of a tropical sky arching overhead. No signs of life were visible, save an occasional deserted village, composed of scattered mud huts, with grass roofs in the last stages of decay and dilapidation; but from the vantage ground all about them the marching men could, of course, be seen from many miles away.

On the 8th September the Regiment caught up with the King's African Rifles, which had dispersed a small party of the enemy. On the 9th September the former, which was still leading the advance, surprised and scattered the 22nd German Company at a place called Donho; and that night, after a very hard day's marching the Gold Coast Regiment camped at Kiringezi at about 4.45 p.m. On the 10th September the Regiment came out upon the main road which connects Tulo and Kissaki, and a stray German Askari was killed by the men of

TAKING UP POSITIONS

G Company, who also captured a few rifles. The 2nd East African Brigade was found to be some five miles ahead, and in the afternoon the Regiment overtook it, and once more joined the reserve.

The advance troops had succeeded in keeping more or less constant touch with the enemy, and as he now showed a disposition to make yet another stand, A and B companies, under Major Goodwin, were sent off at 4 p.m. on the 11th September to reinforce and prolong the extreme right of the British line, which was being held by the King's African Rifles. Meanwhile half of I Company had been sent to the eastern or extreme left of the line in order to form an escort to the Machine Gun Company of the Loyal North Lancashire Regiment. Just before dark half of G Company received orders to advance and take up a position on the left of half I Company. At 8 a.m. on the 12th September further orders were received, and the rest of the Regiment—viz., the Pioneer Company, half of I Company and the Battery—moved up the road toward Nkessa and held itself in readiness to reinforce the left. This the Pioneer Company and half I Company did at 11 a.m., the former taking up a position on the extreme left of the line; and shortly afterwards the Battery advanced to a point immediately in the rear of these companies.

At 2.30 p.m. an advance from the left in a generally south-south-westerly direction was ordered, and the Pioneer Company and half I Company pushed forward to a distance of from 500 to 600 yards, when they were held up by the enemy who were strongly posted in a village ahead of them. Here the men dug themselves in. Captain Poyntz, who was in command, held on to this position for some time, but he was eventually compelled to retire, as he found that all touch with the company on his right had been lost, and as he heard heavy firing from his right rear, he feared that his detachment might be surrounded and cut off.

Meanwhile, G Company, under Captain Macpherson, had barely advanced a hundred yards before it was forced to halt, a very heavy fire being opened upon it from a salient in the enemy's line on the right flank. The fire was so close and continuous that one gun of the Battery had to be retired; and when, subsequent to the action, the grass was burned off and the true position revealed, it was found that the contending forces had here been within fifty or sixty yards of one another.

The enemy's position was astride of the Tulo road, to which his trenches and rifle-pits ran at right angles for a distance of about four and a half to five miles, his extreme right being thrown slightly forward in the neighbourhood of the village against which the Pioneer Company and half I Company, under Captain Poyntz, had advanced. The country was for the most part grass and thick scrub, with trees interspersed among them; but in the centre of his position on the side of the road opposite the British left, where a patch of young cotton trees afforded him excellent cover, he had pushed forward the salient of which mention has been made above.

Orders were sent to Captain Poyntz to fall back; but his own appreciation of the situation

A FIGHT IN THICK GRASS

had already shown him that retirement was necessary, and he presently lined up alongside G Company, which maintained its position.

Reinforcements were asked for by telephone, and a reply was received from Brigade Headquarters that the 29th Punjabis were being sent up by a road which had recently been constructed to a neighbouring water-supply. A later telephone message stated that the 29th would advance to the relief of the Gold Coast Regiment *viâ* the main road.

Meanwhile, on the right flank, A and B Companies had been sent by Major Goodwin to occupy a position on the extreme right of the British line, with the King's African Rifles on their left. At 8.45 a.m. a brisk action began, but the advance achieved was slow. By 1.30 p.m., however, two hills overlooking Nkessa had been occupied. The edge of this village opposite to A and B Companies was strongly held by the enemy, and though the fight continued while daylight lasted, no further advance was made. At 6 p.m., therefore, outpost positions were taken up for the night, and the men slept in the rifle-pits which they had dug. Intermittent firing continued during the night.

On Wednesday, 13th September, patrols were sent out at dawn, and it was eventually established that the enemy had retired from the positions which he had held overnight. A company, under Captain Wheeler, was sent from Major Goodwin's force on the right to rejoin the Regiment on the left of the line; and early in the morning the half of I Company, which had been with the guns of the Loyal North Lancashire Regiment, was relieved by the 29th Punjabis, and rejoined the other half of the Company, which was posted between the Pioneer Company on the extreme left and G Company.

The Regiment then advanced, the Pioneers entering the village which they had attacked the day before, without opposition, where they were later joined by I Company. G Company, which had to advance through very dense elephant grass, lost touch with the rest of the force, as can so easily happen in country of this description, and communication with it was not re-established until the afternoon.

From the village which the Pioneers had occupied, patrols were sent out to locate the river, and this accomplished, the Pioneers, leaving I Company in occupation of the village, crossed the stream, which was only a few feet in width, and advanced in the direction of Nkessa, holding both banks. At first only a few snipers were encountered, but eventually the enemy was found to be in occupation of a position, with his left resting on a village on the river's bank, and his right thrown slightly forward. The enemy promptly attacked, and Captain Poyntz retired the Pioneers about 200 yards, and having dug himself in, held on to his rifle-pits for the rest of the day. At about 1.30 p.m. one section of A Company, which had been sent to reinforce the Pioneers, came up on their left on the southern side of the stream; and an hour and a half later I Company with two machine-guns and the Battery came into action and bombarded the villages held by the enemy on the left and right fronts.

NKESSA OCCUPIED

At 4 p.m. an advance was ordered, and after an hour's fighting, B Company and three sections of A Company reinforced the left of the Regiment, and, night coming on, were halted and dug themselves in. The thick elephant grass in which these operations were conducted rendered the exact location of the enemy's position a matter of great difficulty during the whole of this day.

On the morning of the 14th September, the enemy was found to have once more evacuated his positions, and the Gold Coast Regiment, having been relieved by the King's African Rifles, marched into Nkessa, where the brigade camp had already been formed.

The casualties sustained by the Regiment between the 11th and the 13th September numbered four killed and thirty-three wounded, including Captain Greene, Lieutenant Bray, Colour-Sergeant May, and Lieutenant Arnold. The last named died in Tulo hospital on the 16th September of the wounds which he had received on the 12th September. Lieutenant Isaacs, who had been sent forward to reconnoitre, stumbled into an enemy patrol, and was captured.

On the 19th September the Battalion moved to a spot on the banks of the Mgeta River, where a camp was formed. The Mgeta is a branch of the Ruwu, which falls into the sea at Bagamoyo, opposite to the southern extremity of the island of Zanzibar. Here the patrols and outposts of the Regiment were in frequent touch with the enemy, and a good many casualties were sustained; and on the 22nd September the Battalion returned to the brigade camp at Nkessa. On the 30th the

Regiment moved to a new outpost camp, between the Mgeta and Nkessa; and while here a section of I Company, under Lieutenant Berry, was sent out to demolish a wooden bridge over the Mgeta. Just as the work was nearing completion, this small force was suddenly fired upon by an enemy patrol posted in thick bush, while many of the men were standing waist-deep in the stream, five soldiers being killed and four wounded.

The following day the Battalion, having been relieved by the 130th Baluchis, was moved to Tulo, whence a couple of days later it was sent back to Nkessa, an attack upon that place being anticipated. Here the outposts had frequent casual encounters with the enemy, and on the 16th October two different patrols found mines on the Kissaki road, which had been laid as a trap for troops advancing by that route. These were constructed by embedding a four-inch shell in the earth at the depth of a few feet, with a friction-tube attached to one end of a plank, the other end of which slanted upward to just below the surface of the road. This plank, at a spot about one-third of its total length, measuring from the shell, was supported upon a fulcrum in such a manner that, when any weight was imposed upon the portion near the surface, the lower end jacked up and caused the shell to explode.

On the 17th October the Battalion was once more moved to Tulo, where it remained until the 7th November, upon which date the Second Brigade broke camp and began a march to the coast at Dar-es-Salaam. The way led to the banks of the Ruwu River, of which the Mgete is a right affluent,

MARCH TO DAR-ES-SALAAM

and from Magogoni, the point at which the stream was struck, down its valley to Mafisa. The country traversed—a green and fertile valley, dipping gently toward the coast—was perhaps the most attractive area seen by the Regiment in the lowlands of East Africa during the course of the whole campaign. The rivers, of course, were shrunken to their lowest levels, and many of the tributary streams were dried up; but water was obtainable along the whole line of march, and in spite of the tropical heat, which increased in intensity as the coast was approached, the nine days occupied by the journey to Dar-es-Salaam were less trying than were most of the marches undertaken by the Regiment during this campaign.

At Mafisa the main road, which runs from Kidugato on the railway to Dar-es-Salaam, was struck; and here the valley of the Ruwu was quitted, the Brigade marching in an easterly direction, almost parallel to the railway, which was struck in its turn at Kisserawe on the 15th November. Although this line had now been for some time in the hands of the British, so much damage had been wrought to it that it was not yet open to traffic; and the Brigade, to which the Regiment was still attached, accordingly continued its march to Dar-es-Salaam by road. The last-named place was reached on the 17th November, and the Regiment forthwith embarked on the steam transport *Ingoma*, the men, with their baggage, stores, etc., and a number of carriers being conveyed from the landing stage to the ship's side in lighters. All were got on board by 6.30 p.m., and a rather comfortless night was spent, the *Ingoma* being crowded to the gunwales with the men of the Regiment, their carriers and details belonging to other units. Very early in the morning of the 18th November the ship got under way, and set off on her two-hundred-mile journey down the coast to Kilwa Kisiwani.

CHAPTER IV

IN THE KILWA AREA—GOLD COAST HILL

THE reason for the transfer of the Gold Coast Regiment, from the region lying to the north of the Rufiji to a scene of operations situated to the southward of that river, can be explained in a few words.

The enemy having been driven, in the course of the 1916 campaign, first across the Dar-es-Salaam-Lake Tanganyika railway, and thereafter through the hilly country to the south of that line to the southernmost fringe of the Uluguru Mountains, it was the object of the British command to confine him, if possible, to the lowlying valley of the Rufiji during the coming wet season. He, on the other hand, it was thought, would try to establish his winter quarters in some convenient spot on the southern side of the valley, and it was believed that two of the places which he had selected for this purpose were the mission stations of Kibata and Mtumbei Juu, which are charmingly situated among the group of mountains that rises from the plain within a mile or two of the seashore between the Rufiji and Matandu rivers. In order to frustrate any such intention, Brigadier-General Hannyngton had been dispatched some weeks earlier to conduct the operations in the area above described, and it was for the purpose of acting as a reserve to General Hannyngton's Force that the Gold Coast Regiment was now being dispatched to Kilwa Kisiwani. Another factor in the situation was the great difficulty which the supply of the troops operating to the north of the Rufiji would present during the rainy season. It had become evident that their number must be reduced, and that even when this had been effected so far as safety allowed, the maintenance of the remainder, in a country which ere long would become water-logged, would be no easily solved problem.

The Regiment arrived at Kilwa Kisiwani on the 19th November, and disembarking during the afternoon, marched to Mpara, where it encamped. Here on the following day the Battalion was joined by the Depôt Company, which had hitherto remained at Korogwe, on the Tanga-Moschi Railway under Major Read; but owing to the difficulties of transport, its stores did not arrive with it. On the 24th November the Regiment marched up the coast, along a sandy track within sight of the sea, to a camp situated four miles to the west of Bliss Hill near Kilwa. Arrangements were made for forming a Depôt Company and store accommodation at Mpara as a regimental base, and G Company was broken up, the men composing it being posted to other companies.

On the 25th November the Regiment began its march along the road which leads in a westerly direction from Kilwa to Chemera, but owing to the late arrival of the transport-carriers and water-

A THIRSTY MARCH

carts a start was not made until the afternoon. The Regiment halted for the night in the bush, six miles from their starting-point and a like distance from Ngeri-geri, about six miles down the road; and on the following day it moved on to a camp about two and a half miles to the east of Mitole.

The line of march this day led across a villainous arid flat, covered with mean and dusty scrub and coarse rank grass, wilted and sun-dried. There was not an atom of shade to be found during the whole day's march; the heat from on high was great, and was vied with in intensity by the heat refracted from the ground; and across this weary expanse officers and men plodded painfully, ankle-deep in the sandy surface of the road, and racked with unappeasable thirst. In spite of the assurance given to the Regiment that water would be procurable along the route, not a drop was to be obtained until the camp was reached late in the afternoon. The Gold Coast soldier is a toughish fellow, and as a rule is not greatly affected by extremes of heat. Like all Africans, however, he is blessed with very open pores, and an insufficient supply of drinking-water hits him peculiarly hard. On this day no less than forty men fell out, and sank exhausted on the line of march, and it would have gone hard with them had not some motor-drivers hurried to the rear and returned, after an absence of some hours, with a supply of water. Many of these exhausted men did not get into camp until the following day, and all of them, together with eight officers—for they, too, were "foot-slogging it" with their men—had forthwith to be sent to hospital as the result of this one day's march.

None the less, on the 27th November, the Regiment shifted camp to a spot lying three miles to the west of Mitole; and on the following day it moved on to Chemera, where it relieved the 2nd Battalion of the 2nd Regiment of the King's African Rifles. As soon as this had been effected, I Company with 2 officers, 1 British non-commissioned officer and 182 rank and file, marched off to Namaranje to occupy an outpost position at that place.

The strength of the Regiment at this time was already very considerably reduced, as the breaking up of G Company and the distribution of its *personnel* among the remaining Companies indicated. The field-state on November 28th — the day upon which the Regiment went into camp at Chemera—showed that only 19 British officers were present, as against the 86 who had started from Sekondi at the beginning of the preceding July, and that during the intervening period, the number of British non-commissioned officers had been reduced from 15 to 10, and that of the rank and file from 980 to 715. The principal battle casualties have been noted in the course of this narrative, but much greater havoc had been wrought to the *personnel* of the force by ill-health occasioned by exposure, over-exertion, bad food, and water insufficient in quantity and often vile in quality.

It was hoped that on its arrival at Chemera a period of rest would be enjoyed by the Regiment, but before it had been in camp a week word was

A TEMPORARY RIVER

received that a force composed of a battalion of the King's African Rifles and the 129th Baluchis, which was in occupation of the mission station at Kibata, was being very hard pressed by the enemy, and ran some risk of being surrounded.

On the 9th December, therefore, the Regiment left Chemera and marched in a northerly direction to Mtumbei Chini, and thence on the 10th December to Kitambi at the foot of the mountains, in the heart of which the mission stations of Mtumbei Juu and Kibata are situated. It should be noted that the words "chini" and "juu," which will be found so frequently to occur in place-names in East Africa, signify respectively "low" and "high." Thus "Mtumbei Chini" means "Mtumbei on the Plain," and "Mtumbei Juu" means "Mtumbei on the Hill."

A mile from Kitambi a river was met, through which the advanced guard, under the command of Captain Harman, had to wade with the water up to their necks. The officer commanding the rear-guard reported that when he crossed it, the river was only knee-deep; while Captain A. J. R. O'Brien, R.A.M.C., who passed the same place next morning, found no river at all, but only a partially dried-up river-bed—rather an interesting instance of the eccentricities of tropical watercourses. They, indeed, can rarely be relied upon for very long together, either to furnish drinking-water or to refrain from impeding transport.

From Kitambi onward only mule-transport and head-carriers could be used, the path up which the Regiment was climbing being at once too narrow and too steep for the passage of motors.

The precipitous track was difficult for the men, and still more difficult for the pack-animals; and though the distance from Kitambi to Mtumbei Juu mission station was only eight miles, the mule transport took three-and-twenty hours to make the journey, and in the course of the day three mules were lost by falling over precipices.

The position at Kibata mission station—which lies a few miles to the east and slightly to the north of Mtumbei Juu, and is separated from it by a fairly deep valley—was approximately as follows at the time when the Gold Coast Regiment arrived at the latter station. One battalion of the King's African Rifles and the 129th Baluchis had occupied Kibata, which is situated upon a prominent hill surrounded by an amphitheatre of commanding mountains, and this force had forthwith become the object of very severe bombardment. The Germans had brought up one of the 4·1 naval guns, rescued by them from the *Koenigsberg*, and having placed it in a position on the other side of the mountains at some spot slightly to the northwest of Kibata, were shelling the mission station heavily. They evidently had an excellent observation point concealed somewhere on the surrounding mountains, for they were making very good practice; and the enemy had also established himself upon the slopes overlooking Kibata in a roughly semicircular position, with his left to the east and his right to the west of the mission station. A ridge, which runs parallel upon the east to the hill upon which the mission station stands had been occupied by the garrison; and it was from this point alone that they were able in any degree to

SITUATION AT KIBATA

retaliate upon the attacking force. For the rest, the King's African Rifles and the Baluchis, who had no means of locating the position of the 4·1 gun, and who, even if they had done so, possessed no artillery with which to make an adequate reply to its fire, could only endure the punishment they were receiving with such patience as they might command. The position, in fact, was rapidly becoming untenable; and on the after noon of the 13th December General Hannyngton made a careful examination of the ground from a height in the neighbourhood of Mtumbei Juu, and decided to attempt to turn the enemy's right flank.

Between Mtumbei Juu and Kibata, at a point near the base of the valley which divides the hill upon which the mission station stands from that occupied by the Kibata mission buildings, a hill slopes upward in a long spur, trending in a northerly direction. Its surface, covered with grass and strewn with outcrops of rock, is broken by many minor crests, till the summit is reached at its most northerly extremity. Near the top a spur juts out to the east and south, shaped somewhat like the flapper of a seal, its slopes separated from the main hill by a semicircular valley. The crest, on which there are a few trees but no cover of any kind, to-day bears the name of Gold Coast Hill. The outlying spur is called Banda Hill. From a point near Mtumbei Juu mission station and almost directly to the north of it, a ridge of mountains runs first north and later with a curve to the east overlooking and commanding Gold Coast Hill. It was General Hannyngton's hope that if the latter could be captured while this ridge still remained unoccupied, it would be possible thence to get round behind the enemy and so to outflank his right. The task of capturing this hill was assigned by him to the Gold Coast Regiment.

Accordingly, at 6 a.m. on the 14th December, B Company, under Captain Shaw, was sent forward along the mountain track which connects Mtumbei Juu with Kibata, to get into touch with the force at Kibata, which a day or two earlier had been reinforced by another battalion of the King's African Rifles, and which was now under the command of General O'Grady. He reported that the road between the two missions was open, and at dusk the rest of the Battalion moved along the road for a distance of two to two and a half miles, and there camped for the night.

At dawn on the 15th December, the disposition of the Regiment was as follows :—

The main body lay encamped about two miles along the Mtumbei Juu-Kibata road, with an outpost line, consisting of 50 rifles and one machine-gun, of B Company, under Captain Kelton, thrown out about a mile to the east. Captain Wheeler, with half A Company and one machine-gun, was posted on a line immediately in front of the main body, with a picket on the main road, and another on Harman's Kopje—a small hill to the north-west of the camp. The other half of A Company, under Captain Harman, with one machine-gun, was in occupation of a hill about 1000 yards north of Harman's Kopje, with an outpost on a small hill to the left of a path which led to Kibata, and another picket some 600 yards along

CAPTAIN POYNTZ'S ADVANCE

this path at its point of junction with a track leading west.

At 5 a.m. the Pioneer Company, under the command of Captain Poyntz, moved forward out of camp, and three-quarters of an hour later, Captain Biddulph, at the head of the advanced guard, passed the post which was being held by half A Company, under Captain Harman, and came under fire from the outlying spur on the right which bears the name of Banda Hill. Captain Biddulph was dangerously wounded, and Lieutenant Duncan was killed; and the vanguard then withdrew to the main body, while the Battery came into action from a hill to the north of Harman's Kopje, loosing off a dozen rounds across the valley at Banda Hill, whence the enemy's fire had come.

At about 8 a.m. Captain Poyntz continued his advance, and working round the small hills on the left of the main road, reached Gold Coast Hill, the summit of which was the main objective of the Force, at about 11 a.m. During this advance he encountered no further opposition, though he occupied Banda Hill and another eminence situated somewhat to the north-west of it, and left small detachments to hold each of these points.

While this advance was in progress, the enemy brought his big naval gun into action, shelling very heavily the main road, behind the hill whence the Battery had opened fire. During this bombardment, one of his shells pitched almost at the feet of Colonel Rose, who was sitting under the lee of the hill with the Adjutant, Captain Pye, by his side, and with an orderly standing near. Both

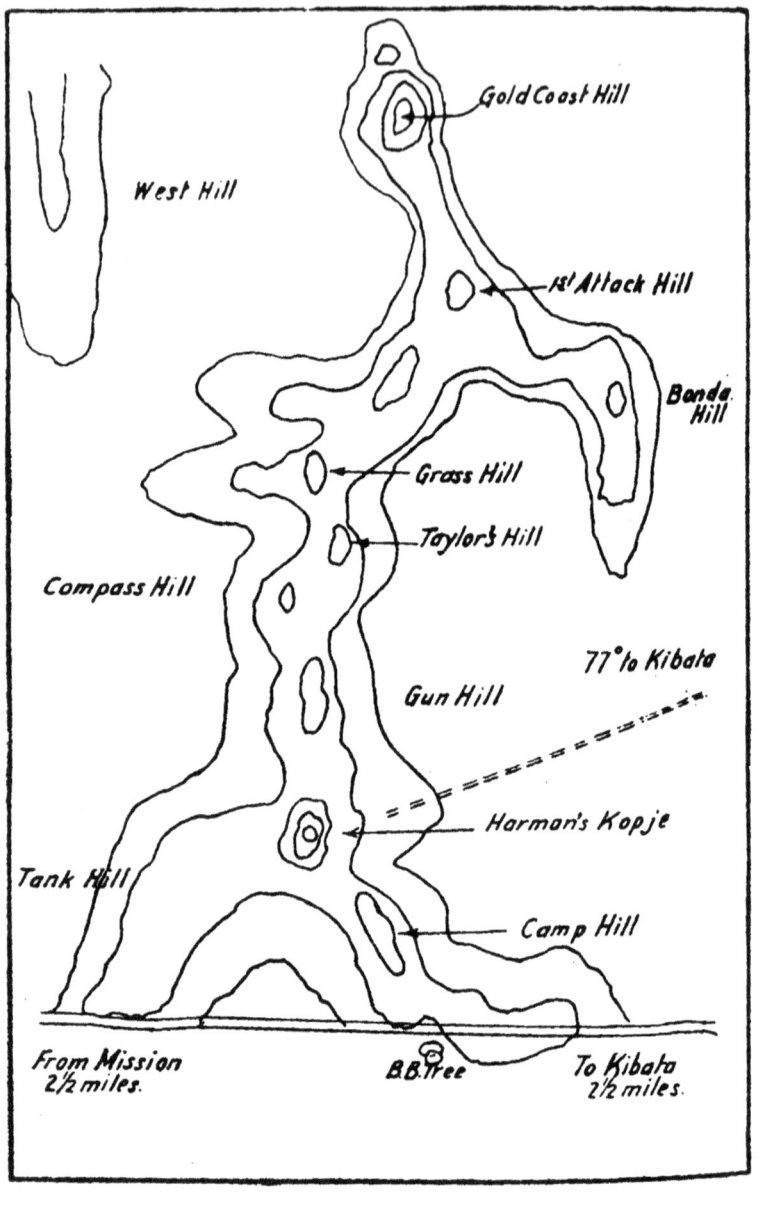

Captain Pye and the orderly were killed instantly, and Colonel Rose was flung backward from this seat to a considerable distance, but was otherwise unharmed.

At one o'clock a heavy counter-attack began on Gold Coast Hill, and upon a small ridge in advance of that position, which was held by Lieutenant Shields with 30 rifles and one machine-gun; and the violent shell, howitzer, rifle and machine-gun fire concentrated upon these points quickly caused many casualties.

By this time the remaining companies of the Regiment, under the command of Major Goodwin, were in reserve upon Banda Hill, and upon the hill to the north-west of it, which had originally been occupied by Captain Poyntz in the course of his advance; and half of A Company, led by Captain Wheeler, was sent forward in support of the Pioneers. They were shortly followed by Lieutenant Piggott with one of B Company's machine-guns, who took up a position on the right flank of the crest of Gold Coast Hill. Lieutenant Piggott was almost immediately wounded, but he contrived none the less to continue in the firing-line.

At 2.30 p.m. Captain Poyntz was dangerously, and Captain Wheeler severely wounded, leaving Captain Harman—who had himself been slightly wounded—alone to command the main position, with Lieutenant Shields and Lieutenant Piggott, the one on the ridge in advance, the other on the right flank of the crest of the hill.

Shortly afterwards Lieutenant Kinley with one machine-gun and Lieutenant Taylor with the rest of A Company came up in support; but Lieutenant Taylor was severely wounded almost at the moment of his arrival on the crest of the hill.

About 3 p.m. the enemy again opened heavy shell fire upon Gold Coast Hill, once more causing many casualties; and Major Goodwin went forward with the remainder of the reserves—about 50 rifles of B Company, under Captain Shaw—who took up a position to the right of Lieutenant Piggott's machine-gun post.

For two and a half more hours the Gold Coast Regiment clung to the position which it had occupied, and in which it had sustained such heavy and continuous losses since 11 o'clock in the morning; but at 5.30 p.m. the 40th Pathans began to relieve it. The relief was effected without serious loss just before darkness fell, and the Gold Coast Regiment took up outpost positions for the night between the hill, which ever since has been known by its name, and the main road from Mtumbei Juu to Kibata.

It was estimated that the enemy fired 180 high explosive shells from his naval gun from the time the hill was occupied until dark; and the men were throughout terribly exposed, as the concentration of his rifle and machine-gun and occasional howitzer fire was such that they were unable to dig themselves in. Effective retaliation was impossible, yet the behaviour of the men throughout the day was magnificent. Those who were in occupation of the hill clung to it during more than six hours with dogged resolution. Those who successively advanced to their support, moved forward with alacrity, and never showed a trace

FINE BEHAVIOUR UNDER FIRE 55

of wavering or hesitation. It was about as severe a test as any to which a body of native troops could be subjected, but the Regiment passed splendidly through the ordeal, the severity of which may be judged from the following casualty list.

During this day—December 15th, 1916—the Regiment sustained no less than 140 casualties. It lost 2 officers killed and 7 wounded; 1 British non-commissioned officer wounded; 26 soldiers killed and 87 wounded; and 5 gun and ammunition carriers killed and 12 wounded,—approximately 15 per cent. of the men engaged, and nearly 50 per cent. of the officers.

On the 16th December the Regiment remained in camp reorganizing its shattered forces; on the 17th and 18th December it was held in reserve; and though during the 17th detachments were moved forward in support of the 40th Pathans, who had been retired from Gold Coast Hill to the kopjes near its foot, they did not come into action. On that day, too, Captain Kelton, with 75 rank and file of B Company, were sent back to Kitambi. On the 19th December the Regiment was withdrawn, and went into camp at the foot of Mtumbei Juu Mission Hill. On the 21st of December the Regiment took up positions upon a roughly semicircular ridge on the left of the road to Kibata and lying to the north-east of the mission, and here it remained for some days, occasionally using the Battery to support the 40th Pathans on Harman's Kopje, and sending out patrols, some of which had slight brushes with the enemy. On the 24th Captain Kelton, Captain D'Amico, R.A.M.C.,

Lieutenant Percy, Colour-Sergeant Beattie, and 78 rank and file, with other details, rejoined the Regiment from Kitambi; and on this day intelligence was received that Military Crosses had been awarded to Captain Shaw and to Captain A. J. R. O'Brien of the West African Medical Staff, which they had earned at Kikirunga Hill.

On the 27th December Captain Kelton, with 80 rank and file, took over Harman's Kopje from the 40th Pathans, and on the 29th December, a German camp having been located on the northern slope of Gold Coast Hill, the Battery opened fire upon it at 11 a.m., but found the target beyond its range. The enemy replied, and quickly found the position of the Battery, which Captain Foley at once removed to another prepared position. This movement had hardly been completed ere a shell burst within seven feet from the spot which had been vacated only a few moments earlier—a striking illustration of the excellence of the enemy's observation and of the accuracy of his fire.

At 9 a.m. on this day Captain Wray arrived in camp with welcome reinforcements from Kumasi and a party of Volunteers from Accra in the Gold Coast. These reinforcements consisted of 160 men of D Company, who were all Fulanis, and 90 Jaundis, who had originally been recruited in the Kameruns, under Captain Wray and Lieutenant Downer, 150 men of the Gold Coast Volunteers under Captain Hellis, and 200 Sierra Leone carriers.

At 1.35 p.m. Captain Biddulph died from the wounds which he had received, when in command of the advanced guard, early in the morning of the 15th December.

THE REGIMENT REINFORCED 57

On the 29th the reinforcements were paraded and allocated to the various companies; and on the following day General Hannyngton held a parade of details from all companies that could be spared from the firing-line, and decorated 3926 Regimental Sergeant-Major Manasara Kanjaga, 4388 Battery Sergeant-Major Bukari Moshi, and Sergeant Palpukah Grumah with Distinguished Conduct Medals which had been awarded to them for services rendered in the Kamerun Campaign.

The strength of the Regiment on the 31st December, 1916, after the reinforcements above mentioned had been received, amounted to 19 officers, 14 British non-commissioned officers, 10 clerks and dressers, 860 rank and file, 444 gun, ammunition, and transport carriers, 34 servants, and 48 stretcher-bearers, making a total of 1429 officers and men of all ranks.

During the first week of January, 1917, the Regiment continued to occupy the ridge to the north-west of the Mtumbei Juu mission station, and on the left of the road leading to Kibata, sending out frequent patrols, which collected some useful information, and came on more than one occasion into touch with the enemy. The latter, meanwhile, had sustained a fairly severe check at the hands of General O'Grady's force, which, from the ridge occupied by it to the eastward of the Kibata mission station, had delivered a very successful night attack upon the extreme left of the enemy's position.

On the 8th January, information having been received that large bodies of the enemy had left and were leaving the area by the road to Mwengei

—a village over the hills directly to the north of Kibata—Colonel Rose decided to make a reconnaissance in force in order to try to reach this road, and to retake Gold Coast Hill. At an early hour of the day, therefore, he proceeded with 250 rifles from A and B Company, with the Battery and with the 24th Mountain Battery, along the high ridge overlooking Gold Coast Hill, of which mention has already been made, starting from the north-westerly extremity of the ridge which the Regiment had been holding. Owing, however, to the extremely difficult character of the country through which his way led, he was not able to reach a suitable place from which to begin operations until late in the afternoon.

At 6.30 on the following morning Major Goodwin began to push forward along the ridge which commanded Gold Coast Hill from the north-west. No opposition was met with, and a patrol which was sent out to reconnoitre Gold Coast Hill reported that it had been evacuated by the enemy. This was later confirmed by Lieutenant Downer, who had reached Gold Coast Hill by the old route from Harman's Kopje, which the Regiment had followed on the 15th December.

Other patrols were sent forward and reached the Mwengei road, effecting a junction with the 2nd King's African Rifles and the 129th Baluchis, who had been operating from Kibata. The fact of the enemy's retreat was now established, the whole area being clear of hostile forces; but the day being far advanced, Colonel Rose camped for the night at One-Stick Hill, so named from a conspicuous white palm-tree on its crest, in a position of extraordinary

MAJOR VON BOMPKIN

strength which had been established by the Germans, and from which it was obvious most of the heavy howitzer, rifle, and machine-gun fire poured upon Gold Coast Hill on the 15th December had come.

On the 10th January the reconnoitring party returned to Regimental Headquarters *viâ* Gold Coast Hill and the main road from Kibata to Mtumbei Juu Mission, while active patrolling of the Kibata-Mwengei road began.

On this day word was received that Captain Poyntz had been awarded the Military Cross, Colour-Sergeant Campbell the Distinguished Conduct Medal, and Lance-Corporal Sully Ibadan the Military Medal for their meritorious services in the engagement on the 15th December.

During the next few days points of strategic importance were occupied, and patrols were sent out in various directions. By one of these, which was furnished by the 40th Pathans, two white German prisoners were brought in, one of whom was a certain Major von Bompkin, and the other a gunner from the *Koenigsberg*, decorated with the Iron Cross. Major von Bompkin had been second-in-command to von Lettow-Vorbeck, but after the British had forced their way into the Uluguru Mountains at the beginning of the preceding September, he had headed a deputation to the German Commander-in-Chief, representing to him that enough had been done for honour, and that further resistance was useless and a mere waste of human lives. Von Lettow-Vorbeck's reply was forthwith to degrade him to the rank of a mere patrol commander; and at the time of his capture von Bompkin was in charge of a party of only six men. He had apparently taken the harsh treatment meted out to him in a fine soldierly spirit, and as a patrol leader had shown great daring and enterprise. For instance, on one occasion he had passed the greater part of the night in the middle of the camp occupied by the 40th Pathans, sheltering himself from the rain in the officers' latrine. At dawn he had run into a very sleepy officer of the regiment, who failed to recognize him as an enemy in the uncertain light, and he had thereafter made good his retreat, carrying with him the detailed information of which he had come in search.

On the 20th January the Regiment moved down the mountain by the main road to Kitambi, Colonel Rose returning to Mtumbei Juu mission station in the afternoon. He came back to Kitambi on the following day with the staff of the 3rd East African Brigade, to the command of which he had been temporarily appointed; and on the 22nd January he left for Ngarambi Chini, a place situated some twenty miles due west of Kibata. Major Goodwin took over the command of the Gold Coast Regiment with effect from the 21st January.

CHAPTER V

IN THE KILWA AREA—IN THE SOUTHERN VALLEY
OF THE LOWER RUFIJI

ON the 26th January, 1917, the Regiment, under the command of Major Goodwin, left Kitambi for Ngarambi Chini, and reached its destination next day, after camping for the night on the road at Namatwe, a spot distant fourteen and a half miles from the former place. From this point the roads in the neighbourhood were regularly patrolled; and on the 31st January the Regiment moved to Kiyombo — a place some six miles north of Ngarambi Chini—where the brigade camp was established. From the 29th January to the 6th February A and B Companies were detached from the Regiment, and were stationed first at Namburage and later at a place on the banks of the Lugomya River, to which the name of Greene's Post was given. From all these points, the work of patrolling the roads in the vicinity was regularly carried out; and on the 3rd February Lieutenant Shields, with Colour-Sergeant Nelson, 50 rank and file and 1 machine-gun, were sent out on this duty from Njimbwe, where the Pioneer Company was then on a detached post, along the road leading to Utete. It should be noted that the Utete here mentioned is not the largish town on the right bank of the Rufiji River which bears that

KIBATA AND NGARAMBI AREA

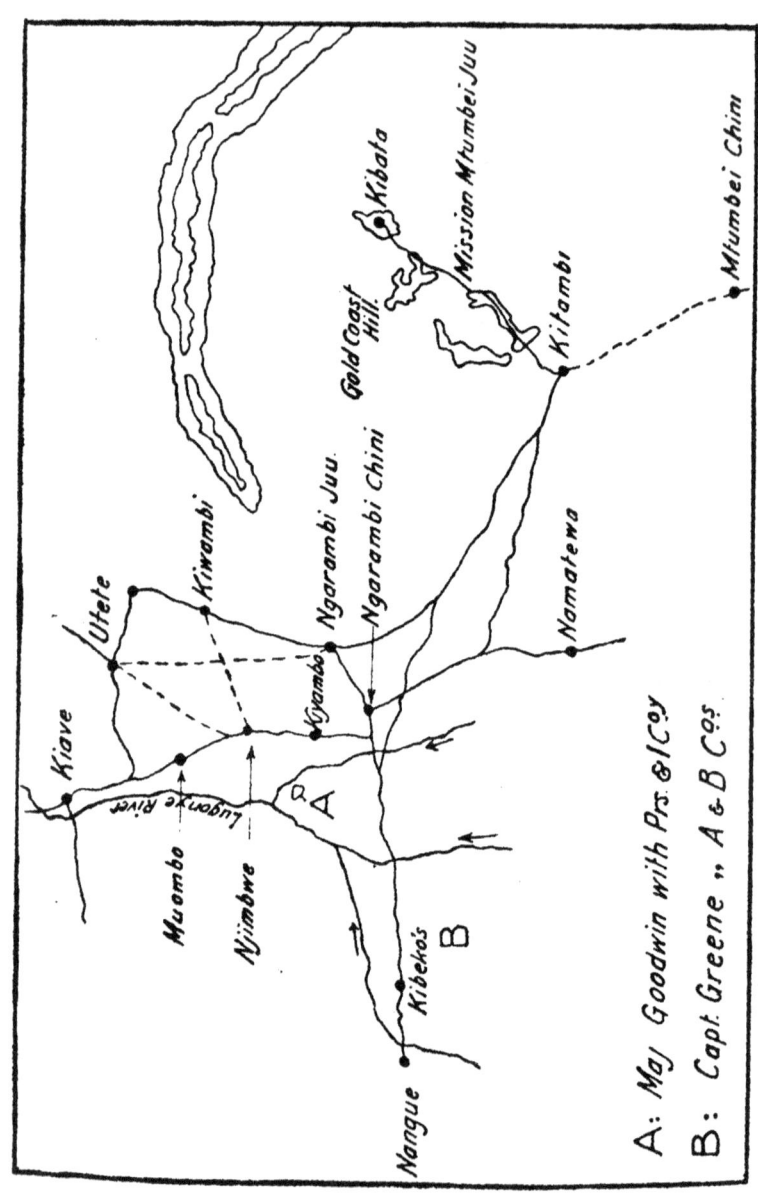

name, but a much smaller place situated about eleven miles north of Kiyombo.

The patrol under Lieutenant Shields had orders to meet a patrol of the King's African Rifles from Kiwambi at a point some nine miles from Njimbwe, but he had proceeded along the road leading to Utete for a distance of only about a mile and a half when the advance point sent back to report that they had seen a group of about ten German *Askari* on the eastern or right side of the track. It was a favourite trick of the Germans at this time to dress themselves and their native soldiers in kit belonging to the British which had fallen into their hands, and thus to occasion confusion as to who was friend and who was foe. The country through which Lieutenant Shields was patrolling was for the most part of a fairly open character, though it was covered with rank grass, set pretty thickly with trees, and studded here and there with patches of underwood. The party of the enemy had only been glimpsed for a moment, but as Lieutenant Shields went forward at once, followed or accompanied by Colour-Sergeant Nelson, a white man, dressed like an officer of the King's African Rifles, appeared at a little distance ahead of the advance point, crying out in English, " Don't fire! we are K.A.R.'s." Lieutenant Shields, who was very short-sighted, taken in by this treacherous ruse, bade his men not fire, and the enemy, who appear to have been about 200 strong with many Europeans among them, thereupon poured a volley into the patrol from the bush at very short range. This was followed by the blowing of bugles and an assault. Lieutenant Shields and Colour-Sergeant

Nelson were both shot, as also was the corporal in charge of the machine-gun while trying to bring his piece into action. A German who attempted to approach Shields as he lay on the ground was shot by a man of the Gold Coast Regiment, and the rest of the machine-gun team managed to get their gun away safely. The patrol, however, had to retire in disorder, and in addition to the casualties already enumerated 8 rank and file were missing and were afterwards ascertained to have been killed, while 2 stretcher-bearers were wounded, and 1 machine-gun carrier, 1 transport-carrier and 2 stretcher-bearers were also missing. The patrol further lost 3 boxes of small-arm ammunition, 6 machine-gun belts, 2 stretchers and a medical haversack.

It was Lieutenant Shields, it will be remembered, who held the advanced post on the ridge beyond the summit of Gold Coast Hill during those soul-searching hours between 11 a.m. and dusk on the 15th December. It seemed a tragedy that this gallant young officer, who had come unscathed through the ordeal of that day, and who had earned for himself a high reputation for coolness and courage, should lose his life in the paltry wayside ambush above described.

George Hilliard Shields was at the outbreak of war a member of the Education Department of the Gold Coast, and held the post of headmaster of the Government Boys' School at Accra. He had earlier filled a scholastic post in Raffles' Institute at Singapore: and in the Gold Coast he distinguished himself by passing the very difficult interpreter's examination in the Ga

PATROL SKIRMISHES

language. Like so many Gold Coast civilians, Mr. Shields early volunteered for active service, but it was not found possible to release him from civil employment until the Regiment was ordered to East Africa in the middle of 1916. He will long be remembered in Accra for the excellent and manly influence which he exerted over the boys who were under his tutelage.

At 1.30 p.m. a standing patrol was sent forward to the Kibega River on the Unguara road, where it entrenched itself. Shortly afterwards a small enemy patrol appeared on the road to the south of this post and was fired upon. The men composing it bolted into the bush, their porters dropping their loads, which turned out to be part of the small-arms ammunition lost by Lieutenant Shields earlier in the day. Later in the afternoon the enemy returned and, supported by three maxims, attacked the post. The patrol of the Regiment held on for a while, but finding itself outnumbered, retired through the bush to the camp at Njimbwe, losing one man.

On the 4th February, the Regiment left the camp at Kiyombo and moved forward to Njimbwe, which lies about five miles to the north, where the 40th Pathans presently joined them; and from here, as usual, small patrols were daily sent out along the roads in the neighbourhood.

On the 5th February the Pioneer Company and the Battery left Njimbwe at 5.30 a.m., in the midst of a terrific thunderstorm, for the purpose of supporting the 2nd Battalion of the 2nd Regiment of the King's African Rifles, who were about to deliver an attack upon two German camps, both of which overlooked the Ngarambi-Utete road. They came in contact with an enemy post, which was quickly dislodged, and they subsequently joined up with the King's African Rifles, only to learn that the elusive enemy had abandoned his camps.

The detachment camped for the night with the King's African Rifles at the junction of the road to Utete with another track; and as a token that the dry season was now fairly over, heavy rain fell with melancholy persistency during all the hours of darkness. The men, of course, had no shelter save such as they had been able to improvise for themselves on the preceding evening; and there are, perhaps, few more dreary or depressing experiences than that of lying out all night under the relentless beat of a steady tropical downpour. The cold felt has little in common with the brisk, keen cold of a frosty day or that met with at a high altitude; but it has certain raw and penetrating properties, and the discomfort becomes hourly more acute, while at every moment the puddles suck and squelch beneath you, and fresh streams of colder water flow in from unexpected directions to chill you to the bone.

At 8 a.m. on the following morning—February 6th—the detachment left its comfortless bivouac, and marched and waded back to Njimbwe over a shockingly bad track, which the heavy rain of the night before had reduced to a quagmire and in places had flooded to a depth of two feet. The detachment had hardly got into camp when some carriers, who had been out searching for fuel, ran in with the news that the enemy was approaching.

AN ENEMY ATTACK

An attack quickly followed, the enemy taking up a line from south-east to west, and approaching in places to within 200 yards of the camp. The surprise was complete, and some of the men of the 40th Pathans, who were outside the perimeter when the attack began, were unfortunately injured by their own machine-gun fire. The enemy, however, was not in any great strength, and he had evidently not realized that he was attacking so large a force. When he discovered the situation he drew off somewhat hastily, and was hotly pursued for over a mile. Only a few of the attacking force were seen, but among them an European was observed wearing a King's African Rifles hat and flash, and two *Askari*, one with a turban and one with the green knitted cap which is part of the service kit of the men of the Gold Coast Regiment. The casualties sustained by the latter were 1 man killed, 3 wounded, 1 gun-carrier and 5 transport-carriers wounded, and 1 Gold Coast Volunteer missing, of whom nothing was ever subsequently heard. The 40th Pathans lost 6 men killed and 18 wounded, while the known enemy losses were 10 men wounded, including 1 European. Immediately after this incident, Captain Harman took out a patrol to repair the telephone-line, which had been cut, while for some time previously it had been frequently tapped by the enemy.

The next few days were occupied in patrolling the roads in the neighbourhood of the camp; and on the 9th February the bodies of Lieutenant Shields, Colour-Sergeant Nelson, and of eight soldiers, who had been killed on the Utete road

68 IN THE VALLEY OF LOWER RUFIJI

on the 3rd February, were discovered. A burial party was sent out, and the bodies of Lieutenant Shields and Colour-Sergeant Nelson were brought back to the camp, where the burial service was read by the Rev. Captain Nicholl, and Holy Communion was celebrated.

For some weeks past the men of the Regiment had been suffering very acutely from lack of sufficient food. Not only was the supply inadequate, but much of the stuff sent up had to be condemned as quite unfit for human consumption. Many of the men were terribly emaciated, and some eighty of them were subsequently sent to hospital suffering from starvation. Had the Regiment not had the good fortune to find a few food plots planted with cassava, things would have been even worse than they were. The officers would have fared no better had not some of them chanced to possess a slender stock of European provisions, which they shared in common; but the officers of a neighbouring mess had to live for weeks upon nothing but mealie porridge, which they consumed at frequent intervals throughout the day, as they found it impossible to eat at a sitting enough of this filling but unsatisfying stuff to allay their hunger for more than a few hours.

The discipline of the men of the Gold Coast Regiment under this prolonged and trying ordeal was beyond all praise. They had followed their white officers across the sea to this unknown land, where they had endured cold such as they had never dreamed of, where they had been grilled by the sun and parched by unappeasable thirst. They had plodded manfully up hill and down dale, across

CAMP AT NJIMBWE 69

barren, arid flats, and had waded through a waterlogged country. Whenever and wherever they had met the enemy they had fought him like the fine soldiers they are, until the saying, "The green caps never go back," had passed into a proverb in the German camp. Now in the heart of a dismal swamp, they were slowly but surely starving. Yet never once did they murmur or blame their officers.

During the next fortnight the Regiment remained in the camp at Njimbwe, sending out patrols, some of which had difficulty in preventing themselves from being cut off by the suddenly deepening swamps, when a more than usually heavy downpour flooded the low-lying land; squabbling with enemy forage-parties for possession of the rare patches of cassava; taking an occasional prisoner; and sustaining a few attacks upon its outposts. During one of the latter incidents, on Valentine's Day, Machine-gun Corporal Tinbela Busanga behaved with great gallantry, working his gun, after he had been badly wounded in the arm, until he was too faint with loss of blood to carry on. On this day, though the enemy was driven off without difficulty, two men of B Company were wounded. On another occasion, a patrol of six men, under Corporal Amandu Fulani 4, was ambushed and killed to a man, though not until they had made a hard fight of it. Amandu Fulani, who was a very smart and gallant young soldier, had been orderly to the Governor at Accra, but when D Company was ordered to East Africa, he insisted upon accompanying "his brothers." When his body was found, it had been stripped of his uniform, but a gunshot wound in the abdomen had been bound up with his *kamar-band*. Though the enemy had removed his casualties, there were abundant signs that the little patrol had sold their lives dearly.

And during all this time the entry in the War Diary of the Regiment, "Half Rations," sounds its reiterated and despairing note.

On the 23rd February the Gold Coast Regiment moved out of Njimbwe camp at daybreak, marched to Ngarambi Chini, which was reached at 2 p.m., and where an hour's halt was called. The march was continued till 6 p.m., at which time Namatewa was reached. The distance traversed was a good twenty miles, which at any time is a tough bit of work for a body of marching men, but though a few swamps were met with the road was drier than might have been expected. None the less, the men, in their then half-famished condition, arrived very tired, and were glad to find that the Pioneer Company, which had gone on in advance, had got a comfortable camp ready for their reception, and had succeeded in finding excellent water. This latter feat had been performed, not for the first time, by Corporal Musa Fra-Fra, a native of the North-Eastern Province of the Northern Territories of the Gold Coast. This man seemed to possess some strange instinct which enabled him unerringly to discover water if such were to be obtained anywhere by digging or otherwise; and though he obstinately refused to reveal his secret or to show any one how to perform similar miracles, frequent use was made of his strange faculty by the officers of the

PROMOTION OF COLONEL ROSE 71

Pioneer Company during the campaign in East Africa.

From this point the Regiment marched by fairly easy stages to Kitambi, at the foot of the hills, to Mtumbei Chini, Chemera, and Mitole, where it arrived on the 27th February, and went into camp to reorganize and recuperate. The men had richly earned a period of rest, for they had been continuously on the march or on active service ever since their arrival at Kilindini, in British East Africa, exactly seven months earlier.

Colonel R. A. de B. Rose, D.S.O., who had actively commanded the Regiment ever since the end of August, 1914, who had served with it throughout the Kameruns campaign before bringing it to East Africa, and who since January 20th had been in command of a column, was made a Brevet Lieutenant-Colonel with effect from the 1st January, 1917, to the great satisfaction of the officers and men.

This pause in the Regiment's activities, though it was not destined to prove of any long duration, may be taken as providing a convenient opportunity briefly to review the general military situation as it stood at the end of the wet season of 1917. The rains in the lower valley of the Rufiji River began this year early in February, and in the ordinary course they might be expected to last until late in May, the commencement of the dry season in tropical East Africa usually synchronizing more or less accurately with the breaking of the south-west monsoon upon the shores of Ceylon on the other side of the Indian Ocean.

IN THE VALLEY OF LOWER RUFIJI

As we have seen, the drive from north to south, which had been begun in earnest in the preceding August, and for participation in which the Gold Coast Regiment had arrived just in time, had had the effect of expelling the enemy first from the country between the Tanga-Moschi and the Dar-es-Salaam-Lake Tanganyika railways, and later from the country between the last-named line and the Rufiji. Once across this river, a further retreat to the south became for the enemy almost a necessity; and when he found that he could not establish his winter headquarters in the highlands about Kibata mission station, he seems to have broken his forces up into comparatively small parties, and while keeping in touch with the troops on the southern side of the Rufiji, who were under General Hannyngton's command, to have worked steadily south, living on the country as far as possible, and gradually making his way out of the water-logged areas amid which he had been overtaken by the break-up of the dry weather early in February.

Von Lettow-Vorbeck, the German Commander-in-Chief, who throughout was the living soul of the resistance offered to the British, was not a man who believed in doing things by halves, and when he found that the valley of the Rufiji was untenable, he established his main headquarters nearly two hundred miles further to the south of that river, at a place lying within thirty-five miles of the Rovuma, which is the boundary between erstwhile German and Portuguese East Africa. The spot chosen was the mission station at Massassi, which is pleasantly situated at a height of 1500 feet

INFLUENCE OF SEA-POWER

above sea-level, and is a point at which the principal roads running through the south-eastern portion of the territory cross one another. The main road from the port of Lindi, which runs in a south-westerly direction to Makotschera on the Rovuna, and there effects a junction with the main road which skirts the northern bank of that river from Sassaware to its mouth, crosses at Massassi the main road from Newala on the southeast, which runs in a north-westerly direction to Liwale, and thence almost due north to the Rufiji River at Mikesse. From Liwale, moreover, another main road runs in a north-easterly direction to the sea at Kilwa Kivinje, and west by south to Songea —itself a point of junction of an elaborate road-system—and thence due west to Wiedhafen on the shores of Lake Tanganyika.

Even in this campaign, it should be noted, the influence of British sea-power made itself felt, for though some supplies are known to have reached the enemy in spite of the naval blockade, the command of the sea had enabled General Hannyngton's force to be slipped in behind the retreating Germans *viâ* Kilwa, and had shown to von Lettow-Vorbeck the danger he ran of being cut off or surrounded by troops rapidly transported by sea to some spot south of the scene of his land operations. Apart from the commanding position which Massassi occupied as 'the key-point of the main lines of communication by land in this part of the country, and from its convenient proximity to the German-Portuguese boundary, its selection as von Lettow-Vorbeck's main headquarters during the 1917 campaign was probably due to the fact that it could not easily be outflanked by troops conveyed further to the south by sea. With his main headquarters established at this point, moreover, and with all the principal highways in this part of the country at his immediate disposal, he could freely raid the districts to the north in which the scattered British forces were strongly established, and could occupy and hold, as long as it paid him to occupy and hold them, points of vantage such as Liwale, which could conveniently be used as his advance bases.

The German troops must have suffered considerably during the months immediately following their expulsion from the country north of the Rufiji, though it is doubtful whether they were called upon to endure a greater measure of physical discomfort or more acute starvation than that which fell to the lot of the Gold Coast Regiment and the 40th Pathans in their water-logged camp at Njimbwe, or to that of the Nigerian Brigade—which had now arrived in East Africa—and which, while holding with other troops the northern bank of the Rufiji during all that dismal rainy season, went lamentably short of everything save water, of which there was always an odious superfluity.

The fidelity of the German native soldiers at this period, and the fact that so few of them voluntarily surrendered to the British, have been quoted in certain ill-informed quarters as providing a striking testimony to the affection which the Germans are alleged to have inspired in the native population of East Africa. Subscription to any such opinion argues a complete misunderstanding

THE GERMAN *ASKARI*

of the military system which the Germans erected in their African colonies. It had for its basic principle the establishment among the native population of an isolated caste, whose members were not only allowed, but were actively encouraged, to assert their superiority over the rest of the inhabitants of the country, who, where a soldier was concerned, ceased to have any rights of person or of property, and could look for no redress when it was an *Askari* who had maltreated them. It will be remembered that in the German mind, as it was revealed to a disgusted world in August and September, 1914, there existed a strange confusion of thought, which drew no distinction between fear of physical violence and the respect inspired by noble qualities. Thus it was openly declared by the German High Command that the organized bestialities practised in Belgium would cause the whole world "to respect the German soldier." It was this characteristic confusion of ideas which led the Germans in their African colonies to seek to inspire the native population with a proper spirit of "respect" for their white rulers, by placing every ruffian who wore the Kaiser's uniform above the law, and by bestowing upon him a free hand in so far as the treatment of the rest of the native population was concerned. An example may be cited, which is drawn from the personal knowledge of the present writer. In September, 1913, a German native soldier in the employment of the Togoland Government shot an old woman—a British subject—for an unwitting breach of quarantine regulations, and having shot her, proceeded to club her to death with the butt-end of his rifle

Protests were duly made to the then Governor of Togoland, Duke Adolf Freidrich of Mecklenburg, and assurances were given that suitable notice had been taken of the incident. Yet when the British occupied Lome, the capital of Togoland, less than a year later, the culprit was found not even to have been sentenced to a term of imprisonment.

During the earlier part of the campaign, and as far as possible up to the very end, everything was done to mark the superiority of the *Askari* over the rest of African mankind. They were provided with carriers who were, to all intents and purposes, their bondsmen and body-servants, their very rifles being carried for the soldiers when on the line of march and at a secure distance from the enemy. For their use a commando of women, under military escort, was marched about the country—a luxury with which the German officers also were for the most part plentifully provided; and, in fact, no stone was left unturned to impress upon the men themselves and upon the rest of the native population that the *Askari* were a Chosen People in whose presence no dog must presume to bark.

The inevitable effect of this system was that the hand of every civilian native throughout the German colonies in Africa was against the *Askari*, and when war broke out these native soldiers were unable, even if they had been willing to risk so hazardous an experiment, to melt back into the native population from whom they had been completely differentiated and isolated, and whose undying hatred they had earned in good measure, shaken together, pressed down, and running over.

CAPTURED *ASKARI*

Their only safety lay in holding together, and in maintaining as long as possible the tottering military system to which they owed alike their past privileges and their present imminent danger of death at the hands of an enemy, or of still worse things if they fell into the clutches of their outraged countrymen. Toward the end of 1916 a number of captured *Askari* were sent back to British East Africa, and were there incorporated in a battalion of the King's African Rifles. The reputation which they there won for themselves is instructive —excellent on parade, but a most violent and undisciplined crew when off duty, who in their relations with the native population respected the laws neither of God nor of man.

It was due to the German system, it is true, that the *Askari* remained faithful to their white masters, but the reasons which inspired this fidelity are to the last degree discreditable to Germany and to her conception of the manner in which an European nation should " co-operate in the work of civilization "[1] among a primitive people in a distant land.

[1] It was a British Prime Minister who declared, speaking during the early eighties of the nineteenth century, that if Germany desired colonies, "Great Britain would welcome her co-operation in the work of civilization."

CHAPTER VI

IN THE KILWA AREA—MNASI AND RUMBO

DURING the month of March, 1917, the main body of the Regiment lay in camp at Mitole, undergoing company training, and sending out frequent small patrols along the roads in the neighbourhood. The Depôt Company still remained at Mpara, between Kilwa Kivinje and Kilwa Kisiwani, the latter being the port at which the Regiment had landed when it was transported south by sea from Dar-es-Salaam in the preceding November. B Company was dispatched to hold a post at a place variously called Kirongo and Nivanga, which lies almost due west from Mnasi a few miles up a track that leads from the main Kilwa Kivinje-Liwale road, to Njijo, whence the main road from Kilwa Kivinje runs northward to Kitambi. A post consisting of one officer and twenty men of the Pioneer Company was also established at Nigeri-geri, near the junction of the main roads from Kitambi and Liwale, and on March 26th the whole company was sent there. On the 25th March the post at Nivanga, which was protecting a party working on the Chemera road, was attacked by an enemy patrol, which was driven off without difficulty, but two men of A Company were wounded.

AFFAIR AT MAKANGAGA 79

On the 3rd April, the Regiment left Mitole, and marching across country along a vile track till the main highway leading from Kilwa Kivinje to Liwale was encountered, reached Mnasi on the following day, and proceeded to establish a camp there. Mnasi lies on the main road above mentioned and is distant about three-and-twenty miles from Kilwa Kivinje. Here two wells, dug by the Germans and cased with brick, were found, but they contained no water. B Company was separated from the rest of the Regiment at this time, being still stationed at Kirongo.

Very early in the morning of April 11th, a bush native came into camp and reported that another native, who had come into Makangaga from the south on the preceding evening, had brought word that the enemy was at Likawage, rather more than thirty miles [to the south of Mnasi, and that two companies, over two hundred strong, were marching down the road to that place. Makangaga lies south-east of Mnasi and is distant barely four miles from that place. Accordingly Lieutenant Kinley, with seventy-five rank and file and one machine-gun, was at once dispatched to make an attempt to ambush the advancing enemy.

This little band proceeded up the road to Makangaga, and passing through that village, sought some point of vantage from whence to attack the enemy as he marched down the road. For once men of the Gold Coast Regiment, whose patrols had so often been harassed by an elusive and invisible enemy, were to have a chance of subjecting a German force to a similarly unpalatable experience.

The country, however, was for the most part a dead flat, broken only by gentle undulations, and now, toward the end of the rains, it was covered with a new growth of tall grass, very thick and lush. In these circumstances, it was not possible to find any spot which actually overlooked the road and was at the same time securely concealed from the observation of the enemy's advanced points. Lieutenant Kinley, however, took careful note of the lie of the land, and led his little force into the high grass, where he drew it up in as compact a line as possible in a position parallel to the highway, and distant some sixty or seventy yards from it. Here the machine-gun was set up, and the men, breathless with expectation and excitement, lay down and waited.

Presently the sound of a large body of men marching down the road became audible; and Lieutenant Kinley, reserving his fire until he judged that the main body of the enemy was in his immediate front, let the Germans have it with rifle and machine-gun for all his little force was worth. An indescribable uproar ensued, while enemy bullets whistled in every direction above the heads of Kinley's men; and presently it became obvious that the Germans were rushing into the long grass upon a wide front to counter-attack their assailants.

Fearing to be enveloped by the greatly superior force which he had had the hardihood to ambush, Lieutenant Kinley ceased fire, rapidly moved his men to the rear and toward one of the enemy's flanks, and from thence repeated his former tactics. Another wild hooroosh was the result, and for

LIEUTENANT KINLEY'S ACTION 81

perhaps a quarter of an hour, the Germans and the little band of Gold Coasters played an exciting game of hide and seek, each being completely hidden from the other by the ten-foot screen of grass, and being compelled to trust purely to the sounds that reached them to determine the direction of their fire. At the end of that time a luckless band of Germans, composed of Europeans and natives, wandered into view, walking along a path within a few yards of a spot in which Lieutenant Kinley and his breathless men were lying. Very few of the enemy survived this encounter; and Lieutenant Kinley considering that he had now done as much damage as he would be able to effect without running too great a risk of himself being enveloped and cut off, extricated his small force with considerable skill, and led it back to the camp at Mnasi.

In this brilliant little encounter six men of the Gold Coast Regiment were killed, six were wounded, and one fell into the hands of the enemy. The latter lost three white men and fifteen *Askari* killed, and over thirty wounded; and the Gold Coast Regiment, remembering the fate of Lieutenant Shields and Colour-Sergeant Nelson and their men, had the satisfaction of feeling that, to use the phrase of the officers' mess, "they had got back some of their own."

On the 13th April the enemy sent in a flag of truce, and restored to the Gold Coast Regiment four of the men who had been wounded during Lieutenant Kinley's action on the 11th April. The bearer of the flag of truce admitted the heavy losses which the enemy had sustained on that occasion. For his daring little exploit, Lieutenant Kinley was recommended by Colonel Rose, who was still commanding the 3rd East African Brigade, for a Distinguished Service Order.

On the 15th April, the Regiment made a nine hours' march over a villainous track to Migeri-geri, which is situated on the main road thirteen and a half miles from Kilwa, where a new camp was established; and on the 17th of April Lieutenant Beech with a patrol of fifty rank and file and one machine-gun marched along the Mnasi road to investigate the cutting of the telegraph wire. He met a patrol of B Company, with whom was the agent of the Intelligence Department, and they shortly afterwards had a brush with an enemy patrol, B Company losing one man killed and one wounded; but the enemy was driven off and the telegraph line repaired.

On the same day, Captain Foley with the Battery and an escort of thirty rank and file of A Company, joined a force, commanded by the Colonel of the 40th Pathans, which was operating in the direction of Mnasi; the Gold Coast Regiment took over the outposts hitherto held by the Pathans; Captain Greene and the Pioneer Company joined the Regiment in camp; and at 7 p.m. a cable party was sent out to restore communication with the Officer Commanding the Pathans at Rumbo, a place about five miles south by east of Migeri-geri.

On the following day the Battery and its escort, under the command of Captain Foley, came in for a pretty hot engagement at Rumbo, where they were in action with the 40th Pathans and 150 men

THE 40TH PATHANS

of the 2nd Battalion of the 2nd Regiment of the King's African Rifles. It was the 40th Pathans, it will be remembered, who took over Gold Coast Hill from the Regiment at dusk on the 15th December, and throughout the campaign they had fought with steadfastness and courage. Their casualties, both in the field and from sickness, had been very severe, however, and their numerical strength had recently been made up by large drafts of raw recruits from India, the bulk of whom were not drawn from the strata of the population which, in the past, have always supplied men for the 40th Pathans. Precisely what happened on this day does not concern us here. That the veterans of the 40th Pathans fought gallantly is attested by the fact that of one of their machine-gun teams every man was killed at his post, but the rest of the story can best be confined to the experiences of the Battery of the Gold Coast Regiment and of its commander.

On the 18th April Captain Foley got his guns into position, in order to cover and support the infantry advance, at a point across the Ngaura River in the neighbourhood of Rumbo. The stream, in which the water was on that day nearly chin-deep, was behind him, and the camp of the force which Colonel Tyndall of the 40th Pathans was commanding lay in the bush on the further bank. The country was covered by pretty dense trees and scrub, and all that the guns could do was to shell the area in which the enemy was believed to be concealed. After this had been going on for some time, the Battery trumpeter, Nuaga Kusasi, approached Captain Foley and reported that there were no British soldiers in front or on the flanks of the Battery, and that the men moving in the bush, barely thirty yards ahead, were the enemy. Captain Foley was incredulous, but Nuaga Kusasi insisted, and stating that he could see a German officer, put up his rifle and fired at him. Immediately the bush ahead of the guns was seen to be alive with enemy *Askari*.

The men of the Battery, and the thirty men of A Company which formed its escort, behaved admirably, and Bogoberi, one of the gun-carriers, drew his matchet and declared that he and his fellows would charge the enemy with those weapons before the guns should be touched. His example was followed by all the other gun-carriers, who were enlisted men drawn from the same tribes as the soldiers.

These things happened in the space of a few seconds, and already Captain Foley had taken complete charge of the situation, his fluency in Hausa making it easy for him to give his orders clearly and rapidly. He bade the Battery Sergeant-Major retire the two guns and all the ammunition across the river, and then dividing his small force, which was composed of the thirty men of A Company and about a dozen men of the Battery, he placed half under the Sergeant-Major of A Company and the rest under Sergeant Mahmadu Moshi of the Battery. These non-commissioned officers successively led charges into the bush, whence, barely twenty yards away, the enemy were firing upon Foley's men. This had its immediate effect, and Foley next retired half his little party a few yards to the rear, while the rest emptied their

A DIFFICULT OPERATION

magazine rifles into the bush occupied by the enemy. The party in advance then retired at the double through the men behind them, and in their turn took up a position from which to cover the retreat of their fellows. In this manner the enemy, who were in greatly superior force, were successfully kept at bay, while Sergeant-Major Bukare Moshi retired the two guns to the further bank of the river, an operation which was so successfully conducted that, in spite of the deep water, it was performed with the loss of only one box of ammunition. One gunner and three men of A Company were killed, and three gun-carriers were wounded; but the guns were saved, and the great coolness and skill with which Captain Foley handled his men, and the pluck, steadfastness, and resource which the latter showed, won the special praise of Colonel Tyndall of the 40th Pathans. The action of the Battery on this occasion did much to avert what at one time threatened to be a serious disaster. Later in the day Captain Shaw, with two hundred men of A and B Companies, marched to Rumbo to reinforce the 40th Pathans.

The feat thus accomplished was one of quite extraordinary difficulty. The river-crossing at this point, even in the dry season, is by no means easy, for the banks, which are some ten feet in height, rise sheer from the bed and had been worn smooth by the passage of much running water. On this particular day, however, the stream was a raging torrent and the steep banks were as slippery as ice. That, in these circumstances, the passage of the guns and ammunition should have been effected with such expedition and success shows what human effort is capable of achieving in moments of intense excitement.

During the action just described, Lieutenant Murray, R.N., who was in command of a naval Lewis gun section, had all the men of his team either killed or wounded. He then attached himself to Captain Foley, rendering him valuable assistance, and refusing himself to cross the stream until the last of the Battery had passed over in safety.

Captain Macpherson, in command of I Company, was also in action during this day at a place called Beaumont's Post, which was situated near the banks of the Magaura river, on a track that runs parallel to the coast, but well out of sight of the sea, to the east and a little to the south of Rumbo. This post, though of great strength, was very close to the enemy, and it and the patrols sent out from it were frequent objects of his attack. On this occasion Captain Macpherson lost two men killed, two wounded, and two local porters killed.

On the 19th April the rest of the Regiment marched to Rumbo, and there relieved the 40th Pathans; and during the afternoon the enemy, under a flag of truce, sent in five men who had been wounded during the action of the preceding day, and who had fallen into his hands. The bearer of the flag of truce admitted that the enemy had himself lost thirty men in that action, so the veterans of the 40th Pathans and the Battery of the Gold Coast Regiment and its escort had not put up their rather desperate little fight in vain.

During the next two days the surrounding

REGIMENT AT RUMBO

country was patrolled, and the defences of the camp at Rumbo were improved; and on the 22nd April the Brigade Headquarters were established there, and the 2nd Battalion of the 2nd Regiment of the King's African Rifles arrived in camp. Patrolling continued, and on the 25th April Captain Macpherson reported from Beaumont's Post that he had been engaged with the enemy on the 18th April and again on the 20th April; that he had lost in all four men killed, four wounded, and one missing; and that among the killed was Company Sergeant-Major Hassan Bazaberimi.

It was while the Regiment was in camp at Rumbo that von Lettow-Vorbeck planned and carried out one of those daring little ventures which, even though they might have no special military value, helped no doubt to keep up the spirits of his people, and certainly appealed very strongly to his opponents' instinctive love of a good sportsman. He sent a small raiding party through the bush to a point overlooking the harbour of Kilwa Kisiwani, and having got a gun on to a hill in the vicinity, opened fire upon a British transport which was lying at anchor. He actually scored three hits, and, the surprise being complete, this unexpected attack upon the British sea-base caused for the moment a certain amount of apprehension. Even the Depôt Company of the Gold Coast Regiment at Mpara was mobilized under Major Read, and was posted along the northern shore of the harbour; but the Germans were not in a position to deliver any serious attack, and when a British cruiser appeared on the scene they prudently withdrew.

For the rest of the month the Regiment remained at Rumbo, daily patrolling the country, improving the defences and the water-supply of the camp, and having frequent slight brushes with the enemy, in the course of which a few casualties were sustained.

The strength of the Regiment on the 1st May 1917, was only 9 officers, 6 British non-commissioned officers, 7 clerks, 2 dressers, 786 rank and file, 381 carriers, 18 servants, and 41 stretcher-bearers, or 1250 men of all ranks. As compared with the *personnel* of the force which had left Sekondi for East Africa on the 6th July, 1916, only one-fourth of the *cadre* of officers was now available; the British non-commissioned officers were reduced by 9; the rank and file by 194; and this in spite of the reinforcements from the Gold Coast which had reached the Regiment on the 27th December. Notwithstanding the prolonged and trying experiences to which the men had been subjected, they were as keen and as staunch as ever; but the strength of a native force must ever depend in a great degree upon European leadership, and now there were only 7 company officers and 2 British non-commissioned officers all told, to be distributed between the Battery and the four Companies of the Regiment, two of the other British non-commissioned officers being members of the Royal Army Medical Corps, and one being in charge of the transport. It may be accounted no less than marvellous that, in these circumstances, the corps continued to exhibit so great a measure of energy and vitality.

During the whole of May, however, the Gold

Coast Regiment remained in camp at Rumbo, making the usual daily patrols, and on one occasion taking part in a reconnaissance in force, in conjunction with the garrison at Mnasi and I Company at Beaumont's Post, on a thirty-two-mile front, during which, however, the enemy was not brought to action. A few casualties continued to occur during the month to men belonging to the detachment at Beaumont's Post; but by the end of May there were eleven combatant and two medical officers with the Regiment,—a material improvement, but still little more than one-third of the proper establishment. The combatant British non-commissioned officers still numbered only four. During the month news was received that Lieutenant Kinley had been awarded the Military Cross for his action on 11th April, and that a similar distinction had been conferred upon Captain Foley, commanding the Battery, for services rendered in the engagement at Rumbo, when supporting the 40th Pathans, on the 18th April. A Distinguished Conduct Medal, and four Military Medals were also awarded to the Battery and to the sections of A Company which supplied its escort for the fight they had put up on that day.

On the 29th May, half the Pioneer Company, under Lieutenant Bray, went to Migeri-geri to form part of the garrison at that place.

On the 1st June, 1917, Major Goodwin was appointed an Acting Lieutenant-Colonel, and was also awarded the French *Croix de Guerre*. Intelligence was also received that Lieutenant Piggott had been awarded the silver medal of the Italian Order of San Maurico.

During the first nine days of the month nothing occurred beyond the usual patrols, and an occasional interchange of shots with the enemy; but on the 10th June, the Pioneer Company reliefs, returning from a post two and a half miles west of the camp, were ambushed at about 7.30 a.m. by a party of the enemy of great numerical superiority. The returning patrol extended in the bush, opened fire on the enemy, and compelled him to retire. The body of one German *Askari* was left on the ground, and some blood spoor was seen in the bush. The Pioneers lost one man killed and one wounded.

On the 11th June information was received that, on the occasion of His Majesty's birthday, the Distinguished Service Order had been conferred upon Lieutenant-Colonel Goodwin and upon Captain Harman, the Military Cross upon Lieutenant Piggott, and the Distinguished Conduct Medal upon Sergeant-Major Medlock.

On the following day, Captain Macpherson with three of the sections of I Company which, with a company of the 33rd Punjabis, had been occupying Beaumont's Post, where they had had so many brushes with the enemy and had sustained such frequent casualties, rejoined the Regiment at Rumbo. Lieutenant Biltcliffe, with another detachment of I Company, remained at Beaumont's Post, and on the same day he reported that a mixed patrol, composed of his men and of the 33rd Punjabis, had been ambushed by the enemy, and that one man of the Regiment had been killed and seven others wounded. The Punjabis lost one European officer and six Indian soldiers killed. On the 13th June Lieutenant Biltcliffe returned

COLONEL SHAW IN COMMAND

to Rumbo from Beaumont's Post with the rest of I Company, after patrolling the Mgaura River, a small stream that empties itself into the inlet of the sea which forms a deep and narrow bay slightly to the north and west of Kilwa Kisiwani.

On the 15th June 987 men of the Sierra Leone Carrier Corps came into camp and were attached to the Gold Coast Regiment, whose officers, with a sigh of relief, saw these sturdy West Africans replace the much less efficient and reliable local porters.

Captain Shaw was appointed Acting Major, and second in Command of the Gold Coast Regiment on the 16th June, and on the 28th June he was appointed Acting Lieutenant-Colonel, and took over the command, Major Goodwin having been invalided to the base. Shortly before Colonel Rose had been struck down with dysentery and had also been invalided to Dar-es-Salaam, the command of the 3rd East African Brigade being taken over from him by Colonel Orr. General Beves had succeeded General Hannyngton in the command of the Division.

A camp on Lingaula Ridge, a few miles to the south of Rumbo, which had been evacuated by the enemy, was occupied by Lieutenant Bray with I Company on the 28th June; and the same day the Regiment received orders to move on the morrow to Ukuli, a place to the south and only slightly to the east of Rumbo, whence it returned on the 30th June, without having succeeded in bringing the enemy to action. On this latter date the detachment at Linguala Ridge was attacked by an enemy patrol, which was driven off with the loss of one European killed, I Company having two men wounded.

Thus ended the month of June, 1917. The dry season might now be regarded as fairly established, and the country, covered by a luxuriant growth of elephant grass and of fresh green bush into which the recent rains had infused a new life, was already beginning to dry up. The *cadre* of officers was still far below strength, but it now numbered thirteen combatants, with two medical officers and three officers attached to the Sierra Leone Carrier Corps. The rank and file only totalled 771 men; but the little force now possessed 1264 sturdy West African carriers, 42 stretcher-bearers, and five interpreters, and was perhaps more really mobile than it had yet been since its arrival in East Africa. In all Colonel Shaw had under his command 2156 men; and after the comparative stagnation and the constant harassing patrol work of the past six months, the Regiment looked forward with eager anticipation to the resumption of more active campaigning.

MAJOR G. SHAW, M.C.   CAPT. E. G. WHEELER, M.C.   MAJOR H. READ.

To face p. 92.

CHAPTER VII

IN THE KILWA AREA—NARUNGOMBE

GENERAL BEVES was now preparing to take the offensive, his plan being to divide his force into three columns which, working southward, but describing segments of a circle on the west and on the east, might perhaps get in behind the enemy and contrive to envelope him. As usual the difficulties of maintaining sufficient supplies of provisions, ammunition and water obtruded themselves from the outset; but the force was well equipped with motor transport, and it was hoped that, by cutting tracks eight feet wide through the bush, a passage might be made for these vehicles in the rear of the advancing columns.

In order to deceive the enemy as to the main line of his advance, Colonel Orr decided to make a feint along the road past Lingaula Ridge due south of the camp at Rumbo, and this duty he assigned to a company of the Gold Coast Regiment. Colonel Shaw selected B Company for the purpose; and when at 10 p.m. on the 4th July the Regiment left Rumbo with the No. 1 Column, B Company, under the command of Lieutenant Eglon, remained behind at Langaula Ridge.

There was an eclipse of the moon on the night selected for the start, and the darkness was intense, and it was not till noon on the 5th July that

Beaumont's Post was reached. No. 1 Column, which was commanded by Colonel Orr, consisted of the Gold Coast Regiment, the 33rd Punjabis, the 2nd Battalion of the 2nd Regiment of the King's African Rifles, the famous Indian Mountain Battery from Derajat, which goes by the name of the "D. M. B.," and the 8th South African Infantry, which joined the Gold Coast Regiment at Beaumont's Post. No. 1 Column was to make the sweep southward on the left of the advance. No. 2 Column was composed of the 1st and 2nd Battalions of the 3rd Regiment of the King's African Rifles, the 7th South African Infantry, and the 27th Mountain Battery, under the command of Colonel Grant. Its sweep was to be made on the right of the advance. A third column was operating still further to the left of No. 1 Column. This column consisted of the 3rd Battalion of the 3rd King's African Rifles, and the 40th Pathans. On the day before the engagement at Narungombe it was reinforced by one and a half companies of the 8th South African Infantry from No. 1 Column. No. 3 Column was under the command of Colonel Taylor. The 129th Baluchis were in reserve at Makangaga.

No. 1 Column left Beaumont's Post at 7 p.m. on the 5th July for Ukuli, and at midnight the men bivouacked in column of route. At dawn the march was resumed, and at 4 p.m. the Gold Coast Regiment took over the advanced guard from the King's African Rifles, who had been heavily engaged all day, and had succeeded in dislodging the enemy from a prepared position.

As soon as this relief had been affected, the Pioneer Company advanced and engaged the

NGOMANIA AND MNINDI

enemy's rear-guard, which it found some 300 yards up the road, and which it drove back to a distance of about a mile. Here the Pioneer Company bivouacked, remaining all night in its advanced position as outpost company, the rest of the Regiment rejoining No. 1 Column in camp. One man was killed and one wounded in the advance by the Pioneer Company.

On the 7th July, the Gold Coast Regiment marched as advanced guard to the column which was now heading in the direction of Ngomania. This place was occupied by the Regiment, after encountering slight resistance, and the rear-guard of the column came into camp there at about 3 p.m.

On this day, however, No. 2 Column had a serious engagement with the enemy in which many casualties were sustained on both sides.

On the 8th July, the Gold Coast Regiment, which had received orders to march to Mnindi, there to join up with No. 2 Column, left Ngomania at 4.30 a.m. It was accompanied by a section of the D.M.B., and the little force marched to Makangaga—the scene of Lieutenant Kinley's exploit—where at 9 p.m. it bivouacked for the night.

Meanwhile B Company, which had been left behind at Lingaula Ridge under the command of Lieutenant Eglon, had carried out the duty entrusted to it with great dash and brilliancy. On the 7th July Lieutenant Eglon, pushing southward down the road from his camp at Lingaula Ridge, found no less than three companies of Germans in front of him, and promptly attacked. Though the enemy hopelessly outnumbered the men under his command, Lieutenant Eglon managed to drive them from three successive positions, making as great a display of B Company as possible, and evidently impressing the Germans with the idea that they were about to be attacked in force. During these operations Lieutenant Scott was seriously wounded, Sergeant Awudu Arigungu, who had had long service both with the Northern Nigeria Regiment and with the Gold Coast Regiment, was killed, and eight other men of B Company were wounded.

Having effected his purpose, Lieutenant Eglon, in accordance with his instructions, fell back to Lingaula Ridge, and on the 9th July rejoined the Regiment at Makangaga.

From this place No. 2 Column cut across country, almost due west, to Kirongo, on the main Liwale-Kilwa road, leaving Makangaga at 6.30 a.m. on the 10th July, Colonel Shaw commanding the column on the march. Kirongo was reached at 1.30 p.m.; and on the following morning at 6 a.m. the column pushed on five miles to some water-holes in the dried-up bed of a stream called Kirongo-Ware, where it camped at 1.30 p.m. On this day Colonel Ridgeway assumed the command of No. 2 Column.

At 6 a.m. on the 12th July No. 2 Column resumed its march down the track leading in a south-easterly direction to Kilageli, and at 10 a.m. its patrols came into touch with enemy scouts, with whom a few shots were exchanged. An enemy camp at Kilageli, ahead of the column, was located and bombarded by the D.M.B., and the column deployed and occupied this camp without resistance at about 4 p.m. Here the column rested for

KIHENDYE AND RUNGO 97

the night, and on the 13th July at 1.30 p.m. it continued its advance, and at sundown reached Minokwe, which lies four miles further along the road south by west of Kilageli. At 4 a.m. on the 14th July, the column again moved forward in the direction of an enemy position some six miles to the west of Mtanduala, from the advanced trenches of which a hot fire was opened upon it. The D.M.B. came into action and shelled the enemy position, and the 1st and 2nd Battalions of the King's African Rifles and the 7th South African Infantry joined in the fight, in which the Gold Coast Regiment also engaged at about 11 a.m. The enemy, fighting a rear-guard action, retired, and two hours later the engagement came to an end. The casualties were few, and the column bivouacked for the night in the prepared position from which the Germans had been ejected.

On the 15th July, the column marched in a south-westerly direction to Kihendye and thence to Rungo, a few shots being exchanged during the day between the King's African Kifles and enemy scouts. The former lost one man killed and three wounded.

During this day the work of cutting a path, designed for the use of motor-lorries, across country and through the thick, tall grass began, two companies of the Gold Coast Regiment being sent forward for this purpose; and during the whole of the next two days this work was continued. It was a very toilsome job, hacking an eight-foot track through elephant-grass and occasional patches of thorn-thicket, with a merciless sun smiting down from above, with nought to breathe save the stuffy overheated and used-up air peculiar to big grass patches in the tropics, with only a few dry biscuits for food, and a constant, agonising insufficiency of water. The men stuck to it manfully, but one poor fellow died during the day of exhaustion and heat-apoplexy; and in the end this vast expenditure of labour was all in vain. The track had been cut on a compass-bearing, but the only surveys in existence were very roughly approximate, and the path through the grass was eventually brought to a standstill by encountering a steep cliff up which no motor-lorry could conceivably find a way. A little further on, a large main road which runs north and south was struck, and No. 2 Column presently found itself in junction with No. 1 Column, which had advanced down this road to Kipondira. Here the Gold Coast Regiment was retransferred to No. 1 Column,

On the 18th July No. 1 Column left Kipondira at 10 a.m., the Gold Coast Regiment being stationed towards the rear of the force, which was in action with the enemy until about 2.30 p.m., when the Germans retired, and the column camped for the night at Kihumburu. Two miles further down the road from this place the main body of the enemy operating in this part of the country had taken up a strongly entrenched position at Narungombe. The plan for his envelopment had miscarried, as was almost certain to befall in a country such as that through which the columns were operating, where movements of troops were inevitably slow, where difficulties hampered supply, where scarcity of water presented a constant menace to the very existence of the forces in the field, and

SCOUTING DIFFICULTIES

where a few scouts, used with even a modicum of skill, could easily keep the enemy informed of the direction which any hostile unit was taking. No. 3 Column had carried out the task entrusted to it very successfully, for the wide sweeping movement which it had made had enabled it to cut in behind the enemy, who was in occupation of a scarp at Mikikama, where he would have presented a formidable barrier to the advance of No. 1 Column. This was a service of considerable importance; but now all three columns, though their convergence in front of Narungombe had not been intended, were assembled in the vicinity of the main road a few miles to the north of that place. This well illustrates the extreme difficulty of concerted operations when carried out in thick bush or high grass, as soon as ever the roads or paths running through it are quitted.

The 2nd Battalion of the 2nd Regiment of the King's African Rifles, who had borne the brunt of this day's fighting, had rendered a tremendous service to the columns by expelling the Germans from a water-hole at Kihumburu, and thus making it available for the troops. It was evident, however, that the supply so obtained was quite insufficient for the needs of the force for more than a very limited space of time; and it thus became a matter of vital importance that the enemy should be dislodged from the very strong position which he had taken up at Narungombe, where a much larger set of water-holes was known to exist. Orders were accordingly given for an attack to be delivered upon Narungombe early on the following morning.

The position which the enemy had prepared and occupied consisted of a series of breastworks some two and a half feet in height, built of earth stoutly faced with sticks driven deep into the ground and bound together with lianas, with a number of small redoubts and strongly constructed machine-gun emplacements, and a specially strong defensive post for the accommodation of the high command. These works, drawn along the upper slopes of two hills, between which the high-road passes, extended in an irregular but continuous line, with many slight protrusions and salients, for a distance of two and a half miles. The defensive position was particularly strong at the left extremity of the enemy's line. From the British camp at Kihumburu the main road runs due south and almost straight to the centre of the German position, dipping into a valley a few hundred yards in advance of the British camp, and thereafter rising gradually in a long glacis to the hills upon which the enemy was entrenched. The country hereabouts is undulating, and covered throughout with high grass, and patches of thorn-scrub set fairly thickly with rather mean-looking trees; but immediately in advance of the enemy's position, the grass had been cut, leaving stalks about two feet six in height, for a distance of some three hundred yards, and thus depriving the attacking force of any cover. The enemy had four companies in the firing-line, with four more companies in reserve, which, however, arrived too late to take part in the battle. He had two guns of about 2·95 calibre and at least six machine-guns; but above all, he had, as usual, been able to select his own defensive

DEATH OF LIEUTENANT EGLON

position, and could rely upon making the task of his ejectment an extremely expensive undertaking.

On Thursday, the 19th July, the British advance began at 6 a.m., No. 1 Column leading with the Gold Coast Regiment in the centre. It had been reported that no enemy post existed at a point nearer than 1000 yards along the road from the British camp; but before the Regiment had traversed 300 yards, and while they were still in column of route, fire was opened upon them, and two men were killed and three wounded ere ever they had time to deploy. An advance in extended order through high grass is necessarily a rather slow operation, and while the Gold Coast Regiment was working forward, one company of the 2nd Battalion of the King's African Rifles was sent forward out of reserve, and in order to protect the Regiment's advance, occupied a ridge on their right flank which lay to the south-west of the British camp,

At 8.15 a.m. the advance-guard of the Regiment became heavily engaged, Lieutenant Eglon having led B Company to within a short distance of the enemy's well-entrenched and strongly held position. Here this gallant young officer, who had done so well a few days earlier when attacking from Lingaula Ridge, was killed, and B Company suffered many casualties. Colonel Shaw had taken up an advanced position along the road behind a mound, from which he was able throughout the day closely to observe the operations he was conducting; and he now sent I Company to prolong the line on the right of the attack. A few minutes later the Pioneer Company was also sent forward to prolong the right; and at 9.30 a.m. the 33rd Punjabis, who had been held in reserve, were also sent yet further to prolong the right, while the 7th South African Infantry deployed on the left of the Gold Coast Regiment.

At this juncture orders were given for No. 3 Column to attempt a wide turning movement on the right of the enemy's position, the 3rd Battalion of the 3rd King's African Rifles and the 40th Pathans leading the advance, with certain waterholes as their objective. No. 2 Column was ordered at the same time to carry out a similar turning movement on the left. At 10.30 a.m. these troops began to get into position, and at noon No. 3 Column became heavily engaged. The 3rd Battalion of the 3rd King's African Rifles and the 40th Pathans had been pushed forward, without any preliminary scouting, into a valley on the British left, where they presently came under a devastating rifle and machine-gun fire from both forces. By this time the enemy's fire had grown intense along the whole line; and the 8th South African Infantry, the bulk of whom still formed part of No. 1 Column and occupied ground on the left of the Gold Coast Regiment, attempted to advance, but were enfiladed by machine-gun and rifle fire from salients in the enemy's line. They maintained their position for a while, but the troops upon their left failed to make good, and the grass all round them was set on fire by the British shells.

This failure on the left placed the Gold Coast Regiment in a highly perilous position, as its flank was now completely in the air. Moreover, by this time, the grass was well alight along the whole of the front. The men, however, were steady as a rock, and showed no signs of giving way as had the South African and Indian troops on their immediate left. As for the blazing grass, that was a phenomenon to which they had all their lives been accustomed, and they manfully stamped the flames out, in spite of the heavy fire to which they were exposed, and stolidly resumed the fight. On the left of the line, where the danger was most imminent, Colour-Sergeant Campbell very specially distinguished himself, and did much to encourage and confirm the spirit of the men, only too many of whose officers were already *hors-de-combat*. He fought his machine-gun until practically all its team had fallen, and in the end brought it safely out of action.

Meantime the right flank had advanced 800 yards, but at 3.30 p.m. they were strongly counter-attacked by the enemy, and two platoons of the 2nd Battalion of the 2nd Regiment of the King's African Rifles were sent to prolong the right and to get into touch with No. 2 Column, which so far had failed to make its appearance. And all this time the enemy maintained from his defences an intense and relentless fire.

A general advance had been arranged to take place at 2.30 p.m., but the position on the left had by that time become so critical that the movement could not be carried out at the hour fixed; and at 4 p.m. orders were sent to the Gold Coast Regiment not to attempt any further advance. These orders arrived too late, and the Gold Coast Companies on the right, with the

NARUNGOMBE

33rd Punjabis and the 2nd Battalion of the 2nd Regiment of the King's African Rifles, charged and took certain of the enemy's trenches, but were unable to hold on owing to their left being unsupported and to their ammunition running short. They were accordingly retired, but only to a distance of 100 yards from the enemy's trenches, where they dug themselves in and held on. The 2nd Battalion of the King's African Rifles remained on the enemy's flank in a patch of thick bush, and succeeded thence in getting into touch with No. 2 Column. Darkness was now falling, and the Gold Coast Regiment and the troops on its right bivouacked for the night in the rifle-pits which they had dug for themselves.

Meanwhile, the troops on the left had again been led forward into action by Major Hill of the South African Infantry and by the Commander of the Stokes Battery, thus reconsolidating the line on the left of the Gold Coast Regiment.

At dawn on the following day it was found that the enemy had evacuated his position. He had effected his object, and had made the attacking force pay a heavy price for the possession of the water-holes of Narungombe. Now, before he could be enveloped or cut off, he beat a hasty retreat toward the south. The position from which he had inflicted so much damage upon his pursuers had served its purpose, and he had nothing more to gain by attempting longer to hold it.

The casualties suffered by the Gold Coast Regiment, having regard to its strength at this time, were very heavy. Of the greatly reduced

HEAVY CASUALTIES

cadre of officers and of British non-commissioned officers, Lieutenant Eglon was killed, Captain A. J. R. O'Brien, M.C., of the West African Medical Staff, was severely wounded, as also were Captain Leslie-Smith, Colour-Sergeant Baverstock and another colour-sergeant. Lieutenant Bray was slightly wounded. B Company lost its sergeant-major—Awudu Bakano—a very fine soldier, and of the rank and file, 37 were killed and 114 were wounded. The total casualties were thus 158 out of about 790 men engaged, or 20 per cent. of the whole combatant strength of the corps.

Never had the men of the Gold Coast Regiment shown more grit than on this day at Narungombe. They went into action early in the morning of the 19th July after having been marching and fighting, or painfully cutting paths through the bush and high grass — labouring practically without cessation—since the evening of the 4th of that month. They were hotly engaged with the enemy during the whole day, exposed to a fierce sun, with very poor cover, with little to eat and with less to drink, and were exposed throughout to gun, rifle and machine-gun fire, mostly at fairly short range, from 8 a.m. to nightfall. In addition to the enemy, they had constantly to fight the blazing grass, which rendered their position more and more exposed; yet these Africans never wavered, but continued stubbornly to hold their positions, though more than one company had been robbed of all its European leaders and was being commanded solely by its native non-commissioned officers. When towards the end of the day, they had occupied the enemy's trenches on the right, and running short of ammunition and being unsupported on their left, were unable to hold on, they retired only a hundred yards in obedience to orders and with perfect steadiness, and from their new position forthwith resumed the fight. It would be difficult to devise a test more searching that could be applied to native troops, and the triumphant manner in which on this occasion the "green caps" maintained their reputation as men who "never go back" is a striking proof of the Regiment's high quality as a fighting unit.

For the services rendered by him while in command of the Regiment on this day, Lieutenant-Colonel Shaw was subsequently awarded a bar to the Military Cross which he had already earned.

CHAPTER VIII

THE HALT AT NARUNGOMBE

ALTHOUGH the Germans had abandoned their position at Narungombe, the severe losses which they had inflicted upon the British were out of all proportion to any advantages which the latter could claim to have secured. The check, too, impressed the British command with the difficulty of dealing with the enemy unless the pursuit could be rendered not only rapid but continuous, and above all with the fact that an adequate supply of water was the hinge upon which all future operations must turn. At Narungombe the very machine-guns of the Gold Coast Regiment had for a time been put out of action through lack of water wherewith to cool the jackets, and the men in the firing-line had been cruelly tortured by thirst during the greater part of that day. After the fight at Narungombe, therefore, the column under General Beves' command remained in camp at that place to refit. There reinforcements speedily arrived, and General Hannyngton, returning from sick-leave, presently resumed command of the force. A large fortified camp was established; a space to the north of it was cleared and made into an aerodrome; supplies of every description were accumulated; and all things were made as ready as circumstances permitted for a renewed advance. Meanwhile no

THE HALT AT NARUNGOMBE

forward movement was attempted from July 20th to September 17th, a delay during two precious months of the dry season which unfortunately gave the enemy also time to rest and reorganize, to complete his preparations for further resistance to the advance, and to accumulate supplies at his advanced bases and depôts. It was desired, however, that General Hannyngton's new advance should form part of a much larger scheme; and its timing, so as to ensure co-operation with another column whose movements will be described in the following paragraph, imposed perhaps a longer period of inactivity than was necessary merely for the purpose of refitting.

The Nigerian Brigade, which had arrived in East Africa some months after the Gold Coast Regiment, had endured unspeakable things during the wet season of 1916–17 in its camp on the northern bank of the Rufiji. Here the Brigade had suffered from an insufficiency of supplies and the difficulties occasioned by a water-logged countryside. Now three battalions, under General Cunliffe, had been brought round by sea to Kilwa Kisiwani, and were about to operate as a separate column on the right of General Hannyngton's force, at present encamped at Narungombe. The task of these columns would be to endeavour to drive the enemy southward into the Lindi area; and meanwhile a large force, of which the remaining battalion of the Nigerians formed a part, had been landed at Lindi, and was trying to slip in behind the enemy for the purpose of helping to encircle him.

Meanwhile, Belgian troops from the Congo

GENERAL NORTHEY'S ADVANCE 109

were advancing in a south-easterly direction, with Mahenge as their immediate objective,—Mahenge being an important place, two hundred miles due west of Kilwa, on the main road which runs north and south from Songia to Kilossa on the Dar-es-Salaam-Lake Tanganyika railway. Simultaneously, General Northey's force, which had worked through from Northern Rhodesia and had had a certain amount of fighting in the neighbourhood of Lake Tanganyika, was advancing, in a north-easterly direction, upon Mpepo, a place that lies fifty miles south-west of Mahenge. The object of both these forces, and of a third which was advancing southward with its base at Dadome on the Dar-es-Salaam railway, was the envelopment or dislodgment of the German European and native troops which, under the command of Major von Tafel, were operating in the western part of the territory, mostly to the south of the Ulanga, which is an upper branch of the Rufiji River.

The position at Narungombe, which as we have seen is situated on a main road that runs north and south some thirty miles to the east of the highway that leads from Kilwa Kivinje to Liwale, was as follows. The enemy had retired down the former of these roads to Mihambia, which is distant only twelve miles from Narungombe, and where there are another set of water-holes; and he had established here his main advanced position. From the high-road at Mihambia, a footpath leads west to a place called Kitiia, three miles away, where four tracks meet. One of these runs for five miles in a westerly direction till a ravine, which bears the name of Liwinda, is struck; one runs south-east to rejoin the high-road at Mpingo five miles south of Mihambia, and northward to Mikikole, which is some five and a half miles off. At Mikikole the Gold Coast Regiment had an outpost; and from this place footpaths lead, one north-west to Narungombe; one east to a point on the main road four and a half miles south of Narungombe, occupied by the company of the 2nd Battalion of the King's African Rifles, to which the name of Gregg's Post was given; and a third in a south-westerly direction, crossing Liwinda Ravine, and running on to some water-holes nine miles further off near the native village of Mbombomya, and thence to Ndessa. This latter place and Mnitshi on the high-road, some ten miles south of Mihambia, were at this time the principal advanced bases and supply depôts of von Lettow-Vorbeck's forces in this portion of the territory, though at neither of them had any fortification been attempted. On a hill near Mpingo, however, the enemy had established a signal-station.

The country hereabouts is for the most part a wide expanse of undulating flat, studded with frequent trees, smothered in thick, and often tall grass, and broken here and there by patches of dense bush. At this season of the year it was waterless, save for a few ponds spattered very sparsely over the face of the land. Bush-fires had been raging intermittently for weeks, and in many places the country was bare and blackened. Though now and again glades occur among the trees, it is rarely possible to obtain an extended view in any direction; and though the vegetation did not impede the movements of troops so completely as it does in real tropical forest country, the character of the locality gave great advantages to a force whose main object was to fight a delaying campaign, and presented proportionate disadvantages to the force that aimed at enveloping its enemy. The British were further hampered by their ignorance of the district, and above all by the scarcity of water. Aeroplanes were being used, and by them bombs were frequently dropped upon the German camp at Ndessa; but for the most part the efforts of the airmen illustrated the eternal triumph of hope over experience. Even when to the landsman's eye the country appeared to be fairly open, the whole area, seen from above, was revealed as one continuous expanse of grass and tree-tops, devoid of all distinguishing landmarks. It was difficult, in such circumstances, to pick out even well-known localities, while the detection of small posts established by the enemy in the bush, and carefully screened from observation, was for the most part impossible. The infantry patrols had generally to smell out such danger-points for themselves.

A peculiar feature of this district is the Liwinda Ravine, of which mention has already been made. It consists of a natural hollow, some two hundred feet in depth and from four hundred to eight hundred yards in breadth, which traverses the country for many miles from the north-west to the south-east. The ground along its edges differs in no way from the rest of the surrounding areas of bush and orchard-country, except that it is somewhat more elevated than most of them.

Throughout this district ant-bears abound, and

THE HALT AT NARUNGOMBE

their holes, which are ubiquitous, are often large enough to admit of the entrance of a man.

On the 21st July, two days after the engagement at Narungombe, Lieutenant-Colonel Rose rejoined the Regiment and took over the command. He was accompanied by Captain Hornby, who until he had fallen ill had long filled the post of Adjutant, and by four new officers—Captains McElligott and Methven, M.C., and Lieutenants Lamont and S. B. Smith—all of whom were joining the Gold Coast Regiment for the first time. Captain Hornby resumed his work as Adjutant which, during his absence on sick leave, had been successively performed by Lieutenant Downer and by Colour-Sergeant Avenell, both of whom had discharged the difficult duties assigned to them with marked success.

On the 22nd July the Regiment was for the first time supplied with Lewis guns, and the work of training teams for them was forthwith put in hand. On the 28th July, Captains Briscoe, Hartland and Brady, and Lieutenants Baillie, Willoughby and Maxwell joined the Regiment with reinforcements consisting of 354 rank and file and 7 machine-gun-carriers from the Gold Coast. On the 29th July 50 rifles of B Company, under Lieutenant Baillie, with Colour-Sergeant Campbell, joined the detachment of the 2nd Battalion of the 2nd King's African Rifles at Gregg's Post; and a detachment composed of men of B Company, under Captain Methven, was sent out to occupy an outpost at Mikikole.

During the whole of August the Regiment

LIWINDA RAVINE

lay in camp at Narungombe, its duties being confined to vigorous training, more especially of the new drafts, and daily patrolling of the roads from the camp and from the outposts at Mikikole and Gregg's Post. A few more men rejoined from sick leave during the month, and on the 31st August the Regiment was more nearly up to strength than it had been at any time since the very early days of the campaign. There were present 29 officers, including 2 doctors, and 2 officers attached to the transport; 17 British non-commissioned officers, including 1 non-commissioned officer of the Royal Army Medical Corps and 4 belonging to the Transport; 7 clerks, 957 rank and file, 133 enlisted gun and ammunition-carriers, 34 servants, and 1 European and 4 native interpreters—a total of 2130 of all ranks.

On the 7th September orders were sent to Captain Methven to move to Liwinda Ravine with 70 rifles of B Company, leaving a picket of 1 European and 20 rifles at Kitiia *en route*. His instructions were to dig for water on his arrival at the Ravine; to take every precaution to prevent the existence of his camp becoming known to the enemy, and to make systematic reconnaissances throughout the neighbourhood, including the roads leading to the fortified enemy post at Mihambia and to Mnitshi.

Liwinda Ravine was reached without incident, but though pits were sunk to a depth of 20 feet not a drop of water could be found. The establishment of a water depôt at this place formed, however, an essential feature of General Hannyngton's plan for the advance which he was about to undertake; and on the 10th September big water-troughs fashioned of rubber, measuring some 20 feet in length, 3 feet in width, 15 inches in depth, were sent to the Ravine on the heads of carriers. Water was also conveyed thither in the long tins to which in India the name of *pakhal* is given, each of which is a load for two men. Only two of the troughs reached their destination in a water-tight condition; and this attempt to establish a water depôt proved a laborious job which only met with a qualified measure of success.

Meanwhile Captain Methven, with a patrol of twenty men, had gone on a scouting expedition to the south-east, in order to try to ascertain the exact position of the enemy's camp and supply depôt at Mnitshi. This, and two subsequent patrols in the direction of the main road, undertaken by Lieutenant Woods, were perilous little reconnaissances penetrating deep into the country occupied by the enemy, and they were very far from commending themselves to the native headman, who was impressed to act as guide. He was an ancient African, very wizened and emaciated, who in camp sported a soiled Mohammedan robe, to which as a Pagan he had no right, with an European waistcoat worn buttoned-up outside it. In the bush he reverted to a dingy loin-cloth wound sparsely about his middle. His anxiety to preserve his skin intact, amid admittedly adverse circumstances, altogether outstripped his regard for truth; and when he had guided Captain Methven to an eminence overlooking Mpingo, he unhesitatingly declared that place to be Mnitshi, which, as a matter of fact, lies five miles further to the south along the main road which leads from Mihambia to Mpingo. This had for him the satisfactory effect of shortening the distance to be covered by the patrol, and of proportionately diminishing its dangers; but Captain Methven reported to Headquarters that he was uncertain how far his guide was to be relied upon, and expressed doubt as to whether the place identified as Mnitshi was indeed that enemy supply depôt.

On the 13th September Lieutenant Woods took a small patrol through the bush to a point on the main road south of Mihambia, and on his way back he came across water-holes near Mbombomya. As Captain Methven considered it important that a more detailed examination should be made, Lieutenant Woods returned to these water-holes next day. As he approached them, however, and when he and his patrol and the ancient guide were in a patch of grass that was not more than waist-high, the enemy suddenly appeared from a camp which he had in the interval constructed in a cup-like hollow on the top of a piece of rising ground overlooking the water-holes Shots were forthwith exchanged, and Woods, seeing that his small party was in a fair way to be surrounded by the enemy, who were at least one company strong, shouted to his men to disperse and to get back to their camp as best they might. Meanwhile, he himself very pluckily ran at top speed and in full view of the enemy, as straight as he could go for the water-holes and the German camp, secured a good view of both, and then

I

plunged into a patch of thick bush, in which he succeeded in eluding his pursuers. He and all his patrol eventually made their way back to the Ravine, one man and one stretcher-bearer only being missing. Of the soldier nothing more was heard, but the stretcher-bearer was picked up many days later, very emaciated and with a bullet-wound in his leg, having crawled through the bush nearly as far to the south and west as Ndessa. The ancient African, who had vanished the moment the enemy appeared, had slipped into an ant-bear's hole, and had there passed the night. He returned to the camp in the Ravine on the following morning.

On the 14th September a patrol from Kitiia, which had crept to within hearing distance of the enemy camp at Mihambia, had a brush with a hostile patrol as it was returning to its post.

Some native porters, who had deserted from the German Force at the water-holes, also came into camp, and from them a good deal of more or less reliable information was obtained by Captain Methven on the subject of the enemy's numbers and disposition. From this source it was learned that Hauptmann Kerr, with 9 Europeans, 200 *Askari*, and 4 machine-guns had passed through the camp at the water-holes near Mbombomya on the 14th September, from Ndessa, on his way to Mnitshi; that the force at the water-holes consisted of 5 Europeans and 150 *Askari* with 2 machine-guns; that there were at that time only 5 enemy companies encamped at Ndessa; and that the main road and the track to Ndessa had both been mined. It was also stated by the

LIWINDA RAVINE

porters that the enemy were short of food and that the Europeans were living on rations of rice and millet.

On the 18th September the main body of the Gold Coast Regiment moved out of camp at Narungombe, where they had been now for almost exactly two months, and marched along the footpath to Mikikole, and thence to the water depôt which Captain Methven had established at Liwinda Ravine. The men started with full water-bottles, and each carried a little canvas bag of water of the kind known in India as a *chaquat*, with which, moreover, every spare carrier was also loaded. The camp at Liwinda Ravine was reached without incident.

The orders issued to No. 1 Column, to which the Regiment was attached, were that Mihambia should be attacked on the morning of September 19th by the 2nd Battalion of the 2nd Regiment of the King's African Rifles, with one and a half companies of the Gold Coast Regiment, the 27th Mountain Battery and the Stokes Battery. In order to prevent reinforcements reaching the enemy at Mihambia, a force under Colonel Rose, consisting of the Headquarters, the Battery, and two companies of the Gold Coast Regiment, was to proceed on the morning of the attack to the junction of the track from Ndessa and the water-holes, near Mbombomya, with that from Mnitshi, at a spot situated about two and a half miles to the south of the camp at Liwinda Ravine. It was also intended that while, on the 19th September, No. 1 Column was attacking the enemy on the Mihambia–Mbombomya–Mnitshi area, No. 2 Column should take up a position on the right from whence to deliver an attack upon Ndessa on the morning of September 20th, for the purpose of cutting off his retreat toward the south, and this operation would be supported by the reserve of "Hanforce," as the force under the command of General Hannyngton was always called.

The Nigerian Brigade, operating further on the right, was to move to Ruale, a few miles south-west of Ndessa, on the 19th September.

These concerted movements were designed to drive the enemy from his fortified position at Mihambia, from Mnitshi and from Ndessa, and if possible across the Mbemkuru River into the arms of the forces thrusting west, from their base on the sea at Lindi, along the road which leads thence to Liwale.

CHAPTER IX

THE ADVANCE TO MBOMBOMYA AND BEKA

ON the morning of Wednesday, the 19th September, the Gold Coast Regiment quitted its camp at Liwinda Ravine. At 6 a.m. A Company and half the Pioneer Company, with which was the 27th Mountain Battery, set out for Kitiia, under the command of Major Shaw. Kitiia, as has been mentioned, lies five miles to the east of the camp at Liwinda Ravine, and three miles to the west of Mihambia, and is connected with both by a footpath leading through the grass, tree-set scrub, and occasional bush. It was the function of this little force, as soon as it had obtained touch with the 2nd Battalion of the 2nd Regiment of the King's African Rifles, which was advancing upon Mihambia along the main road from Gregg's Post, to move off the footpath into the high grass and bush, and to endeavour to fall upon the left flank and rear of the enemy's position. Major Shaw also had instructions to send sixty rifles from Kitiia to act independently, with the German porters' camp, which was situated to the south of their fortified position at Mihambia, as its objective.

Major Shaw's force reached Kitiia without incident, and shortly afterwards got into touch with the right of the King's African Rifles. It then quitted the track, and working its way through the grass and scrub and between the trees on a compass bearing, advanced toward Mihambia. In traversing country of this description, where no extended view in any direction is obtainable, it is always a matter of great difficulty to strike the exact objective aimed at; and on this occasion, when Major Shaw arrived in the vicinity of Mihambia, it was to find himself in front of the enemy's left, instead of on his flank or to his rear. A Company and half the Pioneers, however, forthwith attacked, and the 27th Mountain Battery came into action. Simultaneously, the King's African Rifles joined in the attack.

The enemy's position at Mihambia very generally resembled that which he had taken up two months earlier at Narungombe. Here, however, the water-holes were in the valley, and the enemy's fortifications were drawn along the crest of the hill which sloped up from them, and lay astride the main road leading from Narungombe. On his left there rose an isolated hill which did not appear at this time to be occupied.

The attack was delivered with vigour, and the water-holes passed at once into the hands of the British. The enemy, moreover, did not make a very stout resistance; and as he began to fall back, Major Shaw sought permission to occupy the isolated hill on the right of the attack, of which mention has already been paid, which commanded the main road. Some delay occurred before leave to execute this movement could be obtained, and when at last the occupation of this eminence was attempted, the enemy was found to be holding it

PATROL WORK 121

in great strength, and the whole of the rest of the day was spent in vain attempts to dislodge him. So stout a resistance did he offer, indeed, that the British advance was definitely arrested, the troops being forced to dig themselves in, and it was not until an hour or two before dawn on the 20th September that the enemy eventually retreated down the main road in a southerly direction.

Meanwhile Colonel Rose, with the remainder of the Gold Coast Regiment, had marched from the camp in the Liwinda Ravine in a southerly direction, and had occupied Nambunjo Hill, overlooking the main road between Mpingo and Mnitshi, and situated some two and a half miles to the west of it. An hour after the Regiment left Liwinda Ravine telegraphic communication with Gregg's Post, and consequently with Colonel Orr, who was commanding No. 1 Column, was interrupted.

At 8.30 a.m. B Company, which was acting as advance guard, reached a path leading to Mbombomya, and an officer's patrol, under Lieutenant Woods, was sent down this track with orders to lay an ambush, and to protect the flank and right rear of the Regiment. A second officer's patrol, under Lieutenant S. B. Smith, was sent forward with orders to attempt to surprise the enemy's signal-station on the hill near Mpingo, and then to push on south to Mnitshi, five miles further down the main road. Lieutenant Woods' patrol came into touch with the enemy within three-quarters of an hour from the time when he left the main body of the Regiment. He shortly afterwards reported that the enemy in front of him were few in numbers, but that they were resisting his advance and were fighting a series of small rear-guard actions. He was instructed that his chief duty was to guard the track from Mbombomya, and that he should dig himself in and endeavour to protect the flank and right rear of the Regiment.

Meanwhile, at 11 a.m. Major Shaw reported by telegraph that he had got into touch with the King's African Rifles at 9.45 a.m., but shortly afterwards telegraphic communication ceased, and it was subsequently discovered that the line had been cut and that about a mile of wire had been removed. The Regiment was now cut off from all communication with the forces with which it was co-operating. This, however, did not long continue, and by midday the telegraphic connection with No. 1 Column was restored.

Nambunjo Hill was reached at 2.45 p.m., and a perimeter camp was established there.

At 5.15 p.m. word was received from Lieutenant Smith that his attempt to surprise the signal-station at Mpingo Hill had failed, and that as the position was too strongly held for his small force to attempt an attack upon it, he had withdrawn, and was lying up in the bush at a spot overlooking the main road in the neighbourhood of Mpingo. Already at 2.30 p.m. ninety rifles of B Company, under Captain Methven, had been sent forward to pick up Lieutenant Smith's patrol, and to try to get astride the main road; and at 5 p.m. his party became heavily engaged with the enemy. Instructions were sent to him to attempt to advance toward Mihambia, as No. 1 Column reported that they had been held up by the enemy,

WOODS' PATROL ATTACKED

posted on the hill already mentioned, and had been compelled to dig themselves in. Meanwhile, however, Lieutenant Smith's patrol had been having a very hot time of it. His position was located by the enemy, his patrol was almost completely surrounded, and he only succeeded in extricating it with great difficulty, and joined Captain Methven, who was then at a spot about a mile and a half south of Mihambia, at about 5.30 p.m. Any further advance in the direction of Mihambia was rendered impossible owing to the thickness of the bush and the rapid approach of darkness. Moreover, like the whole of Colonel Rose's command, this detachment had long ago exhausted its supply of water, and the men were suffering acutely from thirst.

At 6.15 p.m. Lieutenant Woods' patrol on the Mbombomya road was strongly attacked by one full company of the enemy with two machine-guns, and was compelled to fall back, his men, who had been fighting all day, being also much exhausted for want of water. Captain McElligott, with a section of I Company, was sent out at once with orders to entrench themselves astride the track from Mbombomya, and to hold on at all costs, so as to protect the flank and right rear of the Regiment on Nambunjo Hill.

The whole of Colonel Rose's command was now very hard up for rations, but above all for water, and though supplies of both had been wired for to No. 1 Column, nothing reached them that night.

At 3 a.m., on the 20th September, Lieutenant Parker left for the camp at Liwinda Ravine with all the available carriers to fetch rations and water, which No. 1 Column reported it was dispatching from Mihambia at 5 o'clock that morning. At dawn, too, Captain McElligott sent forward a patrol from his entrenched position on the track leading to Mbombomya; an officer's patrol under Lieutenant Baillie was dispatched to the main road, with orders to remain under cover, and to watch the movements of the enemy; and a third patrol was sent out towards Kitiia to try and establish touch with Major Shaw's detachment.

Soon after 8 a.m. it was learned that the enemy had evacuated his trenches at Mihambia, and Colonel Rose was instructed to occupy Mbombomya as soon as water and rations had reached him, and his force was once more in a position to advance.

At 8 a.m. also Captain Wray, with a second section of I Company, was sent to reinforce Captain McElligott and to take over the command of the post, and at about 9.30 a.m. he became engaged with the enemy. Shortly before, word was received that No. 1 Column would advance down the main road from Mihambia at noon for the purpose of occupying Mnitshi; and Lieutenant Baillie, who had crept to the edge of the road at a point distant some two miles east of that place, reported that the enemy and his porters in large numbers were streaming past him from the direction of Mihambia towards Mpingo. The enemy south of Mihambia, however, was covering his retreat by fighting a rear-guard action with his machine-guns.

At 11.20 a.m. rations and water at last reached

the Gold Coast Regiment, but the 350 *chaquals* sent were only half-full, and this was all the water available for a force of 1400 men, who had not had a drop beyond the issue made to them on the night of September 18th before they left the camp at Liwinda Ravine. The rations supplied contained provisions for the fighting men only, and left out of the count gun-carriers, stretcher-bearers and the ammunition column. However, rations were pooled, a portion of the emergency rations of the Regiment was thrown into the common stock, and all the men had something to eat and a few gulps of water to drink, though the ration served out was only half a pint per man. The thirst from which one and all were suffering was very acute, and though the men were chewing bits of bark and roots to try to relieve the dryness that was parching mouths and throats and swollen tongues, numbers of them fell exhausted on the ground during the skirmishes fought on this day, and had to be carried in a semi-unconscious condition out of the firing-line.

As soon as the troops in the camp on Nambunjo Hill had been watered and fed, three sections of B Company, under Captain Methven, were sent to reinforce Captain Wray, who was being heavily attacked. His men had been without water for more than twenty-four hours and were terribly exhausted, but they none the less put up a stout fight, in the course of which Captain Wray was severely wounded, and Corporal Issaka Kipalsi showed great pluck and coolness while in command of a party of bombers. On the arrival of Captain Methven's reinforcements the enemy withdrew.

Meanwhile, the advance of No. 1 Column, with which was Major Shaw and his detachment, had met with considerable resistance, and the position was reported to be "very serious all round." A telegram was also received from the column stating that though rations were being sent out, it was not possible to dispatch any more water to the camp at Liwinda Ravine. Later in the day it was learned that No. 1 Column had succeeded in advancing as far along the road as Mpingo, but that there was no chance of the water-holes at Mnitshi being captured that day; and Captain Methven also found it impossible to seize the water-holes near Mbombomya before dark. No. 1 Column could supply itself with water from the captured holes at Mihambia, but the position of the Gold Coast Regiment was rapidly becoming desperate. Officers and men alike were agonized by thirst, which was intensified by the heat in this dried-up, arid waste of dust-smothered vegetation, and those of them who had been fighting and patrolling all day were reduced to a state of pitiable exhaustion. If a supply of water could not be obtained early on the morrow a considerable portion of the force would almost inevitably perish of drought in that weary wilderness.

At 6 a.m. on the 21st September, the Pioneer Company with a supply of rations and of water left Mpingo and reached the camp at Nambunjo Hill at 11 a.m., the Battery having simultaneously been sent back to join up with No. 1 Column. Of the 15 *pakhals* which the Pioneers had brought with them six were one-third full only and eight were only half full. The ration did not amount to

WANT OF WATER

half the supply of one hundred and sixty gallons which had been promised, and though it relieved the immediate distress in some slight extent, the whole force was still in a pitiable state of thirst.

As soon as the men had been watered, the Gold Coast Regiment quitted its camp, and moved out to join Captain Methven's force on some high ground north of Mbombomya village; and Captain Methven with B Company then moved south, cleared the village, and reached the water-holes which lay one and a half miles to the west of it, occupying both places. The water-holes at the village itself were all dry, and those beyond were found, to the intense disappointment of the men, only to contain sufficient water to supply the needs of one company. Fresh holes were dug, but the evening of the 21st September found the Regiment almost as severely racked by thirst as ever, and during the day numbers of the men had completely collapsed. During the night the Mbombomya water-holes only yielded a pitiful supply of ten gallons.

The Regiment on the 22nd September had no alternative but to remain inactive at Mbombomya awaiting water which No. 1 Column reported it had forwarded to it; but B Company sent out patrols towards Kihindo Juu and Ndessa, and to the main road between Mnitshi and Marenjende, some ten miles south of Mihambia. Information was also sent to Colonel Rose that the Nigerian Brigade had been at a point four and a half miles west-south-west of Mawerenye—a place some seven miles down the road from Marenjende—at 9.30 that morning; and that No. 2 Column was at

Kitandi to the east of them, based upon Ndessa Juu for its water supply, The Gold Coast Regiment was ordered to move upon Ndessa Chini as soon as possible after it had received the supply of water which had been dispatched to it, and to reach that place by travelling *viâ* Marenjende on the main road.

During the afternoon two officers' patrols from No. 2 Column came into the camp of the Gold Coast Regiment at Mbombonya.

Before nightfall some 800 to 1000 gallons of water reached the Gold Coast Regiment from Mihambia, and the long agony which the men had so patiently endured was at last sensibly relieved. There is no physical privation which human beings in the tropics can experience that is in any way comparable in the intensity of suffering which it occasions to lack of water. Such a shortage can only occur in the hot weather, at a season when the atmosphere is so abnormally dry that a man may feel his very eyebrows lift and stiffen as the last, least drop of moisture is sucked from out of them. All about lies a parched and arid wilderness, here and there blackened by bush-fires, where the leafless trees provide no shade, an environment the very dustiness of which alone occasions an abnormal sensation of thirst ; and the air is charged with ashes and with minute particles of dust, that seem to penetrate and dry up every pore of the skin. Perspiration evaporates almost before it has time to form upon your rough and cracking skin ; and your whole body is subjected to a desiccative process that sets nature clamouring for constant artificial irrigation. If water be available men

THIRST IN THE TROPICS

swill it in unimaginable quantities, and repeat the operation at frequent intervals; but if there be no water, the thought of it—the dream and vision of it—presently absorb the whole of your mental faculties. You may nail your attention to other things, may be deeply occupied by work that ordinarily would engross your whole mind, but throughout, at the back of it all, you are conscious of an insistent need that dwarfs all other things, and for the moment is the one agonizing reality. For you now thirst no longer only with parched mouth, swollen tongue, cracking lips and throat that is dry as a lime-kiln, for each individual pore is gaping and aching with drought which every passing minute renders more acute and unendurable. Such trifles as the discomfort of accumulating dirt which cannot be washed away hardly affect you; the craving to drink has blotted out all other physical sensations. You realize that you are treading a road along which, perilously close ahead, madness lies in ambush.

It says much for the discipline of the men, and for the trust which they repose in their officers that, during those appalling days between the morning of the 19th and the afternoon of the 22nd September, none deserted, straying away from the force on an insane quest for water.

On the 23rd September the Regiment left Mbombomya, and on its arrival at Ndessa Juu, which place was reached without incident, it learned that the Nigerian Brigade, which was working its way southward cutting a path through the bush by means of which its mechanical transport could follow it, had on the preceding day been very heavily engaged with the enemy at a place called Bweho Chini, which lies ten miles away from Riale and to the west of the main road. The Nigerians, it was subsequently ascertained, had here come into collision with the main German forces, under von Lettow-Vorbeck, which had attacked their camp in great strength at about 4.30 p.m., and had continued the assault upon it at intervals until midnight. The enemy suffered very heavy losses and drew off just as the Nigerians' supply of ammunition threatened to give out. His defeat did much to shatter his *morale*, and though he subsequently put up some good fights before he crossed the Rovuma River into Portuguese territory, the severe handling which he received at Bweho Chini may be said to have definitely started him " on the run."

At Ndessa Juu large water-holes were found, and the men of the Regiment were able properly to satisfy their thirst at last. Here also some Indian troops belonging to " Hanforce " were met, and touch was resumed with the mechanical transport, which meant that the men and the carriers, who had been on very short commons ever since the 19th September, once more received full rations.

On the 24th September, the Regiment left Ndessa at 2 p.m. and reached Kitandi, where it camped for the night after a three hours' march. No trace of the enemy was seen during the day.

On the morrow the Regiment marched to Bweho Chini—the scene of the big fight which the Nigerians had had with von Lettow-Vorbeck's main force on the 22nd September—where junc-

AT BWEHO CHINI

tion was effected with No. 1 Column. The rest of the Regiment, under Major Shaw, however, was not in camp, as it was holding an outpost some five miles away from Bweho on a track leading to Beka.

During these two days Lieutenants Bussell and Shaw, Sergeants Campbell and Payne and 71 rank and file joined the Regiment from the Depôt Company at Mpara, and Captain Benham, 14 rank and file, and 5 carriers were evacuated sick.

On the 26th September No. 1 Column marched at dawn, the Gold Coast Regiment acting as the advanced guard, with Major Shaw's detachment, which consisted of A Company, working independently in advance of the column. The immediate objective was Nahungu, a place which lies on the main road and on the left bank of the Mbemkuru River, ten miles south-south-west of Bweho Chini. The enemy were known to have a prepared position of great strength at this place, which is a point where several tracks meet and where the main road on both sides is overlooked by hills.

Major Shaw gained touch with the enemy at 7.30 a.m., and from that time onward the Germans fought a series of rear-guard actions, their whole object on this day and during the operations which immediately followed being, as was afterwards made clear, to cover the retreat of their main body with their baggage, train of porters, and the numerous wounded whom they had borne away from the hard-fought field of Bweho Chini.

At 10.30 a.m., B Company, under Captain

Methven, was sent to join up with A Company under Major Shaw, and the latter was instructed to try to push the enemy rear-guard back upon Nahungu. It was expected that the Nigerian Brigade would be at Naiku River, some six or seven miles north of Nahungu.

It presently became evident, however, that Nahungu was too far off for the column to be able to deliver an attack upon it that day; and the advance guard received instructions to select a site for a camp early in the afternoon. Accordingly, No. 1 Column camped at Beka, and the night passed without incident.

Since the 19th September the Gold Coast Regiment had sustained the following casualties: Captain Wray severely wounded, Lieutenant Percy wounded, 8 soldiers killed, 22 wounded, and 1 carrier killed and 3 wounded.

With the arrival at Beka the first phase of the push south which had been begun on the 19th September may be said to have come to an end, a new one opening on the 27th September with the projected attack upon the enemy stronghold at Nahungu. So far, the enemy's right, against which No. 1 Column had been operating, had been driven from Mihambia, some thirteen miles south to the banks of the Mbemkuru River, a few miles north-west of which his main body had come into such disastrous collision with the Nigerian Brigade. He had now fallen back up the valley of the Mbemkuru for a further distance of fourteen miles to Nahungu, the general line of his retreat being in a south-westerly direction. Sixty miles to the east of Nahungu was the port of Lindi, whence a large force under General Beves was fighting its way, through very hilly and difficult country, along the road leading to von Lettow-Vorbeck's headquarters at Massassi, the general line of this advance being parallel to the enemy's line of retreat up the valley of the Mbemkuru River. Massassi itself lay only some five and sixty miles south of Nahungu, and if it could be captured before the end of the dry season, the expulsion of the Germans from their East African possessions would have been practically effected.

CHAPTER X

NAHUNGU AND MITONENO

ON the 27th September No. 1 Column broke camp at 5.30 a.m. and continued its march to Nahungu from the east, the 2nd Battalion of the 2nd Regiment of the King's African Rifles forming the advanced guard, with the Gold Coast Regiment in support. Simultaneously the Nigerians were advancing upon Nahungu in two columns from the north. Very shortly after leaving camp, the King's African Rifles came into contact with the enemy outposts. The latter fell back, and a ridge situated to the east of Nahungu was occupied without any serious opposition, by the King's African Rifles, by the 27th Mountain Battery, and by the Headquarters and two companies of the Gold Coast Regiment with the Battery. The main road here runs east and west through fairly thick trees and underwood, with the river flowing parallel to it a few hundred yards to the south. The road ascends from a boulder-strewn hollow until the crest of the ridge above mentioned, which is in the nature of a long hogsback along the spine of which the road runs, is reached. It is overlooked on the north-west by Nahungu Hill, a bush and tree-covered eminence which the enemy had strongly fortified, and where a gun was now in position; and it is also commanded from the south-

NAHUNGU HILL

west by Pori Hill, a similar isolated eminence on the other side of the Mbemkuru to the left front of the British, upon which another gun was in position. This piece was of Portuguese manufacture—how obtained no man could say—and its fire proved completely ineffective. The shrapnel burst in the right spot with exemplary regularity, but thereafter pattered down through the trees with less violence than hail, exciting much derision from the men subjected to this innocuous bombardment. The gun at Nahungu Hill was more formidable, but it was put out of action by the 27th Mountain Battery at about 5 p.m.

The King's African Rifles deployed along the crest of the hill, as soon as its summit was nearly reached. The position which they took up was roughly the segment of a circle, with its convex side toward the enemy, and the road bisecting it at right angles. The Pioneers and I Company of the Gold Coast Regiment reinforced the firing-line of the King's African Rifles, which was extended on both sides of the road; and Colonel Rose, realizing that his left flank was exposed, posted a section of I Company with one machine-gun under Captain McElligott, halfway down the hill to the left rear of the firing-line, and there made them dig themselves in. He also sent an officer's patrol furnished by the Pioneer Company, under Captain Buckby, down to the river to watch the movements of the enemy from that direction. Meanwhile A Company under Major Shaw, and B Company under Captain Methven, were held in reserve behind the shelter of the rising ground, and a few hundred yards to the rear.

The moment the presence of the British was discovered, the enemy guns on Nahungu and on Pori Hill both opened fire, and though the gun on the latter did no damage, it was recognized that this hill commanded the left of the Regiment's position, and an officer's patrol under Captain Buckby, as has been mentioned, was sent to the river at 4 p.m. to watch any movement that might be made from that direction. At 5 p.m. the troops on the right got into touch with the Nigerians, but shortly afterwards touch with them was again lost; and half an hour later the Pioneer Company joined up with the firing-line of the King's African Rifles on the left. About the same time B Company, under Captain Methven, was brought forward from the reserve and was halted in the hollow at the base of the rising ground, on the crest of which the fighting was going on.

Though it was hardly anticipated that B Company would be called upon to take part in the action, Captain Methven sent out one native non-commissioned officer's patrol to supplement Captain Buckby's patrol which, earlier in the day, had been dispatched to the river on the south of the position, and he also established a picket of ten men, under Colour-Sergeant Naylor, to guard B Company's left flank. At dusk he went forward to this picket with ten more men to see how the former was faring, and to tell them that they would have to remain for the night in the shallow excavations which they had made. Just as he reached them one of the men of the picket drew attention to a considerable commotion in the bush in the direction of the river, and presently an irregular line of men was seen to be scuttling through the trees and underwood. In the uncertain light the impression at first formed was that they belonged to the King's African Rifles. One of them was carrying a machine-gun on his shoulder, which he set up with extraordinary quickness, and forthwith opened fire at Captain Methven, at a range of not more than thirty yards. He missed him, however, and the men of B Company, who were squatting down barely a hundred yards away, and who, clumped together as they were, presented at that moment an absolutely fool-proof target, were able to fling themselves flat upon the ground and to crawl into a line, whence they opened a hot fire upon the advancing enemy over the head of Captain Methven and his picket of twenty men.

Darkness was now falling, and the movement of the enemy presently developed into a strong attack, the object of which was to outflank the British left, and to work in to the rear of the positions on the ridge. In this attempt he very nearly succeeded, and might well have done so had it not been for the prompt action taken by Major Shaw, who, with A Company, was a hundred yards or more further down the road than the spot occupied by B Company. He rapidly deployed the men under his command, having in the darkness practically to assign his place to each individual, and he in an incredibly short time joined his line up with that formed by B Company, thus presenting a united and continuous front on the British left to the enemy's determined and well-timed counter-attack, upon which A and B Companies now poured a heavy and sustained fire. The section of I Company which, with one machine-gun under the command of Captain McElligott, had dug themselves in earlier in the day on what was now the left of the enemy's line of attack, also came into action with great effect.

Meanwhile Captain Methven's picket had been joined by both the patrols that had been posted near the river, they having contrived to evade the advancing enemy, The little party, however, had a very hot time of it. From their rear, B Company was firing over their heads with machine-gun and rifle. Ahead of them, less than fifty yards away, the enemy was in considerable force and was busy with rifles and machine-gun; while the men of the picket, exposed to this double fusillade, and being compelled to lie as flat as they could to avoid British, no less than German, missiles, threw the bombs, with which some of them were provided, with a wonderful recklessness that caused many to explode in a manner more dangerous to their friends than to their opponents. The fire, too, was very rapid, and its maintenance was essential if the picket were to avoid being rushed and overwhelmed by the enemy; yet it presently became evident that the supply of small-arms ammunition in the men's possession would speedily become exhausted. No one with the picket, except Captain Methven, knew precisely where the Headquarters of the Regiment had been fixed, or could undertake to strike it in the dark; so Captain Methven decided to attempt to find it himself. It was a really desperate venture to try to make one's way through the scrub, with the enemy firing from in front and B Company blazing away from the rear, but

Captain Methven crawled and crouched and ran, now on his feet, now on all-fours, tearing his way through the underwood and scratching and bruising himself from head to foot until, luck befriending him, he contrived to reach headquarters. Here he procured some boxes of ammunition, and managed to impress a couple of Mendi carriers, with whom, dragging a box of ammunition in each hand, he returned to the picket by the perilous route whereby he had left it. It was a gallant deed dashingly done, and it saved the picket; and the prompt action taken by Major Shaw, combined with the pluck and steadiness of the men of B Company, prevented what might well have been an enemy success of some magnitude. On this occasion Corporal Bila Busanga especially distinguished himself by his steadiness and courage, and by the admirable manner in which he kept the men together. As it was, the attack was beaten off at the end of an hour; a perimeter camp was formed; and the night passed without further incident.

Considering the character of the fighting, and the confusion caused at dusk and in the darkness by the enemy's attack upon the left flank, the casualties sustained by the Regiment on this day were light. They amounted to 1 soldier and 2 carriers killed, 21 men wounded, of whom 1 shortly afterwards died, and 13 carriers wounded.

Patrols sent out at dawn on the 28th September reported that, as usual, the enemy had retired during the night; and Pori Hill was forthwith occupied by a patrol of the Gold Coast Regiment under Captain McElligott, and Nahungu Hill by the 2nd Battalion of the King's African Rifles. The rest of No. 1 Column moved forward and occupied the ground between Nahungu Hill and the river.

Two officers' patrols of the Gold Coast Regiment were sent out, one along the road to the west, and one along the north, or left, bank of the river. The former reported that a gun had been retired by that route.

During the afternoon some officers belonging to the Nigerian Brigade, with about fifty men of that corps, came across from their camp to the north to call on the Gold Coast Regiment, they having now joined up with General Hannyngton's force. In the mess great cordiality prevailed, and the incidents of the Nigerians' big fight at Bweho Chini were discussed with eager interest; but among the rank and file of the Gold Coast Regiment this encounter created the greatest excitement and delight. They had long known by report that a host of "their brothers" from West Africa were co-operating with them in the fight against the common enemy; but this was the first time that they had actually seen any of them in the flesh. Many of the men composing both forces belonged to the same tribes, spoke the same language, and had innumerable memories and associations in common. Some may even have been personally known to one another; and this unexpected meeting in the dreary waste places of German East Africa with their kinsmen—men of the familiar types of whom they had seen no representatives for more than fourteen toil-laden months—held for the homesick men of the Gold Coast Regiment something of the reassurance and comfort which is felt at the sight of the welcome face of an old

CAPT. G. M. DOWNER.   CAPT. S. T. LAMONT, M.C.   LIEUT. D. BISSHOPP.
LT.-COL. R. A. DE B. ROSE, C.M.G., D.S.O.   CAPT. E. B. METHVEN, M.C.

To face p. 140.

friend and by his warm hand-grip. Moreover, the rank and file of both corps were comfortably convinced that but for the West Africans the enemy would have had a comparatively easy time of it.

On the 29th September, A, B, and I Companies, under the command of Major Goodwin, left camp at 8 a.m., the rest of the Regiment remaining at Nahungu. This force had instructions to push forward to Mihomo, viâ Kihindi; along the north bank of the Mbemkuru. This river is at Nahungu about forty yards in width, but now, at the height of the dry season, the actual stream was greatly shrunken and ran for the most part little more than two feet deep, though here and there big still pools were occasionally met with. The banks of the river are covered with fairly high trees and bush. After the experiences in the waterless waste to the west of Mihambia, the men of the Regiment had greeted the sight of running water with enthusiasm, and during the preceding day had revelled in a bathe, by means of which the accumulated dust and dirt of ten laborious, parching days were at length scrubbed away.

The function assigned to Major Goodwin's force was that of backing up the South African Cavalry, which had last been heard of at Mihomo Chini; and simultaneously an officer's patrol of 20 men was sent out along the southern, or right, bank of the river with instructions to keep in touch with Major Goodwin if possible.

After advancing about seven and a half miles along the northern bank of the river, Major Goodwin was held up by an enemy party of about 70 rifles and a machine-gun; and on this being telephoned through by him to Headquarters, he was instructed to find a suitable position in which to camp for the night. This he did about half a mile further on. Later in the afternoon the enemy attacked this camp with about 80 rifles and 2 machine-guns. They were driven off without difficulty, but one man of the Gold Coast Regiment was killed and two were wounded.

On the morning of the 30th September the remainder of No. 1 Column marched from Nahungu along the north bank of the river to Major Goodwin's camp; and from the latter place, before the arrival of the column, two officers' patrols were sent out, one to Kihindi Hill and one to reconnoitre the crossings over the river in the direction of Mitoneno on the south bank. These two places are situated nearly opposite one another, with the river separating them, at a distance of about nine miles upstream from Nahungu.

When No. 1 Column arrived in camp, the enemy was found to be still in position on the hills in front of the camp, and the 1st Battalion of the 3rd Regiment of the King's African Rifles were sent to attack him. By nightfall, however, the enemy had not been dislodged.

On the following morning the 1st Battalion of the King's African Rifles, supported by the 27th Mountain Battery, renewed its attack on the enemy's position in front of the camp, while the rest of No. 1 Column, which had now been reinforced by the 129th Baluchis and one section of the 22nd Mountain Battery, attempted a turning movement *viâ* Kihindi and Mitoneno. The patrol

ADVANCE FROM NAHUNGA 143

sent to Kihindi Hill on the preceding day had left there a small picket of one officer and twelve men.

No. 1 Column marched at 6 a.m., the advance guard being formed of the Pioneers and I Company of the Gold Coast Regiment, with the Regimental Headquarters and the Stokes Battery. On reaching the main road, which here runs to the north of the river and parallel to its course, the picket at Kihindi Hill, which reported that the night had passed without incident, was relieved, the relieving party being instructed to remain on the hill till 5 p.m., at which hour it was to rejoin the column.

On reaching the river, patrols were sent out to scout the high ground on the southern bank, and when this was reported clear of the enemy, it was in due course occupied by the Gold Coast Regiment. These movements had resulted in No. 1 Column having slipped in behind the enemy's rear, while his front was still being engaged by the 1st Battalion of the 3rd King's African Rifles and No. 27 Mountain Battery. He was not, however, completely encircled, as a gap still existed toward the south, by means of which he was able later to extricate himself from the dangers that threatened him.

At 2.30 p.m. orders were received to push on towards Mitoneno by the main path running from the east along the south bank of the river, and the 2nd Battalion of the 3rd Regiment of the King's African Rifles were at the same time ordered to advance by a track leading along the right bank. As Mitoneno was approached the King's African Rifles became engaged with the enemy, and the Pioneer Company of the Gold Coast Regiment was pushed forward to get into touch with the right of their line, to achieve which the Pioneers had to cross to the north bank of the Mbemkuru.

At 4 p.m. it was ascertained that the enemy was in position on the south bank also, and two sections of I Company, under Captain McElligott, were sent forward to get abreast of the Pioneer Company and to attempt to envelope the enemy's left. At the same time the rest of I Company and A and B Companies were brought up to be in a position to launch an attack when the exact disposition of the enemy's forces were more clearly known, as, owing to the thick bush, the precise situation remained very obscure. Half an hour later the rest of I Company, under Captain Dawes, was sent forward to join up with the detachment under Captain McElligott, on the right. The 129th Baluchis had in the meantime dug themselves in to the right rear of the Gold Coast Regiment, and as a consequence a large gap was left between I Company's right and the left flank of the Baluchis.

At 4.40 p.m. Captain Dawes reported that he was heavily engaged; that the enemy were working round his right flank; and that he required support. A Company was accordingly sent forward to his assistance, Major Goodwin assuming the command of the firing-line.

The firing all along the front was now fast and furious, and the reserve of small-arms ammunition with the Gold Coast first line was accordingly sent forward, and an urgent message for more was dispatched to the ammunition-column. It was then ascertained that the latter was a long way to

ENGAGEMENT AT MITONENO

the rear of the column and that no further supply of ammunition could be expected for some time to come. This rendered the position one of considerable anxiety, for the firing continued to be very heavy.

Two sections of B Company, under Lieutenant Woods, were now sent forward to reinforce and prolong Captain Shaw's right. A little later a detachment of the 129th Baluchis, a corps which at that time had been almost depleted of its officers, were also sent to prolong the right; but pushing too far forward, and losing their sense of direction after they had come into contact with the enemy, they passed across the front of the right extremity of the firing-line, and as a consequence they suffered a number of unnecessary casualties. About 80 of them, however, eventually joined B Company on the extreme right, and were later joined by 40 more men of their regiment. The two remaining sections of B Company, under Captain Methven, had a little earlier been sent to reinforce the right, but very soon two sections, under Lieutenant Woods, had to be sent back to fill a gap between I and A Companies.

The position with regard to small-arms ammunition was now very serious. The transport-carriers had vanished to a man, and no word could be gained of the ammunition column. However, 20 boxes of cartridges were borrowed from the Baluchis by the Gold Coast Regiment and were taken to the firing-line by the battery carriers—trained men who had stuck to their duty—under the leadership of Captain Foley. Later, when at last a supply was received from the long-lost ammunition column, Lieutenant Baldwin, in charge of the carriers attached to that body, rendered great service in bringing ammunition up and taking it forward to the firing-line.

By 5.30 p.m. the Gold Coast Regiment had thrown the whole of its reserves into the firing-line, and the Pioneer Company, which had been sent to the left, was urgently recalled, but considerable delay inevitably occurred before it was able to rejoin the rest of the Regiment. On the arrival of the Pioneers, just as darkness was falling, one section was at once sent to reinforce Captain Shaw, the remainder being held in reserve.

At 6.15 word reached Colonel Rose that the King's African Rifles on his left had been withdrawn, and Major Goodwin was accordingly instructed to draw in his left. The firing had now died down, only occasional shots being heard. The firing-line was therefore drawn in; a perimeter camp was formed; and the night passed without incident.

On the 2nd October, scouts sent out reported that the enemy had retreated; and patrols from the Baluchis and the 2nd Battalion of the 2nd King's African Rifles were dispatched to the west and the south-west to try to pick up his spoor. The rest of No. 1 Column closed upon the camp formed overnight by the Gold Coast Regiment, where it duly dug itself in.

The casualties sustained by the Gold Coast Regiment in the fighting on the 1st October amounted to 5 men killed, and 3 Europeans, 50 rank and file and 10 carriers wounded.

On the 3rd October, the men of the Gold Coast

A DAY OF REST

Regiment enjoyed that, to them, unusual experience—a day of rest. Ever since leaving the camp at Narungombe, now more than a fortnight earlier, they had been incessantly on the march or in action, and during that time they had had scant leisure to devote to matters of even an essential character which merely concerned their personal comfort. Now at last, during all the hours of daylight, they were free to do as they chose, and to complete their well-being the shrunken stream of the Mbemkuru exhibited in the midst of this thirsty land the rare phenomenon of running water. The day of rest, therefore was converted into a monster washing-day, the men revelling in a succession of baths such as had not been enjoyed by any of them for months, and thereafter, subjecting their clothes and other belongings to an energetic washing and scrubbing and sun-drying till the whole camp was one large *dhobi*-green. It was real refreshment after all their labours and privations, and by evening the men, new-washed, cool and comfortable once more, were in high spirits and were thoroughly ready to resume their duties on the morrow.

CHAPTER XI

RUANGWA CHINI TO MNERO MISSION STATION

THE operations which have formed the subject of the three preceding chapters were designed to drive von Lettow-Vorbeck's main force in a south-easterly direction, until its progress should be stayed by "Linforce." This latter column, in the face of stubborn resistance, and hampered, too, by the inadequate harbour facilities available at Lindi, was fighting its way mile by mile down the road which leads from that place to Massassi, where, as we have seen, von Lettow-Vorbeck had established his General Headquarters. As must inevitably happen in fighting of this character, all the British columns engaged occupied the anomalous, one might almost say the paradoxical, position of attacking forces which were incessantly and perpetually on the defensive. For them were combined all the risks of the attack upon prepared and unreconnoitred positions with all the moral and actual disadvantages which ordinarily attach to the defence. They were, indeed, only properly to be described as attacking forces because it was they that were advancing, the enemy which was retreating before them; but in the daily conflicts with the enemy, in which they were so constantly entangled, the actual attack was usually delivered by the latter. It was he, not the British, who selected the spot where fighting should take place; to him, not to them, were secured, in practical perpetuity, the advantages of surprise and of being the first to open fire; and while he could concentrate all his attention upon the task of hampering, embarrassing and resisting the advance of his opponents, the commanders of British columns and units alike were for ever distracted from the actual fighting by a knowledge of the extreme vulnerability of the formation in which they were compelled to move, and by the precautions necessary to protect it, as far as possible, from assaults upon its flanks. In this rough country, where an advance was only possible along the main roads or along well-worn paths, each column, with its inevitable train of pack-animals and loaded carriers, sprawled down the tracks for miles in the rear of the advancing force, men and beasts alike being often compelled to go in single file. The pace of such a column is that of the slowest man in it, for it is essential that straggling should, as far as possible, be prevented. It is fortunate if the progress made averages a modest two miles an hour—it will much more often approximate to half that rate of advance; yet the actual fighting force, which can be spared from the work of mere protection, cannot abandon the transport and press on ahead for any great distance without the risk of becoming paralyzed for lack of supplies and ammunition, or without exposing the long, snake-like column of unarmed men and terrified animals to an attack that may work in a few moments its complete disintegration.

The circumvention or outflanking of an enemy in these circumstances and in such country, and still more the envelopment of him, are for the most part impossible military feats. Such movements are generally dependent upon the rapid manœuvring of troops, and upon the enemy being kept in complete ignorance of the strategy which his opponent is adopting ; but rapidity of movement was the one thing which could not be insured in the East African bush, save only where a very small body of men was concerned ; and the forces at von Lettow - Vorbeck's command were sufficiently numerous to expose any weak unit, temporarily detached from the main body, to imminent danger of being cut off or overwhelmed. As for secrecy, that was unattainable in country where the enemy's scouts could creep up to within a few yards of a British column without running any save the most slender risk of being observed, and where, when once the main roads were quitted, the passage of any large body of men through the bush inevitably caused an amount of noise and commotion that was nicely calculated to advertise its presence to even the least watchful and suspicious of enemies. When to these things are added the fact that the British attack was always delivered upon an opponent who was perfectly familiar with the geography of the country in which the operations were being conducted, and to whom it was a matter of complete indifference which point of the compass he should select as the direction of his temporary retreat, the handicaps under which the British commanders laboured can be to some extent appreciated.

Where possible mechanical transport was used, and this fact alone served in a great measure to anchor the British columns to the main roads. Sooner or later, however, there came a time or a place at which it was no longer possible to depend even mainly upon motor transport, and thereupon hosts of pack-animals and of head-carriers became the machine of military supply, and the clamorous, snake-like column thus evolved wriggled, with incredible slowness and clamour, into the wilderness of grass and bush. Of the transport mule much has been written, and much more has been said—most of it being unprintable. As for the East African carrier, the late Sir Gerald Portal said the last word about him a full quarter of a century ago. "As an animal of burden," he wrote, "man is out and out the worst. He eats more, carries less, is more liable to sickness, gets over less ground, is more expensive, more troublesome, and in every way less satisfactory than the meanest four-footed creature that can be trained, induced, or forced to carry a load."

The men who took part in the East African campaign are louder than any in the expression of their admiration for von Lettow-Vorbeck, for the pluck and grit and resource which he displayed, for his dogged resolution, and for the fine resistance which he put up, and which may justly be attributed to his individual energy and force of character. Members of the British public, who happily for themselves have no personal experience of bush-fighting, would do well to realize, however, how heavy was the balance of the military advantages which he throughout enjoyed, how completely these discounted any that could be derived by his opponents from mere numerical superiority, and how practically impossible is the task of rounding up in the bush a well-armed and elusive enemy, which had been entrusted to the British commanders. It may even be said that von Lettow-Vorbeck did not really make the most of his opportunities, and that, given the superiority of his armament, he played this game of bush-fighting less skilfully and successfully than it had been played in their time by the Burman and by the Malay. Had he realized, as the Burmese and the Malays both realized, how small a force is needed to check and delay the advance of an enemy column through the bush, and had he thereafter devoted most of his attention to constant harassing attacks upon the terribly vulnerable transport trains, it would have been altogether impossible for the British to drive him, in the course of two dry-weather campaigns, steadily southward from the country north of the Dar-es-Salaam-Lake Tanganyika Railway to beyond the Rovuma River into Portuguese territory.

When all the facts above noted are borne in mind, therefore, it ceases to be in any degree wonderful that von Lettow-Vorbeck's forces—which from first to last never numbered more than five or six thousand *Askari* and perhaps a thousand to fifteen hundred white men—were able to keep their British pursuers chasing them to and fro and up and down the jungles of East Africa for nearly four years, with all the grotesque lack of success with which a dignified middle-aged person runs after his hat upon a windy day.

On the 4th October the Gold Coast Regiment, rested and refreshed, and above all clean once more, took the field again.

As far as could be ascertained, the enemy appeared to be holding positions on the right bank of the Mbemkuru River on the road to Namehi, approximately four and a half miles to the west of Mitoneno. Patrols sent out on the preceding day had drawn fire from him from the hills to the south of the river, and it was General Hannyngton's intention to attempt to hold the enemy by a frontal attack delivered by one battalion drawn from No. 1 Column, while the remainder of that force worked round his right and sought to possess itself of the hilly country to the south. The reserve of "Hanforce" was simultaneously to detail a weak battalion to hold the enemy's left flank, the rest being held ready in support. Meanwhile, across the river on the British right, the 25th Indian Cavalry were to remain at Kihindi, holding themselves in readiness to move, at fifteen minutes' notice, in any direction in which their services might be required.

At dawn on the 4th October No. 1 Column moved out of its camp at Mitoneno, and speedily found itself in action with the enemy. The Gold Coast Regiment, however, was in reserve on this day, and so did not take part in the action. The column fought its way forward for a distance of four miles, and when, fairly late in the afternoon, the Regiment arrived at the place where it was proposed that a perimeter camp should be formed for the night, B Company, under Captain Methven, was sent to hold a flat-crested hill upon the south, from which the camp was commanded. At dusk the enemy fired a few shells over the camp, but the night passed otherwise without incident.

At Ruangwa Chini, which is the name of the place in the neighbourhood of which No. 1 Column had been held up all day, the road at the spot near which the camp was being established runs east and west and roughly parallel to the river, which is distant from it a few hundred yards on the north—the right of the British advance. On the left the country was very difficult, the road being overlooked by a succession of red, laterite hills, for the most part bare of vegetation, though long rank grass sprouted wherever there was a foothold for its roots. The slopes of these hills were covered and strewn with outcrops and boulders of the same red rock, the colour of which is the deep, rich hue that in England is associated with the coombs and lanes of Devon. The principal feature was the high hill which, late in the afternoon, B Company of the Gold Coast Regiment was detailed to occupy in conjunction with the 129th Baluchis. This hill, of naked red rock, rose in an almost precipitous slope, from near the southern edge of the road, to a flat summit, barely fifty yards in breadth, but extending in a position parallel to the track for perhaps ten times that distance. Its southern and western slopes, which were both accessible to the enemy, were much less abruptly graded; but the approach from the east was again very steep. Near the western extremity of this hill the road curved about its foot in a south-westerly direction; and in the thickish bush, which lay between the road and the river on the right front of the British advance, the enemy had got a gun into position, whence it shelled the head of the column from a safe distance. Early in the day the Germans had contrived to shoot down a British aeroplane into the tree-tops in that locality; but the pilot and the observer both escaped without any serious injury, and were able to make their way back to No. 1 Column.

When that morning the British were advancing along the road from their camp at Mitoneno, the 129th Baluchis had scaled the eastern face of the flat-topped hill above described, and had worked along its summit to a point near to its western extremity. Here, however, they had come into contact with an enemy post, which had opened fire upon them with a machine-gun. The Baluchis had twice retired, but later in the day they had dug their way from the road to the base of the northern face of the hill, and thence had climbed the steep ascent to its summit, where they had dug themselves in in a line of rifle-pits drawn across the flat top at a point about halfway along its length.

Meanwhile Lieutenant Foster of the 27th Mountain Battery had climbed with his orderly up the eastern face of the hill, and from there was engaged in observing for his unit the German fire from the gun posted in the bush on the right front of the British advance. He presently became aware that a party of the enemy was working its way up the gentle slope on the southern side of the hill at a spot to the rear of the place where the Baluchis were dug in ; and Lieutenant Foster and his orderly, taking cover behind a boulder, opened fire upon the enemy with revolver and rifle, and for a time actually succeeded in staying or delaying his advance.

This was the position of affairs when B Company, under Captain Methven, who had been ordered to dig himself in at a spot near the foot of the eastern extremity of the hill, in order to guard the left and left rear of the column, was instructed to quit his entrenchments and go to the assistance of the Baluchis on the summit. He and his men scaled the steep eastern face of the hill, which the Baluchis had climbed in the course of their first advance that morning, and were in time to relieve Lieutenant Foster and his orderly, who were still maintaining their plucky lone-hand fight. B Company then worked along the southern edge of the crest until it had lined up abreast of the Baluchis in their shallow rifle-pits, and thence pushed forward to the western extremity of the hill, from whence the enemy was already retiring down the slope leading to his main position. Here B Company dug itself in for the night, having effectually relieved the camp from the menace to which the occupation of this summit by the enemy had exposed it.

In the course of this operation B Company lost 1 private killed, 5 wounded, and 1 machine-gun carrier wounded.

On the 5th October, patrols sent out at dawn came almost immediately into touch with the enemy, who was estimated to have some five companies in position at Ruangwa Chini, about two miles to the west—namely, in the direction of the column's advance. The 129th Baluchis, the

NO. 1 COLUMN MOVES

1st Battalion of the 3rd Regiment of the King's African Rifles, and the 2nd Battalion of the 2nd Regiment of that corps were dispatched to attack the position, supported by the 27th Mountain Battery and the Kilwa Battery. This hilly and rocky laterite country was very difficult, however, and by 3.30 p.m. so little progress had been made that Colonel Orr decided to break off the attack, and to withdraw the units that had been engaged in it to the camp which the column had occupied on the preceding afternoon.

The Gold Coast Regiment was not engaged during the day, but one of its carriers was wounded by a stray bullet.

On the 6th October, No. 1 Column marched at dawn, working through the bush in a southerly direction for the purpose of outflanking the right of the enemy's position, and of cutting off his retreat, should he attempt to make use of any of the paths leading toward the south. The troops in reserve remained in camp to hold the enemy in front, and to be ready to thrust forward if the flanking movement proved successful. The 27th Cavalry, meanwhile, had instructions to co-operate from the left bank of the Mbemkuru.

No. 1 Column was able to get into a position well to the rear of that which the enemy had occupied on the preceding day, but the Germans had retired from it during the night, leaving only a party of some forty men to watch and delay the movements of the British troops. On the approach of the latter this small band dispersed, and a part of it, which had apparently got "bushed," consisting of one German and ten *Askari*, was captured.

No. 1 Column, suffering somewhat from the disillusionment and disappointment which are the prevailing sentiments that bush-fighting commonly inspires in a pursuing force, accordingly worked its way laboriously back to the main road, where it learned that the rest of the column, which had encountered no resistance, was encamped about two and a half miles ahead of it.

The check at Ruangwa Chini is, in a measure, typical of military operations in the bush. By it the enemy had been able to reduce the advance achieved in the space of three days by a force, greatly its numerical superior, to a matter of seven or eight miles; and in accomplishing this he had exposed himself to no inconvenience and to negligible danger.

On the 7th October No. 1 Column resumed its interrupted march down the main road, which here runs west, with the river parallel to it upon the right. The Gold Coast Regiment, less two companies and the battery, furnished the advance guard. A distance of between eight and nine miles was traversed during the day, and a camp was taken up for the night near Kiperele Chini.

The 25th Cavalry were encamped, with one company of the Gold Coast Regiment, at a spot about a mile and a quarter further down the road.

On the 8th October No. 1 Column marched down the main road, and camped for the night at Mbemba, which is distant some ten miles from Kiperele Chini.

AT MNERO MISSION STATION 159

From this point the road which No. 1 Column had been following more or less continuously ever since it started pushing south from Narungombe, runs on, in a south-westerly direction, still adhering closely to one or another bank of the river. About ten miles from Mbemba it strikes the main Liwale-Massassi road, at a place named Mangano, and here the 25th Cavalry captured large quantities of stores belonging to the Germans. These stores, however, consisted exclusively of native food-stuffs such as mealies, the kind of millet locally called *mantana*, cassava and a little rice—bulky stuff which, since it could not be carried off, was burned to prevent it again falling into the enemy's hands.

On the 9th October No. 1 Column left the main road and the banks of the Mbemkuru River, and turning off to the left along a narrow track, pushed forward in a south-south-easterly direction to Lihonja, distant from Mbemba a matter of some seven miles. Here the main Liwale-Massassi road was struck by the Column for the first time—a really first-class laterite highway, some twenty to twenty-five feet in width, running through grass country and open bush, with a surface consolidated by constant traffic. This road was now followed for a distance of about nine miles, and the Column camped for the night at a mission station named Mnero. This is a pretty little station, with mission buildings and church perched upon a low hill, and with at least a mile square of well-cultivated land lying around it. The church was subsequently used by the British as an advance hospital for their sick and wounded.

During October 9th, as on the two preceding

days, the advance of No. 1 Column had been accomplished without incident.

Eight miles down the road from Mnero Mission Station, to the east and slightly to the south of that place, lies Ruponda, where yet another large food depôt was known to have been established by the enemy, and this was now the Column's immediate objective.

Having quitted the banks of the Mbemkuru, the British troops were once again dependent upon water-holes, but the country was here less arid than it had been further north between Narungombe and Nahunga; and at Mnero itself, and thence all along the line of march eastward and southward, a sufficient, and at times even an abundant, supply of water was available either in existing water-holes or to be obtained by digging.

With the quitting of Mbemkuru Valley and the push to the south upon which No. 1 Column was now embarked, the second phase of the advance may be said to have ended and the third phase to have begun.

GOLD COAST REGIMENT.
Men in marching order.

To face p. 160.

CHAPTER XII

LUKULEDI

THE position at this moment was approximately as follows. After the taking of Nahungu on the 28th September it had become evident to the British Command that it was not possible to feed and supply all the troops assembled in that area, and the Nigerian Brigade was accordingly given a week's rations, and with Major Pretorius acting as its guide, was bidden to march across country, by such tracks as it could find, to join up with "Linforce" on the Lindi-Massassi road. This was a somewhat perilous adventure, for, though the Nigerian Brigade carried with them only a week's rations, it was anticipated that this cross-country march would probably occupy a period of at least ten days. The area about to be traversed, moreover, was very little known, and no exact information was forthcoming concerning the numbers or the disposition of the enemy's troops between the Mbemkuru River and the Lindi-Massassi road. In Major Pretorius, however, the Nigerians possessed a tower of strength. This remarkable man, who in peace-time had been a professional elephant-hunter, not only knew the highways and byways of British and German East Africa more intimately than any other living soul, but had established over the native population a species of hypnotic influence. Though von Lettow-Vorbeck had placed a price upon his head, and though from time to time some unusually daring person had the hardihood and the imprudence to attempt to earn it, the gang of native toughs and scalawags whom he gathered around him and who aided him in his scouting, regarded him with an almost superstitious reverence and served him with unshakable fidelity. On this occasion he piloted the Nigerians across country, by footpaths and through the bush, for a distance of more than fifty miles as the crow flies, and brought them safely to their destination, though in the course of their march they had one very severe encounter with the enemy in which one of their battalions sustained heavy casualties.

Ever since they began their march inland from Lindi, the troops composing "Linforce," with which the Nigerian Brigade had now joined up, had experienced persistent and very effective resistance from the enemy in the difficult, hilly country through which the Lindi-Massassi road runs; and at the time of the arrival of the Nigerians they had only succeeded in progressing along this highway for a distance of about thirty miles from their base. The enemy troops opposing them, like those which were resisting the advance of "Hanforce," were based upon von Lettow-Vorbeck's General Headquarters, which, as we have seen, were established at Massassi; and to the security of this place the advance of the converging British columns was now presenting a constantly increasing menace.

Von Lettow-Vorbeck, at the time of the arrival of No. 1 Column at the mission station at Mnero,

ADVANCE ON RUPONDA 163

was reported to be at Ruwanga, a spot in the centre of the base of a roughly isosceles triangle whereof the sides are formed respectively by the Mbemkuru River and the road from Mbemba to Ruponda. He was said to be occupying a strongly fortified position, and to have with him not less than ten companies of troops. The nearest British force was No. 2 Column of " Hanforce," which was operating to the left and east of No. 1 Column; and it was confidently anticipated that von Lettow-Vorbeck would reinforce Ruponda now that that important food depôt was threatened by the occupation of Mnero.

On the arrival of No. 1 Column at the last-named place, on the 9th October, the 25th Cavalry pushed on towards Ruponda, and at 8 p.m. the Gold Coast Regiment followed in their wake, with orders to support them and to get as near to Ruponda as might prove to be possible. The rest of the Column was to march at 2 a.m.

At 1 a.m. on the 10th October the native guides with the Gold Coast Regiment reported that Ruponda village, which was said to be occupied by the 8th Schutzen Company, was only a short distance ahead. No trace of the 25th Cavalry was found, however, and it was supposed that they must have left the main road and that they must be camping somewhere in the bush.

At 5 a.m. orders were received by the Gold Coast Regiment to march upon Ruponda at 5.30 a.m., acting as the advanced guard of the column, and about the same time touch was at last obtained with the 25th Cavalry, who reported that Ruponda was occupied by the enemy and was being held against the column's advance. This was confirmed shortly afterwards when the advanced guard of the Regiment was fired upon as it drew near to the village; and I Company and the Pioneer Company thereupon moved forward to the attack, the remainder of the Regiment simultaneously making a flanking movement in order to occupy some high ground on the north-east of Ruponda.

As the attack developed, however, the Germans were found to be few in numbers, and while I Company continued to engage them, the rest of the Regiment pushed round the right flank of the enemy's position to seize some high ground and to prevent any possible reinforcements from Ruwanga joining up with the little force in occupation of Ruponda. This movement was carried out, no opposition being met with, and as the position was found to be a good one for defensive purposes, No. 1 Column advanced and formed a camp upon the high ground which the Gold Coast Regiment had occupied.

I Company was still engaging a small party of the enemy, and the 129th Baluchis were sent to the village to clear up the situation. The Germans then withdrew, and the large stocks of native foodstuffs which had been accumulated at Ruponda fell, practically undefended, into the hands of the British. The casualties amounted to one man of I Company killed.

From the 10th to the 16th October inclusive, No. 1 Column remained encamped at Ruponda, sending out patrols in all directions to reconnoitre the surrounding country, digging water-holes, and performing other similar duties. At noon on the 10th October a small party of the enemy, consisting of about forty men with a machine-gun, sniped the camp for about half an hour, inflicting a few casualties; and once or twice the patrols from Ruponda came into touch with enemy scouting parties.

The German correspondence captured at this place showed that the state of things in the enemy camp was very far from happy. Von Lettow-Vorbeck appears to have inspired all his subordinates with fear, but the admiring affection with which he is believed to have been regarded by his *Askari* does not seem to have been shared by many of even the more senior of his European subordinates. As was to be expected in the circumstances in which the Germans had now so long been living, food bulked big in their thoughts and in their imaginations; and as a topic it filled a wholly disproportionate space in much of the correspondence captured. As the large stocks of native food-stuffs seized by the British at Nangano and again at Ruponda clearly showed, the *Askari* were for the most part well fed and well cared for; but cassava and maize and millet, which will perfectly content an African, form a sadly monotonous and unsatisfying diet for white men who have to make of them their staple for many months on end. The Germans waxed almost lyrical in their correspondence when at long intervals fortune sent a pig or some such infrequent luxury their way; but they devoured them in haste, like the Israelites of old, and wrote in terms of the most explicit dispraise of the disgusting greediness, the gross selfishness, and the predatory character of their Chief. No food was apparently secure when that energetic person had got wind of its existence. For the rest, the correspondence showed that all the European rank and file in the German camp were sick unto death of this protracted and, in their opinion, futile resistance; that their dread of von Lettow-Vorbeck and of the prompt and exemplary punishments to which he on occasion resorted, alone chained them to their duty; and that in spite of their Commander-in-Chief's great influence over the *Askari*, the native soldiers, too, were heartily weary of the war, and had of late been deserting in large numbers. Every one concerned, except von Lettow-Vorbeck himself, appeared, indeed, to be ripe for surrender; and it is a wonderful tribute to the energy, to the force of character, and to the resolution of this man that, with such sentiments prevailing all around him and growing daily more and more intense, the campaign was maintained up to the date upon which, a year later, the Armistice was signed, purely and solely *because he so willed it.*

On the 16th October the 2nd Battalion of the 2nd Regiment of the King's African Rifles, with a detachment of the Pioneers of the Gold Coast Regiment, left Ruponda and marched down the Massassi road, about thirteen miles to Chingwea, there to prepare a camp and develop the water supply in anticipation of the advance of No. 1 Column. No. 2 Column was at this time operating on the left of No. 1 Column, and was reported to be at a place some ten miles north of Ruwanga;

ADVANCE-GUARD WORK 167

and word was also received that "Linforce" had advanced down the Lindi-Massassi road as far as Mtama, which is nearly thirty-three miles from Lindi, and had expelled the enemy from the former place.

On the 17th October, No. 1 Column, to which a company of the Gold Coast Regiment, under Major Shaw, acted as advanced guard, left Ruponda and marched to Chingwea, without incident. On the following morning a start was made at 5.30 a.m., the mission station at Lukuledi, about twelve miles further down the road, being the objective on that day.

The Gold Coast Regiment formed the advance-guard on this occasion, B Company, under Captain Methven, preceding the main body, from which at the outset it was separated by a distance of about 400 yards. B Company at this time was not quite 160 strong, including 4 officers—Captain Methven, and Lieutenants Woods, Baillie and S. B. Smith—and 1 British non-commissioned officer, Colour-Sergeant Cuneen. It was accomplished by Captain Gush, a member of the West African Medical Staff. With B Company there also went the 7th Light Armoured Car Battery, which consisted of two Rolls-Royce cars, each of which was armed with a machine-gun and was manned by an officer and two men, all of whom were Europeans. These cars were surmounted by armour-plated turrets, in which the machine-guns were placed; and the driver was similarly protected, the only vulnerable spot being the narrow window through which he looked when driving the car. The bonnet was also protected by armour, but the wheels, which were furnished with pneumatic tyres, were exposed to any fire that might be brought to bear upon the vehicle. At a later date cars of this description were provided with patent tyres of a special character, which were not capable of being punctured.

At a point about three miles from the camp the 1st Battalion of the 3rd Regiment of the King's African Rifles had overnight established a post, and from here that Regiment now entered the bush on the right side of the road. Its instructions were to make a wide sweeping movement to the west and south in such a manner as to enable it to deliver an attack upon the mission station at Lukuledi from the rear and right flank of that position, which should be timed so as to synchronize with the arrival of the Gold Coast Regiment in front of it.

As soon as the 1st Battalion of the 3rd King's African Rifles had taken to the bush, the Gold Coast Regiment continued its march down the road, B Company being still a few hundred yards ahead. As Captain Methven advanced, he sent out patrols to the right and left to explore the numerous paths which here ran criss-cross on both sides of the main road; and after he had advanced some miles upon his way, he deployed his company, the two armoured cars keeping, however, to the main road. The country through which he was passing is for the most part open bush with low scrub, scattered trees and much grass. All the vegetation was parched and sun-dried, and there were frequent blackened patches where the grass had been burned to stubble and where the trees were charred and leafless.

NATIVE INFORMATION

B Company's advance proceeded without incident until about eight miles had been covered and only four more separated the little force from the mission station on the other side of the dried-up bed of the Lukuledi River. At this point a small black boy, wearing a blue waist-skirt, was met sauntering quite unconcernedly down the centre of the road. Though he was only about twelve years of age, and quite alone, he manifested neither fear nor excitement at finding himself thus suddenly confronted by a body of armed men, and he answered the questions addressed to him with the grave maturity of demeanour that is so often to be observed in native children, and which sits so quaintly upon them. Captain Methven, and many of the men of the Company, had picked up a working knowledge of Swahili during their campaigning in East Africa, so communication with the child was easy enough, and from him it was learned that there were a good many Germans and *Askari* at the mission-station, but that they had packed up their gear and apparently meditated an early departure. He added that there was a small enemy post just across the dried-up bed of the Lukuledi River on the left of the advance. The small boy was passed back under escort to the Headquarters of the Gold Coast Regiment, and B Company resumed its march.

About two miles before the mission station at Lukuledi is reached, the road breasts a fairly steep ascent, the crest of which is perhaps a mile and a half from the mission buildings. From the summit of this rise the road dips in a long slope to the Lukuledi River—a stream some twenty or thirty feet in width, with low water-worn banks, and at this season of the year without a drop of moisture anywhere visible in the cracked, sun-baked mud which composes its bed. At the foot of the hill the road crosses this river-bed, and bending slightly to the right climbs the hill on the summit of which the mission station is situated. The surface of this hill is pitted near its base by a few shallow folds and hollows, and toward the left of the advance there were patches of shortish grass. For the rest, however, the vegetation had been burned off and the grass reduced to blackened stubble not more than an inch or two in length.

On the top of the hill some of the mission buildings were enclosed in a *boma*—a zariba or stockade constructed of impenetrable thorn bushes —which blocked the road. To the left rear of this stockade, as viewed from the front, the road once more emerged from it, and passing a substantial, two-storeyed dwelling-house built of red locally-burned bricks, that occupied a position on its left, it ran on two to three hundred yards to the church, which was built of the same material and was surmounted by a high spire. Behind the station, the country was covered by the same open bush, scattered trees, grass and occasional scrub already described. From the valley of the Lukuledi, which separated the Mission Hill from the hill whence the road led down to the river crossing, some fairly high trees rose to a sufficient height for their tops partially to obscure the depth of the depression in which they were rooted.

The summit of the hill leading down to the river crossing was very bare, the grass on each side having been completely burned away, and on arrival here Captain Methven felt convinced that his little force, which was now nearly two miles in advance of the rest of the Regiment, must be clearly visible from the mission station. Owing to the mass of the tree-tops rising from the river valley, it is doubtful, however, whether he was right in this conjecture; but as he advanced a solitary shot was twice fired from the bush upon his left. Believing himself to be under observation from the mission station, Captain Methven deployed his men on either side of the road in the sparse bush and grass, in order to provide them with such cover as was available, and he then began to descend the hill, the armoured cars moving forward with him, but of course remaining on the highway. Halfway down the hill the rearmost car suddenly developed engine trouble, and had to be left behind.

The section of B Company which was under Lieutenant Woods' command led the advance, and on reaching the river crossing it found that, though an enemy post had been established on the far side of it and to his left, as had been accurately reported by the small boy, it had now been withdrawn. Woods therefore crossed the river, and proceeded up the road until the *boma* was reached. There was no sign of the enemy, and he accordingly went back down the road and reported to Captain Methven that he believed the station to be unoccupied, and that he had sent a small party forward to confirm this fact.

B Company was then deployed along the base of the Mission Hill, the section on the left wing being under the command of Lieutenant S. B. Smith, that next to it being under Lieutenant Baillie, while the centre, with which was the machine-gun, was astride the road, under Captain Methven and Colour-Sergeant Cuneen, with Lieutenant Woods' section upon its right. The formation of the company was thus an irregular semicircular line, the men being in extended order; and it was thus that, at about 2.30 p.m., the advance up the hill was begun.

The few shallow folds and hollows in the surface of the hill near its base had been left behind, and B Company had advanced about a hundred yards into the wide belt of bare and fire-blackened earth which extended thence to the edge of the *boma*, when fire was suddenly opened upon it from machine-guns placed in the bush to the right and left of the mission station, while from behind the *boma* there came a tremendous burst of rifle-fire. The enemy had watched the approach of B Company, and had held his fire awaiting the psychological moment to attack. Now, when Captain Methven's little force had reached a position where no cover was to be found for a hundred yards or more in any direction, the Germans suddenly subjected their opponents to a withering cross-fusillade. Shortly afterwards a party of the enemy, about 150 strong, was seen to emerge from behind the mission house to the right rear of their position, and to run at a double into some long grass with the evident intention of outflanking the left of the line formed by B Company.

The position in which Captain Methven's little force found itself was desperate, no less; but, as usual, the courage, the discipline and the steadfastness of the men were beyond praise. Hugging the bare ground as closely as they might they returned the enemy's fire; but save the *boma*, they had no target at which to aim, while the Germans were firing upon them, as the accuracy of their marksmanship proved, at ranges which had been carefully ascertained in advance.

Captain Methven brought his machine-gun into action, and Colour-Sergeant Cuneen, who was working it, was immediately killed. Sergeant-Major Mama Juma, who took his place, was instantly hit, and though it was now evident that the enemy had the position of this gun "taped," as it is called, and that it was practically certain death for any one to touch it, the gun-team continued to try to serve it until every man among them had been killed or wounded. From end to end of the line the casualties were now very heavy, but retreat was even more dangerous than the continued occupation of this mercilessly exposed position; and B Company maintained its ground, and manfully tried to return the enemy's fire. On the right, Lieutenant Woods was killed early in the action, but Sergeant Yessufu Mamprusi at once assumed command of the section, and continued to direct and steady his men. In the centre, where the casualties were very heavy, Colour-Sergeant Cuneen had been killed and the whole of the machine-gun team had been put out of action, while Captain Methven had been thrice wounded in the same leg—a leg which already bore the scar of a wound received some months earlier on the western front in France.

The foremost armoured car, contrary to orders, had come right up into the firing-line, thus presenting a target to the enemy which caused the men lying to the right and left of it to be subjected to a specially devastating fire. Both this car and its fellow, which had overcome its engine troubles, and had crept up the hill, had had their tyres shot to ribbons; the driver of the leading car had been wounded in the eye, through the window of his vehicle, and the machine-guns with which they were armed were quite unable effectively to retaliate upon the enemy.

On the left of Captain Methven, Lieutenant Baillie had been shot through both feet, and had contrived to drag himself back into an isolated patch of grass and scrub, in which he was now lying. Further to the left again, Lieutenant S. B. Smith alone survived unharmed, but though the grass here afforded a certain amount of cover for his section, his position was being outflanked and enfiladed by the enemy.

Meanwhile the rest of the Regiment had arrived at the summit of the hill leading down to the river crossing, and the Pioneer Company was sent forward to the relief of B Company, with Major Goodwin in command. The slope was descended, the river-bed was crossed, and the Pioneers took cover in such hollows in the surface of the hill near its base and right flank as they could find. It was in one of these hollows that Captain Methven presently met Major Goodwin, with whom the position was discussed; but it was evident that B Company, more than a third of whom were now casualties, could not be with-

LIEUTENANT R. SAUNDERSON 175

drawn, and that any attempt to reinforce their firing-line would only result in a useless sacrifice of life. All that could be done was for B Company to remain where it was, and to endure the terrible punishment to which it had been exposed for more than an hour. The fire continued to be so hot that many of the dead and wounded in the firing-line were being hit over and over again.

Lieutenant Saunderson was sent forward from the Pioneer Company to take over the section, at that time being commanded by Sergeant Yessufu Mamprusi, on the extreme left of the line; and very shortly after his arrival he attempted and led a desperate charge against the *boma*. His men loyally followed him, but the feat attempted was impossible of achievement, and their gallant young leader fell riddled with bullets within a yard of that impenetrable stockade of thorns. Here his body was recovered next day, having during the night been partially buried by the Germans, and several of his section lay dead around him. Sergeant Yessufu Mamprusi, however, who had himself taken part in the charge, led the survivors back to their former position, where they remained during the remainder of the afternoon. This non-commissioned officer, who throughout showed great coolness and courage, and who continued to command his men to the very end of the day, was himself wounded in three places.

Robert de Bedick Saunderson, who here lost his life, was just six-and-twenty years of age. He had been appointed an Assistant District Commissioner in the Gold Coast in January, 1915, served in Ashanti for a few months, and then was attached to the Gold Coast Regiment at Kumasi, being accounted "one of the lucky ones" by his brother officers, in that his application to be seconded for military service had been approved. In April of the following year he returned from leave, and was for a time employed in the Secretariat at Accra; but when in April, 1917, the second draft was dispatched from the Gold Coast to reinforce the troops in East Africa, Mr. Saunderson accompanied it, and was with the Regiment, except when incapacitated by sickness, until he fell at Lukuledi in the manner just described.

Meanwhile Lieutenant Foster, of whose lone-hand fight mention has been made in connection with the action at Ruwanga Chini, had crossed the river and made his way up the hill to the hollow on the northern slope of it where Major Goodwin was halted. His business, as usual, was to try to observe for the 27th Mountain Battery, to which he was attached, and which had now opened fire from the opposite hill upon the buildings in the *boma*, and upon the area between the big dwelling-house and the church. Here he learned from Captain Methven of the position in which Lieutenant Baillie was lying in a little patch of bush to the right rear of his section, most of whom were now casualties. To reach this spot about one hundred yards of burned stubble, in which not a square inch of cover was anywhere obtainable, had to be crossed. This area, throughout the afternoon, had been swept by the enemy's rifles and machine-guns, which had the range to a nicety. Lieutenant Foster was warned by Captain Methven that it was almost certain death to attempt to reach

FOSTER'S GALLANT ACT

Lieutenant Baillie, but this information had no deterrent effect, and Lieutenant Foster not only went out, but actually succeeded in bringing Lieutenant Baillie safely back to the dressing-station without either of them being hit. In any other war this gallant exploit would have won, as it surely merited, the Victoria Cross. As it was, the Military Cross was awarded to Lieutenant Foster for this signal act of heroism. Captain Gush, while dressing Lieutenant Baillie's wounds, was himself shot through the arm.

The remainder of the Gold Coast Regiment had now moved down the hill, and had dug itself in at a spot on the slope above the river crossing; while the rest of No. 1 Column had halted on the crest whence, as has been noted, the 27th Mountain Battery had come into action. How far their fire was effective could not be ascertained, but it afforded the only relief that was to come to B Company during this trying afternoon, and about this time the enemy's fire showed signs of slackening.

From the position which the Regiment had taken up Major Shaw was sent with three sections of I Company to occupy some high ground on the east and south-east, and to gain touch with Major Goodwin and the Pioneers. I Company was at that time the only company in reserve, and the left and right flanks of the Regiment were therefore very much exposed. No information could be gathered as to the whereabouts of the 1st Battalion of the 3rd King's African Rifles, and the orders issued to Major Shaw were therefore cancelled, the left flank of the Regiment being made secure by posting

A Company and three sections of I Company there to guard it.

This movement had hardly been completed before the enemy delivered a vigorous counter-attack upon the left of the Regiment's position. It was carried out with great determination, but it was beaten off without difficulty by Major Shaw, and as the *Askari* exposed themselves much more recklessly than usual, it was thought that considerable losses were inflicted upon the enemy. Such beliefs were, however, throughout this campaign, for the most part mere matters of speculation and conjecture, for the enemy attached great importance to the removal of his dead and wounded, and generally left as little trace as possible of any misfortune that might have befallen him.

Toward dusk the enemy fire died down, and as soon as darkness had fallen the Pioneers, the two armoured cars, and all that was left of B Company were withdrawn from the position on the hill, which the latter had occupied for nearly four hours, and fell back to the slope across the river upon which the rest of the Gold Coast Regiment lay entrenched. The remainder of No. 1 Column lay encamped on the road about a mile further to the rear.

The casualties sustained on that afternoon were Lieutenants Woods and Saunderson and Colour-Sergeant Cuneen killed, and Captains Methven and Gush and Lieutenant Baillie wounded, while 10 of the rank and file were killed and 25 were wounded, and of the gun-carriers 2 were killed and 7 wounded—in all 15 killed and 35 wounded, many

B COMPANY'S CASUALTIES

of the latter being hit more than once. The total casualties thus numbered 50 out of a total of about 160 men actually engaged. The enemy had set their trap with cunning and dexterity. It was one in which, given the circumstances of the advance, it was not possible for B Company to avoid being caught. A detachment of the King's African Rifles succeeded in reaching the neighbourhood of the church during the afternoon, but the place was at that time being shelled by the 27th Battery so heavily that a withdrawal was considered necessary.

Captain Methven, who had already earned a Military Cross on the Western Front, was awarded a bar to that decoration for the gallant service he had rendered from the time he occupied Liwinda Ravine on the 9th August to the 18th October, when he was repeatedly but happily not fatally wounded, in that death-trap on the Mission Hill at Lukuledi.

CHAPTER XIII

EXPULSION OF VON LETTOW-VORBECK FROM GERMAN EAST AFRICA

On the 19th October patrols sent out at dawn reported that the enemy had retired. The 1st Battalion of the 3rd Regiment of the King's African Rifles accordingly occupied the mission *boma* and the church, while the remainder of No. 1 Column camped on the crest of the hill to the north, overlooking the valley of the Lukuledi, from which on the preceding day Captain Methven had caught his first view of the mission buildings. Before this move was made, I Company of the Gold Coast Regiment was dispatched to occupy a ridge to the north-east of the camp in which the Regiment had passed the night; and from here a strong officer's patrol was sent out along the road which runs in an easterly direction from Lukuledi to Chikukwe. At 3 p.m. a detachment of the 1st Battalion of the 3rd King's African Rifles took over this post from I Company; and at 6 p.m. the patrol along the Chikukwe road returned and reported that it had obtained touch with the enemy at a point about four miles down the road.

During the day the Battery rejoined the Gold Coast Regiment, and the 129th Baluchis rejoined No. 1 Column.

ENEMY MOVEMENTS

On the 20th October the enemy delivered an attack in force upon the 1st Battalion of the 3rd Regiment of the King's African Rifles, who were in occupation of the Mission Hill. This attack was the result of certain rapid movements that von Lettow-Vorbeck had made during the past few days, which are of sufficient importance to warrant some detailed description.

As we have seen, he had last been heard of at Ruwanga, a point some sixteen miles north-east of Ruponda; and on the arrival of No. 1 Column at the Mission Station of Mnero, it had been confidently anticipated that he would take energetic steps to defend his food depôts at Ruponda. Instead, leaving perhaps three companies with six machine-guns to resist the British advance at Lukuledi, he marched rapidly eastward, and joined forces with the troops which were opposing "Linforce" near Mtama, on the Lindi-Massassi road. He here fought two severely contested actions with "Linforce," at Njengao and at Mahiwa, which places are only two or three miles apart, the former being about four miles further down the Linda road than Mtama. The brunt in both these engagements was borne by the Nigerians and by General O'Grady's Brigade, which was mainly composed of battalions of the King's African Rifles, who succeeded in inflicting unusually heavy losses on von Lettow-Vorbeck's forces, but themselves suffered even more serious casualties. It was estimated at the time that the enemy lost 800 men killed and wounded, and that the British loss was approximately 2000.

Satisfied that he had now done enough temporarily to paralyse the advance of "Linforce," von Lettow-Vorbeck forthwith set off post-haste down the main road in the direction of Massassi, taking with him four of the companies which had been in action with the Nigerians both at Njengao and at Mahiwa. Pushing on very rapidly to Chigugu, he left two companies there, and picked up three fresh ones which had been in action at Lukuledi on the 18th October.

His plan was to approach the last-named place from the south with the men under his command, advancing from the direction of Massassi, while the two companies which he had left at Chigugu simultaneously attacked the left flank of the British from the east. These concerted movements were timed to be executed on the morning of the 20th October.

On that day the 1st Battalion of the 3rd King's African Rifles, supported by the 25th Cavalry, had orders to advance toward Massassi, and it had actually set forth upon its march when it suddenly found itself confronted by von Lettow-Vorbeck's five companies, with which were two guns. The King's African Rifles took up a position south of the church, which completely dominated the German attack, and though the bulk of the 25th Cavalry failed to support them, they, in the fight which ensued, not only inflicted heavy losses upon the enemy but caused him to abandon two of his machine-guns, and took from him also a number of prisoners.

It is worth noting that during the British attack upon the Mission Hill at Lukuledi, on the 18th October, care had been exercised to avoid

THE ENEMY WITHDRAWS

shelling the church. Von Lettow-Vorbeck's gunners were hampered by no corresponding scruples, and one of their first acts was to bring the tall spire down with a crash.

Meanwhile the two German companies left by von Lettow-Vorbeck at Chigugu had made their way across to a spot north of the main camp and a mile or so up the road, where the 25th Cavalry had their encampment. They found it practically undefended, and they in a few moments reduced it to a woeful state of chaos. The horses left in it were slaughtered, stores and equipment were destroyed, and everything which was spoilable was completely ruined.

The 129th Baluchis had been sent forward to support the 1st Battalion of the 3rd King's African Rifles on the Mission Hill, and the camp was taken over by the Gold Coast Regiment with the 2nd Battalion of the 2nd King's African Rifles in reserve. The enemy force which had demolished the camp of the 25th Cavalry, twice attempted to attack during the day, but on both occasions were beaten off without difficulty. That was all that these two companies were able to achieve, and von Lettow-Vorbeck's main attack having met with no success, the Germans drew off, probably in the direction of Massassi. The enemy's troops had been worked with merciless severity during the past few days. They had fought two severe actions on the Lindi road, and thereafter had covered by dint of forced marches a distance of not less than fifty miles. Without rest or refreshment they had then been launched upon an attack against Lukuledi, where they had encountered very effective resistance from the 1st Battalion of the 3rd King's African Rifles. The prisoners captured were pitifully exhausted; and there can be little doubt that von Lettow-Vorbeck on this occasion subjected his willing troops to a strain beyond their strength.

In these circumstances it is all the more regrettable that at this moment orders were received by No. 1 Column to fall back on Ruponda. This order was dictated not by choice but by necessity. "Hanforce" was still based for its supplies upon Kilwa Kisiwani, which was distant from Ruponda by road very nearly one hundred and fifty miles. It had been hoped that by this time the provisioning of the columns might be supplemented by supplies landed at Lindi, which is only seventy odd miles from Lukuledi; but the very stout resistance which "Linforce" had encountered had prevented it from advancing westward from its base for much more than half that distance. Already, after the fight at Nahungu, difficulties of supply and transport had compelled the British Command to detach the Nigerian Brigade from the troops thrusting south from the Kilwa area, and had caused it to transfer itself to "Linforce." Now, once again, the ever-lengthening lines of communication behind "Hanforce" had imposed upon the machinery of transport a strain which threatened it with a serious break-down. There was no alternative, therefore, but temporarily to shorten those lines, and though it was realized that the moral effect which a retirement would produce at this juncture could not but be deplorable, orders were issued for the column to fall back.

NO. 1 COLUMN FALLS BACK

Accordingly, at 8.30 p.m. on the 22nd October, No. 1 Column began its march back to Ruponda. To the Gold Coast Regiment which, during the advance, had so often acted as advanced guard, the position of rear-guard was now assigned, and it was not till 3 a.m., after the last of the long train of laden men and animals had finally crawled out of camp, that the Regiment, too, set forth upon the road. All fires were left burning, and everything was done to prevent the enemy from detecting the movement which was in progress. Chingwea, twelve miles up the road, was reached without incident, and at 3.30 p.m. the retirement to Ruponda was continued. Ruponda was reached by the Gold Coast Regiment and the perimeter of the camp was taken over by it at 9.40 a.m. on the 23rd October.

From this date until the 7th November the Gold Coast Regiment remained in the standing camp which had now been formed at Ruponda, furnishing patrols which kept in touch with No. 2 Column to the east, drilling the men for three hours daily, and training gun-teams for the Stokes Battery with which it had now been provided.

On the 7th November No. 1 Column resumed operations in the Chigugu-Lukuledi area, and marched without incident to Chingwea. Here it learned that "Linforce," which was still fighting its way down the Lindi-Massassi road, had the day before been in action against eight of von Lettow-Vorbeck's companies, and that after the engagement the enemy had retired in the direction of Nangus, which is on the main road at a spot about twenty miles east by north of Lukuledi, and about the same distance north-east of Massassi.

On the 8th November No. 1 Column marched to Igumi on the left bank of the Lukuledi River, seven miles below the mission station; and on the following day, it pushed on to Chigugu, on the main Lindi-Massassi road. This place is distant only about ten miles south-west of Nangus, where von Lettow-Vorbeck's forces were reported to be encamped.

Meanwhile No. 2 Column had crossed the rear of No. 1 Column and had occupied Lukuledi, whence it made a strong reconnaissance to Ndomondo on the Lukuledi River, two and a half miles up-stream from Igumi. None of these movements met with any opposition from the enemy.

On the 10th November, No. 1 Column pushed on east by south to the mission station at Ndanda, and a high ridge on the south of this place was occupied by the 129th Baluchis and the 55th Rifles, which had now joined the Column. Only slight opposition was met with and four Europeans were captured, and an enemy hospital was found containing 54 sick and wounded German combatants, and 120 *Askari*. There were also at this place a number of civilians and several European women and children.

The 1st Battalion of the 3rd King's African Rifles occupied the village, and the 2nd Battalion of the 2nd King's African Rifles took up a position on the road leading from Ndanda to Nangus. The rest of No. 1 Column encamped at the mission station. Word was here received that

"Linforce" was only three miles to the east of Nangus, and that No. 2 Column had occupied Chigugu, where No. 1 Column had spent the preceding night. Thence they had advanced toward the mission station at Jumbe Nwinama, which lies about two and a half miles to the east, where they had come into collision with the enemy.

It looked at the moment as though von Lettow-Vorbeck's forces were at last in a fair way to be surrounded, and it was anticipated that his main body would try to escape *viâ* Chiwata, leaving strong rear-guards to keep both "Linforce" and "Hanforce" in play, and to delay their advance.

On the 11th November No. 1 Column remained encamped at Ndanda Mission Station, two strong patrols being sent out; the one toward Nangus and the other toward Chiwata. The latter was undertaken by B Company of the Gold Coast Regiment, which went some miles down the track without seeing any traces of the enemy.

On the 12th November No. 1 Column marched back to Chigugu, its objective being Mwiti, which is situated on the right bank of the river of that name—a tributary of the Rovuma—and lies fourteen miles due east of Massassi and about half that distance almost due south of Chiwata.

Moving from Chigugu to Chikukwe on the 13th November, No. 1 Column attacked and occupied Mwiti on the 14th November. The Gold Coast Regiment, however, was in reserve upon this day and took no part in the action beyond sending a patrol, furnished by I Company, to occupy a ridge on the right of the advance of the 2nd Battalion of the 2nd Regiment of the King's African Rifles. This was achieved without opposition from the enemy.

The country in which "Hanforce" was now operating consisted of a succession of hills which rise from the plain to the height of anything from 1000 to 2000 feet, and are grouped about the western and southern flanks of the great Makonde plateau. The latter, which towers above the highest of its foothills by a good 1000 feet or more, is an elevated piece of flat land, roughly circular in shape, situated between the Lukuledi and Rovuma rivers to the north-east of Newala, and measuring approximately forty miles from north to south and again from east to west. The slopes of all these hills and those which lead up to the plateau are covered by grass and trees; and though the latter are sparsely scattered over the hillsides, they grow more thickly in the valleys, which seen from above seem to be choked with vegetation. The foothills are intersected by deep ravines and gorges, and it was through these that von Lettow-Vorbeck's forces were now making their way in the direction of Newala, the last German base in this part of the country.

Word had been received from the War Office on the 9th November that a German airship was *en route* for East Africa, and later it was reported that it had started, that it intended to effect a landing on the summit of the Makonde Plateau, and that it might be expected to arrive on the 14th November. This was precisely the sort of spectacular performance, dear to the German heart, in which the enemy so frequently indulged during the war, and which usually involved him in expense and risk altogether disproportionate to the military value that could thereby conceivably be secured. It was doubtless thought by simple folk in Berlin that the dramatic arrival of a Zeppelin on the battlefields of East Africa would fill the native troops fighting against von Lettow-Vorbeck with awe, terror and despair, and would produce upon them the demoralizing effect which a belief that the Germans stood possessed of supernatural powers might be expected to inspire. But the Oriental and African native of to-day is a thoroughly *blasé* person who has long ago outgrown such childish weaknesses. To put the matter colloquially, he is "fed up" with European inventions, which have almost ceased to amuse or interest him, and have long ago ceased to excite his wonder, much less his fear. The arrival of a German Zeppelin at this juncture would have been welcomed by the men of the Gold Coast Regiment, for instance, as a bright spot breaking the drab monotony of their days; while the British airmen, who by now were heartily sick of the practical inutility of most of the work that they were doing in East Africa, would have hailed its coming with even greater joy. The Zeppelin is believed to have actually made a start from Aleppo, or from some other place in Asia Minor, but if so it was recalled before it had proceeded far upon its journey. Perhaps von Lettow-Vorbeck, who throughout received frequent messages from his Government by wireless, and who may occasionally have been able to communicate with it in his turn, warned the Great General Staff that an airship could produce no effect, military or moral, that it was pretty certain to be wrecked, and that, in a word, the game was not worth the candle.

The mission station at Mwiti, unlike most of its counterparts in East Africa, has been built upon flat land, shut in toward the north and east by a semicircular range of hills; and from this place the Pioneer Company of the Gold Coast Regiment was sent on the 15th November to patrol to Manyambas, six and a half miles to the south-east, which is connected with Mwiti by a track skirting the base of the hills. The Pioneers left half a company at Maruchiras, a place on this track beyond the Miwale River, a left affluent of the Mwiti, which in its turn is a left tributary of the Rovuma; for the enemy had now been driven south of the Mambir, the last river of note in erstwhile German East Africa, and had been definitely pushed into the valley of the Rovuma, which is the northern boundary of the Portuguese possessions.

Meanwhile, at 2 p.m., the rest of the Gold Coast Regiment marched out of camp at Mwiti, and breasting a long slope in an easterly direction, ascended to the summit of a hill lying immediately under the lee of the escarpment which, across a deep valley, leads up to the Makonde Plateau. The latter rising directly to the north of Miwale Hill, the eminence occupied by the Gold Coast Regiment, soared above it to a height of perhaps 2000 feet.

The object of this movement was, if possible, to locate a German camp which was believed to exist at Luchemi, in the ravine between Miwale

CAPTAIN BRISCOE'S PATROL

Hill and the slope leading up to the plateau; but looking down from this height, the valley was revealed as a sea of tree-tops and vegetation to the depths of which the eye could not penetrate. At 6.15 p.m. a camp was selected on a spur jutting out into the valley. To the east, however, there rose yet another and a higher spur, connected with that upon which the camp was pitched by a saddle, the whole covered by grass and trees. This spur was reported by a patrol from a picket of the 55th Rifles, which had taken up a position on the northern flank of Miwale Hill prior to the arrival of the Gold Coast Regiment on its eastern summit, to be held by the enemy. This rendered the position of the camp somewhat precarious, and that night no lights or fires were permitted.

Word was received that evening that the Nigerians had occupied Chiwata, five miles to the north, at one o'clock that afternoon, and that on the morrow they would operate from that place against the enemy camp at Luchemi.

At dawn on the 16th November, Captain Briscoe with twenty rifles drawn from A Company set out from the camp to patrol down into the valley in a northerly direction; and Captain McElligott started at the same time, in command of a similar patrol, to reconnoitre the high spur across the saddle to the east of the camp. Captain Briscoe's patrol was fired upon very shortly after he left camp; and a little later a party of the enemy were seen moving about down in the valley. It was one of the many trials of the campaign in East Africa that even a glimpse of the folk against whom they were fighting was very rarely vouchsafed to the attacking forces. It was the rôle of the former to keep well under cover at all times, to let their pursuers discover their whereabouts if they could, and to make them pay as heavy a price as possible for the knowledge so obtained. The spectacle of a number of German soldiers, visible to the naked eye, and scuttling about in the valley, accordingly created considerable excitement, and fire was at once opened upon them with the Gold Coast Regiment's machine-guns. There are few feats more difficult, however, than accurately to find the range of an object situated far below and aimed at from a considerable height above it. Almost invariably the fire is not sufficiently depressed, and the bullets fly well over the target. It may be doubted, therefore, whether on this occasion much execution was done. The enemy, however, quickly took cover, and was presently seen to be in action with the 55th Rifles, who were working up the valley from west to east.

Between eight and nine o'clock in the morning the rest of No. 1 Column joined the Gold Coast Regiment on Miwale Hill; and the 1st Battalion of the 3rd Regiment of the King's African Rifles was sent south to work round the high spur on the east, which was being patrolled by Captain McElligott and his party.

The latter had reached the spur without encountering any opposition, but he reported that the northern slopes were occupied by the enemy, and that patrols sent out by him in that direction had been fired upon. At 1.45 p.m. Captain McElligott, signalling by flag-wagging from the western slope of the spur, confirmed this report;

THE ENEMY IN THE VALLEY 193

and in the meantime B Company had been dispatched to reinforce his patrol. With B Company also flag-communication was established, and the 55th Rifles and the 2nd Battalion of the 2nd King's African Rifles were sent forward to occupy the spur.

No sooner had Captain McElligott's signaller set to work on the western slope of the spur than the enemy from the bottom of the valley began shelling the British position with quite extraordinary accuracy. The first shot was aimed at Captain McElligott's signaller and scored a direct hit, blowing the poor fellow to pieces. The shelling which followed was no less accurate, and the target this time was the crowded perimeter camp in which No. 1 Column had that morning joined up with the Gold Coast Regiment. As all the carriers and troops were inside the perimeter, the position was rendered peculiarly vulnerable, and great commotion and consternation were caused among the non-combatants by the extreme precision of the enemy's aim. As soon, therefore, as the 55th Rifles and the 2nd Battalion of the 2nd King's African Rifles had established themselves upon the spur to the east, the whole of the remainder of No. 1 Column moved across to that less dangerous spot, where another perimeter camp, sheltered this time from the guns in the valley, was formed. During the night the enemy retired from his positions on the northern flank of this spur.

It is not thought that any large body of the enemy was present on this day, but a strong rearguard—for such it probably was—had been able to check the British advance, and had succeeded in giving von Lettow-Vorbeck's main body the time it needed to escape from a desperate situation, and to slip away in the direction of Newala.

The casualties sustained by the Gold Coast Regiment on the 16th November were 1 colour-sergeant, who had been attached to the Gold Coast Regiment from the South African Infantry, killed, and Captain Dawes and 1 colour-sergeant wounded, 3 soldiers and 1 carrier killed, and 9 soldiers and 8 carriers wounded.

On the 17th November No. 1 Column moved forward in an easterly direction to a camp which had been occupied on the preceding night by the 1st Battalion of the 3rd Regiment of the King's African Rifles; and the latter marched east and occupied a big water-hole near Luchemi. On the following day Luchemi was occupied by No. 1 Column, no resistance being offered by the enemy; and on the 19th November the column pushed on to Mkundi, which lies almost due west of the hills upon which Massassi is situated, and at a distance of perhaps two and a half miles from that station. It will be remembered that Massassi had been chosen by von Lettow-Vorbeck, after he had been driven across the Rufiji, as his General Headquarters. He had now, however, abandoned it and was basing his present operations upon Newala, which is distant only a dozen miles from the Portuguese frontier on the Rovuma River. It was for Newala that the enemy's forces were now believed to be heading; and it was understood that the troops under von Tafel's command, who had been driven in a south-easterly direction by the advance of the Belgians and

GERMANS RETREAT

of General Northey's column, had been ordered to join forces with von Lettow-Vorbeck at this place.

At Mkundi information was received that the Nigerians had captured a German hospital on the previous day, containing 25 British, 2 Belgian and 5 Portuguese officers prisoners, and 250 German and 700 natives, most of whom, however, were believed to be carriers, though there were 100 or more *Askari* among them. Twenty German officers and 242 *Askari*, and 4 European and 10 native non-combatants had also surrendered on this day. Von Lettow-Vorbeck, with the Governor of German East Africa—Herr Schnee—were believed to have with them some 800 to 1200 men, and to be about to quit the erstwhile German colony and to cross over into Portuguese territory.

On the evening of the 19th November the disposition of the British forces operating in this area was approximately as follows. No. 2 Column had reached Nairombo on the left bank of the Mwiti River, twelve miles south of Chiwata. One battalion of the Nigerians was at Mpoto, on the main road from Massassi to Newala, and distant about fourteen miles to the north-west of the latter place. Two Nigerian battalions were at Manyambas, the village to which the Pioneer Company of the Gold Coast Regiment had marched from the mission station at Mwiti on the 15th November; No. 3 Column was halting further north with orders not to advance for the present; and the 25th Cavalry were near Lulindi, fourteen miles east of Mpoto.

On the 20th November No. 1 Column marched from Mkundi, in a south-easterly direction, to

Lulindi, a distance of fourteen miles; and here information was received that Lieutenant Isaacs, who, it will be remembered, had been captured by the Germans during the fight at Nkessa in the Uluguru Mountains on the 12th September, 1916, was among the British officers who had been released by the Nigerians on the 18th November. During his fourteen months' captivity Lieutenant Isaacs had lost about two stone in weight, and had suffered severely from the shortage of all supplies, by which the Germans themselves had for many months been acutely pinched. Apart from these inevitable hardships, however, he and his fellow-European captives appear to have been well treated. The absence of any British native soldiers among the men released was, however, of sinister significance.

On the 21st November No. 1 Column advanced with the intention of making a reconnaissance in force towards Newala for the purpose of attacking and capturing this the last of the enemy's strongholds in his African colonies. The advance was led by the 55th Rifles and the 1st Battalion of the 3rd King's African Rifles, the Gold Coast Regiment following in support. The 55th Rifles, however, occupied Newala without resistance, and it was there ascertained that von Lettow-Vorbeck, with the remainder of his war-worn forces and carrying the unhappy Herr Schnee with him, had early that morning marched south to Nakalala on the northern bank of the Rovuma, where a number of canoes had been assembled, and intended thence to cross over into Portuguese territory.

At Newala 126 Germans surrendered to No. 1 Column.

GOLD COAST REGIMENT.
2·95 Battery.

To face p. 196.

CHAPTER XIV

TRANSFER OF THE GOLD COAST REGIMENT TO PORTUGUESE EAST AFRICA

THE actual movements and whereabouts of von Lettow-Vorbeck and his troops were, as usual, still largely a matter of conjecture, but every base which he had possessed in German East Africa was now in the hands of the British. He was known to be short of supplies, of food, of equipment, and of ammunition; the end of the dry season was drawing near, and the Portuguese were aware that he was approaching the frontier, and were strongly encamped at Ngomano, on the right bank of the Rovuma, about fifty miles upstream from the point at which the German force had crossed the river. The Rovuma is here a fine river, with a bed of sand and shingle, about half a mile wide from bank to bank. At this season, however, it was shrunken to such an extent that the running water measured only a hundred yards or so across, and was easily fordable at many points. The banks of the Rovuma were low and water-worn; the country in the vicinity was flat and covered with vegetation, which owed such fertility as it possessed to annual extensive inundations. In the rainy season the valley of the Rovuma would clearly be even more uninhabitable than the basin of the Rufiji had proved to be in 1916–17.

There were many sanguine people in the British camp who held that with the expulsion of von Lettow-Vorbeck from the territory that had once belonged to Germany the campaign in East Africa—which had already, nearly a year before, been publicly declared to have been practically at an end—was now at last definitely concluded. Since the first pronouncement to that effect was made, the enemy, quite unperturbed by this pious expression of opinion, had kept the field continuously, had fought a series of vigorous rear-guard actions, among which those at Njengao and Mahiwa on the Lindi road were of considerable magnitude, and had incidentally cost the British taxpayer an average of over twelve millions sterling *per mensem*. Now, even if fighting did not cease, the campaign, it was thought, could henceforth be conducted upon a much more modest scale; but most of the men who had fought against von Lettow-Vorbeck, and who had had opportunities of gauging the resolution, the determination, the resourcefulness, and, if you will, the dogged obstinacy of the man, were convinced that he would carry on the fight so long as he had an *Askari* to fire a rifle, and a cartridge to be discharged. It was also regarded as probable that he and von Tafel might still be able to join forces.

On the night of the 21st November the Gold Coast Regiment, which had not entered Newala, camped on the road halfway between that place and Lulindi, and on the following day retraced its steps to the latter. On the 23rd November, No. 1 Column marched from Lulindi to Luatalla, where

BANGALLA AND ROVUMA 199

it was joined by the 55th Rifles and the 1st Battalion of the 3rd King's African Rifles from Newala. Word was here received that von Lettow-Vorbeck's column was moving down the right, or Portuguese, bank of the Rovuma, and it was reported by natives that von Tafel had recrossed the river to the left bank, and was moving slowly and with great difficulty through the bush in the neighbourhood of Miesi, which lies halfway between the Mwiti and Bangalla rivers, both of which are left tributaries of the Rovuma. No. 1 Column was ordered to proceed to the mouth of the Bangalla River, by forced marches, for the purpose of trying to cut off von Tafel, and of preventing him from effecting a junction with von Lettow-Vorbeck. The Cavalry was to move in advance of No. 1 Column, and No. 2 Column was simultaneously to march down the Bangalla River from the north.

At 4 p.m. on the 24th November, therefore, No. 1 Column, with the Gold Coast Regiment leading the advance, set out for the mouth of the Bangalla, and at midnight bivouacked in column of route along the roadside. At 5.30 a.m. on the 25th November, the march was resumed, and the junction of the Bangalla with the Rovuma was reached at 10.30 a.m. During the march a solitary bull buffalo, outraged by this intrusion upon his privacy, savagely charged the column, went through it like a clown through a paper hoop, knocking over two carriers, and so vanished into the bush.

During the march a distance of 24 miles was covered, and it was calculated that since leaving

Ruponda, nine days earlier, the main body of No. 1 Column had marched no less than 174 miles—an average of over 19 miles *per diem*—while many of the units composing it, of which the Gold Coast Regiment was one, had materially exceeded that average. This would have been a sufficiently fine performance anywhere and in any circumstances for a body of infantry impeded at every step by a large number of carriers; but in the East African bush, at the fag-end of the dry season, when everything is at its dryest and hottest, it represented a really considerable feat.

On the 26th November, word having been received that an enemy force, composed of thirty white men and an unknown number of *Askari*, had cut the Column's line of communication to the north-east, the 129th Baluchis were dispatched toward Luatalla for the purpose of dislodging it; and at 9 a.m. the remainder of the column marched from Bangalla to Miesi by the road which it had followed on the preceding day. On arrival here it was learned that the 129th Baluchis, who at this time consisted of only about 130 rifles, had had a sharp engagement with the enemy on the banks of the Mwiti River, that they had had the worst of the encounter, and that they had been compelled to retire, leaving a considerable amount of small-arms ammunition in the hands of the Germans. This, however, was subsequently recovered, the enemy having had no means of carrying it away.

The 2nd Battalion of the 2nd King's African Rifles were sent to a place called Jumbe Nambude, with half of A Company of the Gold Coast Regiment, to form a flank guard to the Column;

LIEUTENANT NASH

but at 6 p.m. this half-company returned to Miesi, having seen nothing of the enemy.

During the night the enemy with whom the 129th Baluchis had come into collision retired, and communication with Lustalla was restored. Half of B Company, under Captain McElligott, was sent to patrol the Mbalawala hills, to the north of Miesi, and thence to send out parties to reconnoitre to the north and north-west. It was thought that von Tafel's camp was near Nambingo, to the west of Miesi, between the Bangalla and Mwiti rivers.

On the 28th November No. 1 Column marched back to Bangalla, at the junction of the river of that name with the Rovuma, where the perimeter camp formed on the 25th November was re-occupied. Here Captain McElligott with his patrol rejoined the Gold Coast Regiment. Very shortly after the arrival of the column in camp, a British aviator effected a landing on the sand and shingle of the Rovuma's dried-up bed, and when he came up to the camp it was found that he was Lieutenant Nash, who, in 1913-14, had been engaged in surveying the line of the projected railway extension in the Gold Coast from Kofori-dua to Kumasi. After he had partaken of such frugal fare as the mess of the Regiment afforded— for at this time the whole force had for some days been on greatly reduced rations—Lieutenant Nash resumed his journey, a squad of Gold Coast men being sent out to give his machine a "push off," as the sand and shingle of the river-bed proved to be rather heavy going. Nash flew down the river for a few miles, and then finding that his stock of petrol was running short and that his machine must be lightened, he dropped all the bombs he had with him into the Rovuma. Thus in a double degree the Gold Coast may claim to have had a special share in the surrender of von Tafel and his forces; for the explosion of Nash's bombs led the German Commander to believe that von Lettow-Vorbeck's troops were heavily engaged with the British between him and Newala. He had already learned that the latter place had been evacuated; his whole force had consumed practically all its supplies; ammunition was running very short; and now it seemed that he was separated from von Lettow-Vorbeck on the left bank of the Rovuma by a British column. This decided him to surrender, and that afternoon he sent in his Chief Staff Officer and another member of his staff with a white flag. They were received by a detachment of the Pioneer Company of the Gold Coast Regiment, and were forthwith conducted to Colonel Orr, the Column Commander.

The German officers, one of whom spoke English perfectly, stated that von Tafel had destroyed his last ammunition and buried or burned all his arms of precision. He asked to be allowed to surrender unconditionally, and suggested that his force should be marched into the British camp, and should occupy near it any area that might be chosen for the purpose. These conditions were approved, and late that afternoon the German force, consisting of 190 Europeans and about 1,200 *Askari*, with their carriers and camp-followers, waded across the Rovuma which they had crossed the preceding evening and came into camp.

The whole movement was carried out with

machine-like precision. The little column marched, as though on parade, to the area which had been allotted to it for its encampment, in which each company at once took up the position habitually assigned to it. Baggage having been deposited in a most orderly fashion, the men of each company instantly set to work to construct bush-huts for their European officers, while the carriers cleared the grass and underwood with their matchets, and prepared less elaborate huts for the *Askari*. The work was done with great rapidity, and on a system which had evidently become so instinctive that each cog knew to a nicety the precise place which it occupied in the elaborate mechanism. But what chiefly impressed the British spectators was not only the discipline and the order, but the almost unbroken silence which prevailed throughout. Silence in the ranks is easy enough to secure among men subject to strict military discipline, but no Englishman has yet learned the secret of imposing a like silence upon a mob of male and female African carriers. The result was impressive, but it may perhaps be hoped that the British never will achieve this particular miracle. Those who know the natives of Africa will agree that it is only to be wrought by means of methods that have always found greater favour in Prussia than they are ever likely to secure in Great.Britain. The cowed and silent carrier was the inevitable adjunct to the German *Askari*, an analysis of whose privileged position has been attempted in an earlier chapter of this book.

Though von Tafel's men did not appear to be at all near starvation, they, and especially the

Europeans, had not been full-fed for many days. In illustration of this it may be mentioned that a Tabora sovereign—the handsome gold coin, bearing the Prussian arms on the obverse and an African elephant on the reverse, and with no bevelling to its edge, of which von Lettow-Vorbeck had caused a few thousand to be coined at Tabora during the early days of the campaign —was freely offered that afternoon for a tin of honest bully-beef. No. 1 Column, however, was itself very hard-up for rations; and on the morrow von Tafel's men, under the escort of the 55th Rifles, were sent up the bed of the Bangalla River to join the Lindi road at a point to the southwest of Massassi, and thence to march along it to the sea. They were fed by means of the consignments of rations which were being dispatched from Lindi for the use of the British columns in the field; and the latter accordingly, for a space, went shorter of supplies than ever.

On the 29th November, orders were received to break up No. 1 Column. All the Indian units were directed to proceed to Massassi, and all the African units—the Gold Coast Regiment, the 2nd Battalion of the 2nd and the 1st Battalion of the 3rd King's African Rifles—to Naurus, where they were to join up with No. 2 Column. The Indian and African troops were designated A Column and B Column respectively; and the command of the latter was entrusted to Colonel Rose, Lieutenant S. B. Smith acting as his Staff Officer.

B Column started upon its march on the 30th

STRENGTH OF THE REGIMENT

November, and moving *viâ* Nambere and Maparawe, reached Naurus, without incident, on the 2nd December.

The strength of the Gold Coast Regiment at this time was as follows. There were actually present in the field 19 British officers, including 2 doctors and 2 officers attached to the transport; 8 British non-commissioned officers, of whom 3 belonged to the transport; 850 rank and file, including 18 signallers and 84 Gold Coast Volunteers, the majority of the latter being employed as orderlies; 106 gun and ammunition-carriers; 35 stretcher-bearers, 21 servants, 5 clerks, and 1305 carriers. The potential strength of the Regiment, however, largely exceeded these figures, for 11 British and 2 British non-commissioned officers were now available at Mpara, Mingonyo or Lindi, some of whom had returned from leave, while others were newly posted for service with the corps; and new drafts having arrived from the Gold Coast, 510 rank and file and 106 gun and ammunition-carriers were in readiness to join the Regiment. The total available force, therefore, at this time, numbered 1360 rank and file and 212 gun and ammunition-carriers, and it was once again very fairly well officered. The Regiment also possessed, in addition to its machine-guns, 2 Lewis and 4 Stokes guns.

On the other hand, the quality of the rank and file was not quite up to the standard of the original force which the Gold Coast had put into the field in July, 1916. The men at that time composing the Regiment were seasoned soldiers, all, or nearly all, of whom had recently seen active service. They were "made" soldiers to a man, and had every one of them been subjected to a long process of training and discipline. Gaps in their ranks, after the arrival of the first fully-trained draft which had joined the Regiment in December, 1916, had been filled, in the first instance, by hastily collected levies of greatly inferior quality, and as early as the fight at Nahungu, at the end of September, 1917, it had not been thought expedient to make use of all of them in the firing-line. Subsequent drafts were far superior to these, and had also undergone a more prolonged training, but they, of course, lacked the experience of the men belonging to the original Exeditionary Force and of those who formed the first draft of reinforcements. On the whole they acquitted themselves very well; but the Gold Coast Regiment at the end of December, 1917, though numerically stronger than it had been at any period during the whole campaign, was not, perhaps, such a homogeneous and thoroughly efficient force as it had been on its first arrival in East Africa.

On the 3rd December, the Pioneer Company of the Gold Coast Regiment, under Captain Arnold, was sent to Wangoni, on the banks of the Rovuma, to relieve the 1st Battalion of the 3rd King's African Rifles, and the rest of the Regiment was employed during the next few days in road-making, in cleaning up old camping grounds, and on other fatigues. On the 5th December a draft consisting of 5 British officers, 2 British non-commissioned officers, and 401 men, nearly all of

MAJOR GOODWIN TAKES COMMAND 207

whom were new drafts from the Gold Coast, reached the Regiment from Mpara.

On the 9th December, Colonel Rose, who had been summoned by General Van der Venter to General Headquarters, which were established at that time at the mission station at Ndanda, handed over the command to Major Goodwin, and set off for his destination by motor-car; and it was announced that the Gold Coast Regiment was about to be sent by sea from Lindi to Port Amelia in Portuguese East Africa. It also leaked out that von Lettow-Vorbeck, having reached a point on the left bank of the Rovuma near Ngomano, had waded across the river, his men having at that time barely fifty rounds of small-arms ammunition per head, and being to all intents and purposes at the end of their resources. He had then surprised the Portuguese camp at Ngomano so effectively that he succeeded in capturing *inter alia* a million rounds of small-arms ammunition, several guns, and a supply of canned European provisions sufficient to meet the requirements of his force for at least three months. Having thus secured to himself a new lease of life, he was now proceeding to make things as unpleasant as possible for the Government of Portuguese East Africa.

On the 9th December the Gold Coast Regiment marched to Bangalla—not the place where the river of that name debouches into the Rovuma, but the spot where that stream is bridged by the road which leads through Massassi from Makochera, on the Rovuma, to Lindi on the sea. From this point the Regiment marched up the main road, reached Massassi Mission Station on the 12th December, picking up at that place a signal section of Royal Engineers, and pushing on to Chigugu the same day. Marching distances which varied from nine to sixteen miles daily, the Regiment, on the 15th December, reached Mahiwa, where General O'Grady's Column from Lindi had fought one of its big battles. On the morrow at Mtama, nine miles further up the road, it was learned that Major Shaw, with Captains Harris and Watts, and Lieutenants Pike, Smith and Biltcliffe and 250 men of the Gold Coast Regiment, had already sailed from Lindi for Port Amelia. On the 17th December Mtua was reached, and Lieutenant Withers, Colour-Sergeant Thornton, and A Company, with two machine-guns and their teams, were then dispatched to Lindi by motor-car to embark for Port Amelia. The authorities were evidently in a hurry, and von Lettow-Vorbeck was reported already to have two companies of his *Askari* within ten hours' march of Port Amelia.

Next day, the Regiment moved on two miles to Mingoya, where it held itself in readiness to embark at Arab House, the landing-stage at Lindi, which lay some six miles further up the road.

Meanwhile Colonel Rose had reported himself to General Van der Venter, the Commander-in-Chief, and to General Sheppard, the Chief of Staff, at Ndanda Mission on the Lindi main road. He was here informed that it had been decided to send a column forthwith to assist the Portuguese at Port Amelia, where much consternation had been caused by the approach of von Lettow-Vorbeck's forces; that the column would be composed mainly of the Gold Coast Regiment; and that the command would be entrusted to Colonel Rose.

The Gold Coast Regiment had now been serving continuously in East Africa since its arrival at Kilindini on the 26th July, 1916. During the seventeen months that had thereafter elapsed the Regiment had been constantly on the march or in action, save when it had been camped, as for instance at Njimbwe, at Mnasi, at Rumbo or again at Narungombe, in close proximity to the enemy, with whom its patrols and outposts had been in almost daily collision. Thanks to the efforts of the Government of the Gold Coast, and to the highly efficient work performed by Lieutenant-Colonel Potter, D.S.O., who had assumed command of the training depôts in that colony, the Regiment had been constantly and regularly reinforced; but after the remainder of the regular force, originally left behind in the Gold Coast, had been sent to East Africa, the quality of some of the drafts had by no means equalled the high standard at which the Regiment had always hitherto aimed. The Nigerian Brigade, which had reached East Africa some months after the arrival of the Gold Coast Regiment, was about to be sent back to Lagos; but the Gold Coast Regiment, which had enjoyed less than three months' rest at Kumasi after the conclusion of the campaign in the Kameruns, was still to be kept in the field.

It was realized by all, however, that a great compliment to the Regiment, and a tacit recognition of the fashion in which it had borne itself, were implied in this selection of it, out of all the available troops, to undertake yet one more campaign; and if there were some who thought that the men were being tried almost too severely, the rank and file accepted the new duties which were about to be imposed upon them with their usual philosophy and good temper.

CHAPTER XV

THE ADVANCE FROM PORT AMELIA TO MEZA

WITH the transfer of military operations from German to Portuguese territory the campaign against von Lettow-Vorbeck assumed a somewhat new aspect. Until now the German Commander-in-Chief had been operating in country that had long been subject to German rule, throughout which German mission stations and German administrative posts had been established, and where every corner and cranny of each district was familiarly known to Europeans or natives resident in the German camps. The enemy troops, moreover, had possessed bases both for military purposes and for the accumulation of supplies; and so long as this continued to be the case points existed here and there which it was important should be maintained as long as possible, and which the movements of von Lettow-Vorbeck's forces were to some extent designed to defend. With the abandonment of Newala, the last of these permanent posts had been evacuated, and with it any prisoners of war he had taken and the German sick and wounded, who had hitherto been under the treatment of their own doctors, had been suffered to fall into the hands of the British. Thereafter von Lettow-Vorbeck occupied a position of complete independence and irresponsibility. He was situated very much as de Wet and his commando were situated during the concluding months of the South African War; and his troops had similarly been transformed from an army in the field into a mobile band of fugitive marauders, whose only objects were to avoid capture, to cause to their pursuers and to all connected with them the *maximum* amount of loss and trouble, and simultaneously to maintain themselves by seizing any supplies upon which, from time to time, they could contrive to lay their hands. The business of the British, on the other hand, was rendered more difficult than ever. The object to be aimed at was to wear down the enemy's forces, to reduce them by gradual attrition, and for this purpose to bring them to action whenever and wherever this could be achieved. There were now, however, no important places, such as Newala, to be threatened by the British advance, and von Lettow-Vorbeck having got rid of all *impedimenta*, and having no preoccupation save that of maintaining himself in the field as long as possible, was able to place his opponents in a very embarrassing position. This he was now about to do, compelling "Pamforce," as the Expeditionary Force dispatched to Port Amelia was officially designated, to extend its lines of communications from the coast into the interior for any distance that he might elect to fall back before it; diminishing by this means the strength of the striking force which it could actually bring against him, since lines of communications have to be garrisoned and guarded; multiplying with every additional mile the difficulties surrounding transport and supply; while he carefully husbanded his own forces, and contented himself with delaying and harassing the advance by means of small patrols whose occasional losses could not seriously diminish his military strength.

The estimate formed of the strength of von Lettow-Vorbeck's troops at the moment when he evacuated Newala—viz. that they only amounted to about 800 to 1200 men—was certainly incorrect, and subsequent operations clearly showed that he had at his disposal not less than 2000 soldiers, 10 per cent. of whom perhaps were white men. These were now nearly as well armed and equipped as they had ever been; and in von Lettow-Vorbeck's able hands they were capable of leading their opponents as tantalizing a dance through the jungle-covered plains and hills of tropical East Africa as de Wet had led the British troops across the veldt to the south some seventeen years earlier.

He in the first instance established his Headquarters at Nanguari, a place on the right bank of the Lujendi River, which is one of the principal right affluents of the Rovuma. The Portuguese camp, which von Lettow-Vorbeck had so successfully surprised, had been pitched at Ngomano, at the junction of the Lujendi with the Rovuma; and Nanguari, nearly a hundred miles up the former river, had for von Lettow-Vorbeck the advantage of being one of the most inaccessible places in the northern part of Portuguese East Africa. From Nanguari, he dispatched raiding parties, some of which threatened Port Amelia, while others penetrated down the coast as far as Nkufi and Lurio, at the mouth of the Luri River, where they gutted the shops and stores of their stocks of European provisions. It is possible that the report which was current with regard to von Lettow-Vorbeck's intention to attack and sack Port Amelia may have been true, but if so, this project was abandoned when word reached him that British forces had landed at that port. He, however, placed some of his forces astride the road which runs westward inland from the shores of Pomba Bay, so as to frustrate any attempt that the British might make to convey troops to the south of him by sea, and so to slip them in behind him, as they had earlier attempted to do by landing a force at Lindi while he was still operating actively in the Kilwa area.

Major Shaw's detachment of 250 men which, as we have seen, had been dispatched from Lindi to Port Amelia in the middle of December, had reached the latter place in time to save it from attack, if an attack upon it indeed formed part of von Lettow-Vorbeck's plans. Major Shaw, however, was not provided with carriers, and none were forthcoming at Port Amelia. His force, therefore, was reduced to a condition of complete immobility, and he was forced to content himself with putting Port Amelia in a state of defence by forming an entrenched camp in its vicinity.

After the arrival of the Gold Coast Regiment at Mingoya, it was joined on the 18th December by Captain Harman, D.S.O., who had been absent for several months on sick leave, with whom were Captain Duck, D.S.O., and 150 details. On the

ON BOARD THE *SALAMIS*

following day, at 3 a.m., A Company marched to Arab House, and thence was ferried across the bay to Lindi. On the 23rd December Colonel Goodwin with the Regimental Headquarters and 620 men, including the Battery, with 4 Stokes guns and 100 *personnel*, marched to Arab House, where they were embarked in lighters. Captain Harman remained behind at Mingoya in charge of details. At 2 p.m. the Gold Coast Regiment was transhipped from the lighters on to H.M. transport *Salamis*, and immediately set off down the coast on their journey to Port Amelia, which is distant from Lindi a matter of 180 miles. They had been joined on board the *Salamis* by A Company, and by Colonel Rose and the Headquarters of "Pamforce."

Shortly after midnight a slight shock was felt, and the *Salamis* came to a standstill with that peculiar sensation of finality which always conveys the impression to those on board a stranded ship that the vessel has of a sudden been welded indissolubly into a neighbouring continent. The *Salamis* thereafter behaved precisely as though this had actually occurred, and every effort to move her proved to be unavailing. There was nothing to be done, therefore, but to await the next high tide, which was due at about 9 a.m.; and at this hour, two whalers having arrived in the interval, fresh attempts to get her afloat were made. The *Salamis* obstinately declined, however, to budge an inch; and late in the afternoon H.M.S. *Lunkwa*, an armed merchantman commanded by Captain Murray, R.N., having meanwhile come upon the scene, it was decided to transfer the Gold Coast Regiment to her. This was accomplished by midnight, and the members of the little force spent a dismal Christmas Day steaming back up the coast to Lindi, mourning their separation from many of their stores and much of their private gear—a great deal of which, as it subsequently turned out, they were destined never to see again; and on their arrival they took up their quarters in the crowded detail camp.

On the 27th December 250 men of the Gold Coast Regiment, with 2 Stokes guns and the 50 rank and file and the carriers attached to them, under the command of Captain Duck, returned on board the *Lunkwa*, and once more set for Port Amelia. For lack of transport the remainder of the Regiment had perforce to be left behind at Lindi, but Colonel Rose and the Headquarters of "Pamforce" accompanied Captain Duck's detachment.

Colonel Goodwin and the Headquarters of the Regiment, with 500 rifles and 300 carriers of the Sierra Leone Carrier Corps, embarked on H.M. transport *Hongbee* on the 5th January, 1918, and followed the two detachments, under Captain Shaw and Captain Duck, which had preceded them.

The Portuguese Estado d'Africa Oriental, like Gaul in the time of Julius Cæsar, is divided into three parts—Lorenço Marquez, Mozambique, and the territory of the Nyassa Company. The last-named, which is really the northern portion of Mozambique, comprises all the country situated between the Rovuma and the Lurio, or Luli, rivers, and between the eastern borders of British Nyassaland and the sea. It is leased to a chartered company, which appoints its own Governor, subject to the approval of some Portuguese authority, and depends for its revenues upon a poll-tax and a hut-tax. Both of these impositions are for the most part paid in kind, and they are collected by agents or revenue-farmers, who occupy the entrenched forts, locally called *bomas*, which are dotted about the country at fairly frequent intervals. The smaller fortified posts, similarly occupied by the native agents of the revenue-farmers, are called *mborio*. The population is comparatively speaking dense, but there is little trade and even less prosperity. It is of the territory exploited by this chartered company that Port Amelia is the capital.

At Port Amelia there is an inlet of the sea, roughly circular in shape, which measures about six miles across at its widest part, and bears the name of Pomba Bay. The entrance to this bay is about a mile broad and on the southern side a cliff, two hundred feet or more in height, juts out, narrowing the mouth of the inlet. It is at the foot of this cliff that the commercial portion of Port Amelia and the native town are situated; and on its summit is the house of the Governor, flanked by the building in which the officers of the Portuguese Government at once live and work, with a rather ramshackle set of police barracks facing it. The landing-place at Port Amelia consists of a short, snub-nosed stone pier, which leads to a sandy beach, beyond which there is a single line of rather mean-looking shops and commercial buildings. These are for the most part constructed of mud, lime-washed or colour-washed, red or blue, fitted with green shutters and roofed with corrugated iron. Near their centre, however, there are two fairly substantial houses built of wood, one of which was subsequently used as a rest-house for British officers passing through Port Amelia. To the left, as you face the town, the native quarter adjoins the commercial buildings—a cluster of squalid mud huts roofed with grass. The total population of the place does not exceed fifteen hundred souls.

From the lower town a steep motor-road climbs the hill till the summit of the cliff is reached, where it passes between the Governor's house and the police barracks. The former is a two-storeyed building, raised on piles, with stone or concrete verandah pillars, but for the rest constructed entirely of wood. The block of Government offices in which the officials live and work is built of similar materials; but the police barracks are a mud structure colour-washed a dull red. All these buildings, like those in the commercial town at the foot of the cliff, are roofed with corrugated iron.

Judged from the æsthetic standpoint, these tin roofs are always an abomination; but in the tropics they are peculiarly hateful. They are most efficient conductors of heat, and with a vertical sun beating down upon them, they produce in the buildings which they cover an atmosphere resembling that of an oven. Moreover, exposure to the sea air causes rapid corrosion, and they speedily cease to be even water-tight. For the rest, the extensive use of corrugated iron roofing in the tropics always marks, in a European settlement, a very primitive stage of development. It proclaims the phase of makeshifts and of temporary expedients—the period of comfortless picnicking—which must always precede, though it is not always followed by, an era of advancement and prosperity. Where corrugated iron roofing is found predominating in any tropical settlement which has been in European occupation for more than a very few years, the fact may be accepted as a sure indication that local enterprise has so far produced very indifferent results.

From the flat ground on the top of the cliff a grassy slope runs down in a long slope to the waters of the Indian Ocean. Turning one's back on this and looking out across the bay, a rather pretty view is obtained of hills rising inland behind the little fishing village of Bandari, six miles away. The shores of the bay are stretches of sand varied by patches of black-green mangroves; and seen from the sea, Port Amelia—a line of mean white and colour-washed buildings, surmounted by glaring tin roofs, and flanked by a cluster of native hovels—devoid of vegetation, and sweltering beneath a tropical sun, appears as undesirable a specimen of a European outpost as it would be possible anywhere to light upon.

Major Shaw's detachment, which had been the first to arrive, had established a camp on the top of the high ridge, which has the sea on one side of it and the waters of the bay upon the other, at a spot distant about a mile from the residence of the Governor.

The motor-road, which ascends to the top of the cliff, runs on, dropping down again to the level of the bay, through masses of very thick, fine grass; and by this route Mtuge, which lies about two miles inland from Bandari, is distant eight and twenty miles from Port Amelia. A quicker means of reaching this place, however, is to sail across the bay to Bandari; but here there is a sloping beach and shoal water which prevent even a rowing-boat being brought close to the shore. The journey to Bandari was usually accomplished by sailing across the bay in *dhows*, such as have plied in the Red Sea, the Persian Gulf, and upon the waters of the Indian Ocean ever since the days of Hippalus and before. When the wind was favourable this was easy enough, but often, in the sheltered area of the bay, these sailing-boats would be becalmed for days at a time, and they still more often had to be warped out from the shore for several hundreds of yards to a point from whence they could catch enough breeze to set them moving. This operation was affected by shipping the anchor and placing it on board a gig, which then rowed ahead of the *dhow* and dropped the anchor overboard. Next all hands and the cook tugged on the anchor-chain, till the *dhow* had been brought short up to her moorings, when the anchor was once more shipped, retransferred to the gig, and the tedious process was repeated. By this means a couple of hours were sometimes occupied in covering a distance of as many hundred yards.

When the *dhow* had at last been got under way, and the six miles of sea separating Port Amelia from Bandari had been crossed, all her contents had to be man-handled to the shore for a distance of about two hundred yards. Between Bandari and Mtuge, whence the main road runs inland in a westerly direction, there lies a swamp

DIFFICULTIES ON ARRIVAL 221

which rendered the two-mile journey a matter of still further difficulty; and at a later period this slough became spattered with derelict motor-lorries which had become engulfed in it past all possibility of salvage. These facts are worth noting as illustrating some of the initial difficulties which impeded the transport and supply of "Pamforce"; for Mtuge was destined to be the base of its operations during its thrust into the interior of the Nyassa Company's territory. Mtuge, as we have seen, could also be reached from Port Amelia by the road which ran round the bay.

Though Port Amelia had been reported to be threatened by von Lettow-Vorbeck's marauders, the arrival of the British troops caused no apparent excitement; but Signor Abilio de Lobao Soeiro, the Governor of the Nyassa Company's territory, was very civil and obliging, and on the day following Colonel Rose's arrival he placed the Portuguese gunboat *Chaimite* at his disposal to transport him and Major Shaw and to tow three or four *dhows* containing 250 men of the Gold Coast Regiment across the bay to Bandari.

Colonel Rose, however, found himself almost as completely paralyzed as Major Shaw had done, for still no carriers were forthcoming; and though alarming rumours were current concerning the doings of von Lettow-Vorbeck's raiding parties at Mkufi and Lurio, it was only possible to send an Intelligence Department agent with forty scouts down the coast to report what was going on. This agent kept in touch with Colonel Rose by telephone, and the reports which he sent back were very far from being reassuring; but as a matter of fact the German patrols sent to loot the coast stores to the south of Port Amelia were never more than thirty or forty men strong, though they brought with them or impressed sufficient porters to carry away everything likely to be of service to them upon which they could lay their hands. This was the report returned from Mkufi by Captain Harris, who, with a party of thirty rifles, was sent to that place from Port Amelia to ascertain the real state of affairs.

The main body of the Gold Coast Regiment reached Port Amelia without further |mishap on the 7th January. It was forthwith disembarked and marched up the hill to the camp which had been established by Major Shaw. On the following day A Company, under Captain Wheeler, marched down the coast road from Port Amelia to Mkufi. Captain Wheeler was instructed to patrol the country in the neighbourhood of the Magaruna River and of Chiure, which lies about forty miles inland from Mkufi. He was also to send patrols south along the coast as far as Lurio and Lurio Bay. A post consisting of thirty rifles, under Captain Harris, had already been established at Mkufi before the arrival of the main body of the Regiment, and it was instructed to remain there with Captain Wheeler and A Company.

On the 9th January two Stokes guns and the Battery, under Captain Parker, were sent across the bay to Bandari by *dhows*, and from that place they joined Major Shaw's detachment at Mtuge. On the following day the Headquarters of the Gold Coast Regiment with I Company and details left the camp at Port Amelia at 6.30 a.m. *en route*

MARCH TO MTUGE

for Mtuge. They marched along the motor-road already described, descending to the level of the bay and thereafter skirting its shores. The grass on either side of the road was impenetrable, the black loam underfoot made heavy going, and the heat and the exhausted atmosphere, which in the tropics is peculiar to a narrow path through grass, rendered the march more than ordinarily trying. The road itself was much overgrown—symptomatic of the decay by which Port Amelia appeared to be stricken; but it was later cleared and repaired, and throughout the expedition to this part of Portuguese East Africa, it was the only route available for the passage of motor-vehicles from Port Amelia to the troops at the front. The Regiment camped for the night at a point fourteen miles along the road, and reached Mtuge next day. The Pioneer Company and two Stokes guns remained at Port Amelia, and the other details left there were formed into a sub-depôt under the command of Captain Watt.

The force at Mtuge, after the arrival of Colonel Goodwin on the 11th January, consisted of the Headquarters of the Regiment, I Company, B Company, and two Stokes guns.

From Mtuge two roads run inland in a westerly direction. Of these one is the main road from Mtuge to Medo, which place is distant about eighty-four miles from Mtuge. The other is a telegraph road, originally designed for motor traffic, but at this time much overgrown, which also runs in a westerly direction, rejoining the main road at Nanunya, a place distant some seven and twenty miles from Mtuge. From Nanunya the telegraph line follows the main road as far as Meza, which is about thirty-four miles further on.

Major Shaw's detachment had been patrolling the country in the neighbourhood of Mtuge since its establishment at that place, but on one occasion only had the enemy been met, a patrol under Lieutenant Robertson having come into contact with a small party of *Askari* on the telegraph road above mentioned.

On the 12th January a party consisting of 145 rifles, 1 Lewis gun and 1 machine-gun, under Captain Dawes, left Mtuge to patrol by native paths to Pumone, a place which is situated about ten miles to the south of the main road and some forty-five miles south-west by west of Mtuge. Here it was known that the enemy had a post, and Captain Dawes was ordered to eject him from it if possible.

On the 13th January Captain Foley reached the camp at Mtuge with two Stokes guns from Port Amelia, and assumed command of the Battery.

On the 14th January a party of fifty men belonging to 1 Company was sent, under Lieutenant Clarke, to patrol toward Sanananga, which lies on the telegraph road about ten miles to the south of the main road and is distant about sixteen miles from Mtuge. At Sanananga Lieutenant Clarke came into contact with an enemy patrol, and a fight took place in which one carrier was killed and two soldiers wounded. The enemy was believed to have lost five killed, the number of his wounded being unknown; and he retired, Lieutenant Clarke remaining at Sanananga and consolidating his position.

A AND I COMPANIES

On the 15th January, A Company, under Captain Wheeler, arrived at Mtuge from Mkufi, having left Colour-Sergeant Hart and thirty rifles at the latter place. No traces of the enemy had been seen in the neighbourhood of Mkufi.

On the same day, I Company, under Captain Harman, was sent up the main road to establish a camp at Mahiba, a place about twelve miles from Mtuge. Here some high ground suitable for the purpose was found, in the neighbourhood of which a sufficient water supply could be obtained by digging in a sort of rocky grotto. The country all around was an undulating expanse of grassy land, set fairly thickly with small trees, and studded with patches of scrub and frequent clumps of bamboos—in a word, the usual featureless, uninteresting bush country so common in Africa beyond the limits of the belts of forest.

The country up the road as far as the Sovar River, about six miles further on, was reported by Captain Harman to be clear of the enemy.

On the 16th January I Company established a post at Sovar River; and Lieutenant Clarke reported from Sanananga that the country was occupied by the enemy as far as Bulu, a village five miles up the telegraph road from the former place.

On the 17th January the Regimental Headquarters were removed from Mtuge to Mahiba, the Pioneer Company and two Stokes guns accompanying it; and on the same day Captain Dawes reported that he had moved toward Pumone at dawn on the 15th January with the intention of attacking it. While still three miles distant from his objective, however, he had encountered an enemy patrol, and though it was driven in, it had succeeded in delaying his progress for a considerable time. Accordingly, Captain Dawes did not come within sight of Pumone till near midday, and he then found that it was a strong post, prepared for defence and with well-constructed entrenchments occupied by the enemy. Having regard to the scanty supply of small-arms ammunition in his possession, and to his distance from reinforcements, Captain Dawes did not consider it advisable to attempt an attack. He consequently withdrew to Koloi, the place from which he had started that morning, and was thence actively patrolling the country in the neighbourhood.

On the 20th January motor transport between Mtuge and Mahiba was established, for all this time every effort was being made to improve the road between Port Amelia and the front; and Lieutenant Barrett who, with twenty rifles, had been sent up the main road on the preceding day to examine Nanunya as a suitable site for a camp, reported that he had found a party of the enemy at that place, and that in the encounter which followed one of the Intelligence Department scouts attached to his patrol had been killed. Lieutenant Barrett had later fallen back to the post at Sovar River.

On the 21st January Lieutenant Bisshopp, with fifteen men of I Company, one Intelligence Department agent and ten scouts, left for Sovar River to reinforce Lieutenant Barrett; and on the same day two officers, a hundred rifles of A Company, one machine-gun and one Stokes gun were dispatched from Mtuge to reinforce Captain Dawes at Koloi. News was also received that the Depôt Company of the Gold Coast Regiment had at last arrived at Port Amelia.

On the 22nd January Lieutenant Bisshopp reached Nanunya without encountering opposition, and he there learned from the local natives that the enemy post at that place had only consisted of one German and five *Askari*. On his way back Lieutenant Bisshopp, in accordance with instructions, left a post consisting of Lieutenant Barrett, twenty rifles and one Stokes gun at Namarala, and brought in the men who had hitherto been stationed at Sovar River.

On the 25th January Captain Dawes, who had advanced to within six miles of Pumone on the previous day, attacked and occupied that place at noon, expelling the enemy without difficulty and capturing and destroying five tons of native foodstuffs which had been accumulated there by him. In the course of this operation one soldier and one carrier were wounded.

On this day the post at Namarala, which had been established by Lieutenant Bisshopp, was strengthened; and a detachment of the newly-formed King's African rifles Mounted Infantry arrived at Mahiba *en route* for Nanunya. Instructions were then sent to Captain Dawes at Pumone to get into touch with the Mounted Infantry, and to patrol toward Ankuabe, which lies twelve miles up the main road beyond Nanunya, for the purpose of finding a suitable position for a camp within striking distance of the former place.

On the 28th January the post at Namarala was moved forward to Nanunya, the former being occupied by twenty rifles of the Pioneer Company under Lieutenant Wilson. On the following day the King's African Rifles Mounted Infantry occupied Ankuabe without opposition, and Captain Dawes next day moved to that place, leaving thirty rifles under Lieutenant Norris to garrison Pumone. On the 30th January the Regimental Headquarters, with the Pioneer Company and I Company, marched up the road to Namarala, and on the following day established their camp at Nanunya. On the 3rd February the Headquarters of the Regiment, with which also was Colonel Rose and the Headquarters of "Pamforce," A and B Companies and two guns of the Battery, moved forward to Ankuabe, leaving the rest of the Battery, the Pioneer Company, I Company and two Stokes guns to garrison Nanunya. The site chosen for the camp at Ankuabe was overlooked by a big bluff of rock, but its sides were so precipitous as to be unscaleable, and it therefore presented no menace to the security of the camp.

On the 4th February the Post at Pumone was withdrawn to the Maguida River, five miles south of Ankuabe; and though reports were received that the enemy were advancing, he failed to put in an appearance, the natives subsequently stating that he had been checked by an unfordable river, and that two of his white men had been badly mauled by lions.

On the 8th February an enemy patrol, consisting of two Europeans and forty *Askari*, came out of the bush on to the main road between

Nanunya and Ankuabe at a point where a post manned by six men of the Gold Coast Regiment, under Lance-Corporal Etonga Etun, had been established. The men of this post opened fire upon the enemy, and led by Etonga Etun, charged him so hotly that the Germans and their *Askari* and carriers did not stop to find out the small numbers by which they were opposed, but dropping some of their loads, took refuge in precipitate flight. Among the articles picked up by Etonga Etun's party were some belts of machine-gun ammunition and a couple of European loads containing among other things a number of official papers. Etonga Etun, who showed such dash on this occasion, was a native of Jaunde, and was originally enlisted during the 1914-16 campaign in the German Kameruns. In East Africa he won both the Distinguished Conduct Medal and the Military Medal.

An attempt was made from Ankuabe to cut off the retreat of this enemy patrol, but the latter made good its escape, dispersing into the bush in great haste when overtaken by the Mounted Infantry. The captured documents showed that the object of this party had been to harass the British lines of communication and especially to capture mails and ammunition.

During the next few days nothing of any interest occurred, but on the 17th February the 22nd D.M.B. arrived in camp, and on the 25th February the Gold Coast Regiment, less one hundred rifles of I Company and two Stokes guns, marched out of Ankuabe with half a section of the 22nd D.M.B., and camping for the night at Muapa, fourteen miles up the road, next day advanced on Meza.

The start was made at 6 a.m., fifty men under Lieutenant Bisshopp being left in charge of all the supply carriers in the camp at Muapa. Just before 7 a.m. an enemy patrol was met, which retired hurriedly, and nothing more happened until one o'clock, when the enemy, posted in some thick bush about three-quarters of a mile east of Meza, opened fire with a machine-gun upon the advancing troops. He retired after an engagement which lasted about half an hour, during which only one man of the Gold Coast Regiment was wounded; and at 2.30 p.m. Meza was occupied. Two camps which the Germans had established a little beyond Meza village were found to be deserted. The supply convoy came into camp at 5 p.m.

On the 27th February a post was established on the main road eight miles beyond Meza, and about 1200 carriers were sent back to Muapa to bring up supplies.

During the first ten days of March nothing occurred, the troops being employed in patrolling the country around Meza, where on one or two occasions they came into contact with small parties of the enemy. The task of accumulating supplies was now chiefly engrossing the attention of the Headquarters staff of "Pamforce," which, on the 11th March, established itself at Meza. Indeed, the question of transport was the hinge upon which at this junction everything turned. The advance was favoured by the fact that no definite break had yet occurred in the weather, though a good deal of rain had fallen since the camp was advanced to

SERGT. GRANDA DIKALE, D.C.M., M.M.   CORPL. SHUMBO LAMBE, D.C.M.
CORPL. ETONGA ETUN, M.M.

To face p. 230.

Ankuabe. Moreover, no difficulty with regard to water had as yet been encountered, though the quality of the supply obtained was not always very satisfactory. For the rest, however, the advancing force was tethered to its base at Mtuge by the sixty odd miles of road along which it had advanced; and though the highway had been improved and motor traffic established, the indifferent landing facilities at Port Amelia, the uncertain sea communication between that place and Bandari, and the fact that everything taken to the latter had to be man-handled from the *dhows* to the shore, caused endless vexatious delays. The deep, black "cotton" soil, moreover, was quickly reduced to a quagmire by even a moderate amount of rain; and eventually it had to be "corduroyed" with small tree-trunks along its entire length. Every advance, of course, added to the distances over which supplies had to be conveyed, and more than two months had been occupied in pushing some sixty-four miles up the main road to Meza, without it having once been found possible to bring the enemy to action.

The German Commander-in-Chief, who was now engaged in playing out time, had so far completely succeeded in attaining the objects he had in view.

CHAPTER XVI

THE ENGAGEMENT AT MEDO

ALTHOUGH the Great War had now been in progress for more than three years and a half, the time-honoured British practice of attempting to effect a military purpose while employing therefor a wholly inadequate force had once more been resorted to. The difficulties which had been experienced in feeding and supplying the columns of "Linforce" and "Hanforce" during the operations which led to von Lettow-Vorbeck's retreat across the Rovuma, probably convinced the British Command that any direct pursuit of the enemy into the country beyond that river, at a time when the beginning of the rainy season was almost due, would be attended by too great risks. The Germans, as they retired, always swept the country clear of supplies of every description and of practically all its able-bodied inhabitants, so an advancing British force would depend entirely upon the provisions that could be conveyed to it from Lindi along many miles of unmetalled motor-road, and thereafter by head-carriage over tracks, most of which would be submerged as soon as the waters of the Rovuma had been sufficiently swelled by the first freshet to cause them to overflow their banks.

Direct pursuit being therefore out of the

question, an advance westward from Port Amelia had been determined upon, but unfortunate delays had occurred, as we have seen, and by the time "Pamforce" had begun its march inland, the enemy had been able to complete his arrangements for its embarrassment and for his own security.

Towards the end of February, therefore, it was decided that "Pamforce" must be strengthened if anything practical were to be achieved, and a second column was dispatched to Port Amelia, the whole force being placed under the command of General Edwards. It was General Edwards, it will be remembered, who, while commanding the lines of communication when the extended attack upon the Dar-es-Salaam-Lake Tanganyika Railway was in progress in 1916, had inspected the Gold Coast Regiment immediately after its arrival in East Africa.

"Pamforce" was now divided into two columns, one, under the command of Colonel Rose, being composed of the Gold Coast Regiment, the 4th Battalion of the 4th Regiment of the King's African Rifles, the 22nd D.M.B., and a body of the King's African Rifles Mounted Infantry, and the other, under the command of Colonel Giffard, comprising the 1st and 2nd Battalions of the 2nd Regiment of the King's African Rifles. The first was designated "Rosecol" and the second "Kartucol."

A good deal of rain fell during March, deepening the swamp between Bandari and Mtuge, which had already caused so much trouble, filling the nullahs all along the road, and reducing the surface to a quagmire which, in many places, made traffic very difficult, even though the track had now been "corduroyed" from end to end. The journey up the road from Mtuge to Meza, though the distance was only some four-and-sixty miles, often took more than a week, and after the striking force had been strengthened by the addition of "Kartucol" the work of moving the new troops up to the front and of accumulating sufficient supplies to render an advance in any degree continuous, when it could at last be undertaken, proved to be at once slow and difficult.

Until the 27th March, therefore, the Gold Coast Regiment remained in camp at Meza, sending out patrols in all directions, doing its best to familiarize itself with the topographical features of the country in its neighbourhood, and having occasional brushes with small parties of the enemy, which more than once attempted to cut its lines of communication.

On the 27th March half the Gold Coast Regiment with the Stokes Battery and half the 2nd Battalion of the 2nd Regiment of the King's African Rifles, marched up the road, and camped for the night at Natovi—eleven miles distant—pushing on the next day to Namarika, some seven miles further on. Heavy rain fell on both days very soon after the camp was formed, and the bush-huts, called *banda* in East Africa, constructed of sticks and grass, afforded indifferent protection from the tropical downpour, which turned the trodden mud of the camp into deep slush.

From Natovi Lieutenant Clarke, with a patrol of thirty rifles, had been sent out to try to intercept an enemy foraging party, and on the following day

Captain Leslie-Smith and fifty men had been left at Namarika, when the rest of the Regiment advanced eight miles along the road to Manambiri. On the 29th March patrols under Lieutenant Chaundler and Lieutenant Beech were sent out, the first along the main road as far as Kitambo, distant four miles from Manambiri, and the other along the Nicoque-Medo road, which branches off to the north-west from the latter place. Neither of these parties found any traces of the enemy, and Lieutenant Clarke's report, when he reached Manambiri the same afternoon, was similarly negative. During the night, however, shots were exchanged between an enemy patrol and an outpost furnished by the 4th Battalion of the 4th King's African Rifles.

On the 30th March Lieutenant Chaundler again patrolled to Kitambo, but found that an enemy camp, which had been established just beyond that village, was deserted. During the day Manambiri camp, which by now had become a mere mud-hole, was rearranged, an endeavour being made to pitch it upon higher ground.

On the 2nd April, an enemy patrol having fired upon a party of sappers and miners near Namarika at about 7 a.m., Lieutenant Bisshopp with fifty rifles was sent out to try to intercept him, marching through the bush on a compass-bearing for a distance of eight miles. It was a toilsome and comfortless task, cutting and forcing a way through dripping-wet bush, but it led to no result.

On the 5th April Captain Harman patrolled along the main road to Medo with half of I Company, and reached Namaaka, which is distant about four miles from Manambiri. From Namaaka he sent out a small party which engaged an enemy patrol, composed of about thirty men and two machine-guns, which retired before it, though two men of I Company were wounded.

On the 7th April the Headquarters of the Gold Coast Regiment, with A and I Companies, advanced to Namaaka. This place was reached without incident, but two miles further on the advanced guard came up against a party of the enemy, about fifty strong with two machine-guns. A fight ensued which lasted for about two hours, in the course of which one man of the advanced guard was killed, and five men, two machine-gun carriers and four carriers belonging to the Sierra Leone Carrier Corps were wounded. The enemy was driven back to a position behind a large swamp, from which it would have been very difficult to eject him unless he could be outflanked. The advanced guard was not strong enough to attempt this, and it accordingly fell back upon the main body. A patrol was then sent round the north side of the swamp, only to find that the enemy had retired.

On the 8th April, half of I Company, under Captain Webber, was sent forward in the direction of Medo, and came into touch with the enemy at a place about half a mile beyond the position behind the swamp which the latter had evacuated on the preceding evening. As usual, the first intimation received on this occasion of the proximity of the enemy was a volley fired from cover, the men forming the advanced point being shot down. This accomplished, the enemy blew his bugles and

FIGHT AT NAMAAKA

sounded the charge. It had been previously arranged that, in the event of a fight developing, the supporting section, under Lieutenant Bisshopp, should move to the side of the road upon which the enemy appeared to be the more numerous, in order to support the leading section, which was under the command of Lieutenant Clarke. As the enemy came on, the shouting and cheering which accompanied his charge indicated that he was strongest on the left of the road, so Lieutenant Bisshopp with his party pushed forward in that direction at the double, receiving a volley in partial enfilade from the *Askari* who were engaging Lieutenant Clarke's section, and whose onset had already been almost stopped by the latter. As Lieutenant Bisshopp's section continued at the double, they presently met the enemy, who were also delivering an attack upon Lieutenant Clarke's flank; whereupon the *Askari* faced about and bolted. Many of them were wearing the green caps which are part of the service kit of the men of the Gold Coast Regiment, and so confused at all times is fighting in the bush, that one of Lieutenant Bisshopp's party, seeing his officers aiming at a retreating *Askari*, pulled his rifle down, crying out that the fugitive was one of their own corps. The next moment, this soldier fell, shot through the ankle, ejaculating many and bitter things about the manners and morals of the "Germani." I Company then attacked and drove the enemy down the road for several miles, and the other half of I Company having been sent forward to reinforce, a strong post was established about two miles west of Namaaka, with a picket thrown out a mile ahead of it. On this day I Company lost three men killed and five men wounded.

In the afternoon the rest of the column arrived at Namaaka, and on the 9th April it went forward through I Company's post, the 4th King's African Rifles being the advanced guard. The enemy were driven back about four miles further down the road, and the column camped for the night at a point to which the name of Rock Camp was given, on account of a large isolated bluff which was situated near to it on the northern side of the road.

From Rock Camp Lieutenant Reid was sent out to try to locate the road to Kimone toward the south, and Lieutenant Cumming took out a patrol in a north-easterly direction to the Montepuez River, which falls into the sea about forty-five miles north of Port Amelia, and on the right bank of which Medo is situated.

This place was now the immediate objective of "Pamforce," the enemy being believed to have occupied it in some strength, and to have accumulated there a considerable quantity of supplies.

General Edwards and his Staff reached Rock Camp at 7.30 a.m. on the 10th April, and at 1.30 p.m. the Gold Coast Regiment moved out towards Medo, which was distant about seven miles.

The *boma*, or entrenched camp, at Medo—originally a stronghold of a Portuguese revenue-farmer—occupied a situation on a piece of rising ground some six or seven miles up the main road from Rock Camp. To the south of the *boma*, and about three-quarters of a mile from it, lay the village of Medo; and the country, which is here

SKETCH TO ILLUSTRATE OPERATIONS AGAINST MEDO.

both rocky and hilly, was for the most part parkland, studded with frequent trees and covered with grass and patches of bush. Though some of it had the appearance of being fairly open, it proved to be what is called "very blind," no extended view being obtainable in any direction.

The main road runs east and west from Rock Camp to Medo, passing through broken country, and flanked on the left or southern side by Chirimba Hill. This is an eminence several hundred feet in height and about two miles in length—a mass of slate-grey rock rising out of a tangle of bush and low forest, which clothes its lower slopes and overflows to the very edge of the road. The summit of this hill is razor-edged and deeply serrated throughout its length, rising into three principal peaks divided by ravines; and its nature was such that no attempt could be made to advance along it. Running parallel to the main road at a distance of only a few hundred yards from it, Chirimba Hill commanded it for a matter of about two miles, and completely dominated the position.

As usual, the enemy had selected a very awkward place in which to offer this, his first serious resistance to the British advance in Portuguese East Africa. He was six companies strong—say about eight hundred men—with twelve machine-guns and one field gun which he had captured from the Portuguese at Ngomano. The whole force was under the command of Major Kohl, the ablest of von Lettow-Vorbeck's lieutenants, to whom throughout the campaign the task of harassing and delaying the British advance, and of fighting rear-guard actions, was most frequently confided by his chief. He had posted men in the thick bush along the base of Chirimba Hill, and had occupied a strong position on high ground astride the road on a very extended front, and most effectually concealed in the bush.

When the Regiment moved forward on the afternoon of the 10th April, Captain Harris with fifty rifles was sent out on the left to try to establish himself on the eastern extremity of Chirimba Hill. This patrol ran into an ambush before it had proceeded far upon its way, Sergeant Flatman and one soldier being killed and several of the party wounded. Though, after this, Captain Harris was at first forced to retire, he succeeded in collecting his rather scattered men, and, advancing again, made good a post on the slopes of the hill which had been his objective.

Meanwhile the advance-guard had come into action about three miles down the road from Rock Camp, and it speedily became evident that the enemy could not be ejected from the position he had taken up until Chirimba Hill had been occupied. The Gold Coast Regiment accordingly camped at a place two miles from Rock Camp, with an advanced post thrown out a mile further down the road. Its further losses during the afternoon were 1 man killed, 10 wounded, and 1 carrier missing, who was believed to have been killed.

On the 11th April the rest of "Rosecol" moved forward to the camp which the Gold Coast Regiment had established over night, and at dawn the advanced guard, consisting of I Company and two

Stokes guns, advanced to the forward post a mile further down the road. From this point an officer's patrol consisting of one section of I Company under Captain Webber was sent out on the left to occupy the peak at the eastern extremity of Chirimba Hill, at the foot of which a post had been established by Captain Harris on the preceding evening. His right rested on the road, the section being thence strung out through the bush to the foot of the hill.

Simultaneously another section of I Company, under Lieutenant Barrett, was pushed out on the right of the road, its left keeping touch with Captain Webber's right. Yet a third section of I Company, under Lieutenant Bisshopp, was deployed on Lieutenant Barrett's right. Lieutenant Barrett's section was the first to come into action, a small party of the enemy opening fire upon it and then retiring. It was also seen by one of the enemy's observation-points posted on Chirimba Hill, for it was shelled by the Portuguese field-gun, which was posted in the bush somewhere in the neighbourhood of Medo *boma* to the right front of the advance. A section of A Company was sent out still more to the right to move along a track to the north which ran parallel to the main road, and was often described as "the telegraph road," as there were vestiges on it of a line which had been constructed by the Portuguese and utilized by the enemy.

Major Shaw, who was in command of the advance, decided that it was not possible to push on further until Chirimba Hill had been cleared of the enemy, and a section of A Company was sent out to the left to reinforce Captain Webber's party. This part of the line came into action early in the afternoon, and was engaged with the enemy, posted in the thick bush and low forest on the lower slopes of Chirimba Hill, until about 4.30 p.m. By the end of the day all that had been achieved was the establishment of a post, occupied by half of I Company under Captain Webber, on the slopes of Chirimba Hill, the eastern extremity of which had been cleared of the enemy; while on the right of the road a small post had been established under a native non-commissioned officer, about four hundred yards in advance of the point reached by Captain Webber on the left of the line.

At 4 p.m. "Kartucol" advanced from Rock Camp through the bush to the south of Chirimba Hill, for the purpose of taking up a position from which to join on the morrow in a general attack upon Medo; and an hour later "Rosecol" received orders to advance at 6 a.m. on the following morning, the attack to be delivered by the Gold Coast Regiment, the 4th Battalion of the 4th King's African Rifles forming the force and column reserve.

On the 12th April the advanced guard, consisting of B Company with two Stokes guns, under Major Shaw, moved forward at 6 a.m., the 22nd D.M.B. covering its advance by shelling the bush in which the enemy was believed to have established himself. The broken, bush-covered country lent itself to defence, and the enemy's machine-gun and rifle fire from the lower slopes of Chirimba Hill was persistent and galling, nor could even his main position be accurately located. Early in the day,

CLEARING THE HILL

however, three or four men of I Company scaled the higher peak of Chirimba Hill, which overlooked that cleared of the enemy the night before, and succeeded in ejecting therefrom a solitary *Askari*, who had evidently been engaged in observing for the enemy's gun.

At this time the advance of "Rosecol" was being opposed by about two companies of the enemy, the remainder being held in reserve, though the movement of "Kartucol" round the southern side of Chirimba Hill had not yet been discovered by Kohl. The resistance offered was, as usual, of a very determined character, and tbe progress made by the attacking force was proportionately slow.

During the whole of the advance the Stokes guns belonging to the Gold Coast Regiment were of the greatest assistance. Under the command of Captain Foley and Lieutenant Lamont, these guns had been almost continuously employed in all recent actions, and while the companies of the Regiment had taken it in turn to bear the brunt of the work, the Stokes gun team and their officers had a record of almost continuous activity. On this occasion they had opened fire as soon as ever the machine-guns came into action, throwing their shells about one hundred and fifty to three hundred yards to the right and left of the advance on both sides of the road. When the line halted to fire, fifteen minutes were allowed the Stokes guns to take up fresh positions, generally about fifty yards in the rear of the firing-line. This worked very well, and the advance, though slow, was practically continuous until about 12.30 p.m., when the enemy developed a very stout resistance, and held the Gold Coast Regiment up for nearly three hours.

At 2 p.m. two sections of A Company, under Captain Wheeler, were sent forward to reinforce Major Shaw, and to extend the line on the right of the advance; and an hour later the Headquarters of the Regiment, with two sections of I Company, advanced, and Colonel Goodwin took over the command from Major Shaw. The latter then went forward and assumed the command of the firing-line, which at this time had worked its way along the northern face of Chirimba Hill, and was getting clear of its western extremity. Simultaneously fifty rifles of I Company, with one machine-gun and one Lewis gun, under the command of Captain Harman, were sent out to the right of the two sections of A Company, under Captain Wheeler, with orders to extend the line to the right and to be prepared to swing the right flank round so as to enfilade the enemy when the advance was continued.

At about 3 p.m. "Kartucol," on the southern side of Chirimba Hill, was heard to be heavily engaged with the enemy, and the resistance offered to the advance of the Gold Coast Regiment perceptibly slackened. Major Shaw therefore worked round the western end of the hill and succeeded in getting into touch with the King's African Rifles, who had dug themselves in in a hastily made perimeter camp. At the moment of Major Shaw's arrival the enemy was delivering a strong counter-attack upon the leading troops of "Kartucol," which were very hard pressed. Major Shaw at

ACTION AT CHIRIMBA

once attacked vigorously, and a very sharp engagement ensued, which resulted in the Gold Coast Regiment and the King's African Rifles driving the enemy back with considerable losses.

Meanwhile half of I Company, under Captain Harman, which, as we have seen, had been sent out on the extreme right of the advance, had met a large open swamp, the negotiation of which caused some delay; and as the firing-line, commanded by Major Shaw, was wheeling steadily to the left, following the configuration of the ground at the western extremity of Chirimba Hill, touch with A Company was presently lost. Captain Harman crossed from the right to the left of the main road, still without regaining touch with A Company; and soon after firing broke out in front of him. Advancing in the direction from which the sound came, touch with the right of A Company was at last regained; but as the whole line pushed forward the wheel to the left became more and more pronounced, Major Shaw being engaged at this time in moving round the western extremity of Chirimba Hill to go to the assistance of "Kartucol." Just as this movement began, fire was opened upon Captain Harman's half-company from the right flank and right rear, the enemy company, which had hitherto been held in reserve, having been sent, it is probable, to join up with the other companies which were delivering a heavy attack upon the roughly made perimeter camp in which "Kartucol" was defending itself. The half-section of I Company on the extreme right of Captain Harman's little party was hastily faced about to resist the attack from the right rear, and the section bombers on its left drove the enemy off from its right front. The attacking party to the right rear, however, was more persistent, and Colour-Sergeant Thornett, with three of his machine-gun team and three carriers, who at the moment when fire was opened upon them had just loaded up in order to move forward, were all hit, Colour-Sergeant Thornett being killed on the spot. These losses were caused by a machine-gun which the enemy had captured from the Portuguese. The reserve gun-team and carriers, however, behaved with their usual coolness, and they succeeded in getting their gun away, only leaving one box of ammunition behind them, which was recovered next day.

Sergeant Mudge was wounded badly in the groin and died in the course of a few minutes, while Lieutenant Barrett was slightly wounded in the thigh.

Meanwhile the half-section of I Company on the immediate left of the party which had been thus roughly handled, had gone on with the main advance, leaving only about twenty-five men to deal with the surprise attack which had been delivered upon them. They succeeded, none the less, in driving the enemy off; but recognizing the necessity of guarding the right flank of the main advance against a possible renewed attack, and hampered in his movements by the number of his casualties, Captain Harman decided to remain where he was, and not to attempt for the moment to regain touch with the troops on his left.

The wounded men were carried back to the place where Colonel Goodwin had established his Headquarters, the work being done in difficult

ACTION AT CHIRIMBA

circumstances, no stretchers or stretcher-bearers being available. Darkness fell, and Captain Harman's little party, having found no further trace of the enemy, gathered together and began to work over to the left with the intention of regaining touch with the men under Major Shaw's command. These had now joined up with "Kartucol," as already mentioned, and had thereafter established themselves in the perimeter camp which had been hastily dug earlier in the day by the King's African Rifles. Here, guided by the bugle-call of I Company, Captain Harman's party presently joined them; and the weary men of both columns dossed down for the night on the bare ground to sleep as best they might, without food or cover of any description.

While the engagement was in progress Colonel Rose and several members of his staff had a very narrow escape. They had been walking up and down the road at some distance to the rear when a loud explosion occurred within a few feet of them, and a man of the 22nd D.M.B., who a few moments before had been coming down the road toward them, was blown into the air, receiving terrible injuries from which he shortly afterwards died. It was a road-mine which he had touched off—a road-mine constructed, as usual, of one of the 4·1 shells from the *Koenigsberg*—and Colonel Rose and his companions, who as it was were only spattered from head to foot with mud, had during the last quarter of an hour repeatedly passed within a few inches of the spot where the slightest pressure upon the surface of the road would have ignited the charge. These road-mines were found with considerable frequency, and the men of the Gold Coast Regiment had a rather embarrassing habit of digging them up, and carrying them to their officers for inspection, live-fuse and all, handling the lethal things with a reckless familiarity which it was hair-erecting to witness. On the whole, however, extraordinarily little damage was done by these man-traps.

Mention has been made of the good work done by the Stokes guns under Captain Foley and Lieutenant Lamont. These guns, one of the notable inventions of the Great War, proved to be the ideal artillery for bush-warfare. Their discharge causes so slight a report that, when rifle-fire is going on, it is practically inaudible, and it was therefore very difficult for the enemy to locate the positions from which the guns were shelling them. On the other hand, the Stokes guns were very handy and could be got into action with great rapidity, while the shells thrown by them burst with a particularly loud report that was not without its moral effect, and threw a very effective charge.

The losses sustained by the Regiment from the 10th to the 12th of April amounted to 4 Europeans —Colour-Sergeant Thornett, Sergeant Mudge, and Sergeant Flatman—killed, and Lieutenant Barrett wounded; 10 men killed and 40 wounded; and 1 carrier killed and 14 wounded—in all 69 casualties. Unfortunately the losses among the rank and file included a number of old soldiers and section commanders, all of whom were at this time doubly valuable owing to the experience which they had gained during nearly four years of almost continous warfare.

During these three days a great strain was imposed upon Captain J. M. O'Brien, of the West African Medical Staff, and upon his assistants; and Captain O'Brien, by no means for the first time, displayed almost reckless courage while attending to the wounded under fire.

On the 13th April scouting parties sent out from the camp found that, as usual, the enemy had retired. His primary object had been to delay and embarrass the British advance, and to make it pay as heavily as might be for its passage over a few miles of road lying through particularly difficult country. This he had achieved; and if indeed the *boma* at Medo had contained any accumulation of supplies, he had also succeeded in removing them before he was compelled to evacuate that place, for none were found when the troops occupied Medo on the 13th April. Meanwhile "Pamforce," which throughout the three days' fighting had been engaged in attacking and being attacked by an enemy who, from beginning to end, remained practically invisible, was no nearer the fulfilment of its purpose—the wearing down or rounding up of von Lettow-Vorbeck's forces—than it had been when, more than three months earlier, it had first landed at Port Amelia.

CHAPTER XVII

THE ADVANCES FROM MEDO TO KORONJE AND MSALU

ALL that remained of the Portuguese *boma* at Medo was the deep ditch by which it had been surrounded, and the mound or earthwork fashioned from the earth that had been excavated from it. Any buildings that these fortifications may have been designed to protect had long ago been burned to the ground, and save for a big red-brick store, with an iron roof, situated outside the ditch, there was no habitable place in the immediate vicinity. It can never have been of much military value, except against attacks delivered by natives armed with primitive weapons, and its capture and occupation by the British conferred upon the latter no material advantage. Medo, however, or rather the place a few miles east of it where Rock Camp had been formed, marks the beginning of a stretch of very blind and difficult country, where big clumps of bamboos are numerous, where bamboo-brakes of considerable extent are not infrequently encountered, and where elephant grass nine feet high is a common feature. Further on along the road, as the columns advanced, more broken ground was met with, and numbers of isolated rocky hills, often fantastically shaped—the solitary

ADVANCE TO MWALIA

curved horn of the rhinoceros being one of the forms most commonly represented—provided the enemy with excellent observation-posts from which every movement of the British troops could be watched and provided against.

On the 13th April the two columns camped at Medo, and on the following day a strong officer's patrol of the 4th Battalion of the 4th King's African Rifles went down the road toward Mwalia, and speedily found itself engaged with the enemy. Von Lettow-Vorbeck and Kohl had allowed the British, very slowly and painfully, to work their way inland from the coast from a distance of eighty-four miles to Medo; and having now drawn them on into a very difficult belt of country, they were preparing to ambush the advance once or twice daily, to make the troops fight as often as possible and in disadvantageous circumstances, for the camping-ground and for their supply of water, and to withhold from them any chance of dealing a very effective blow at their ubiquitous and elusive enemy.

The campaign was at once more harassing and less hopeful than had been the advance from Narungombe to Lukuledi in the preceding year, for then "Linforce" had been working its way inland from Lindi, and there had always been a chance of the enemy being enveloped by the converging columns; and the country, though thick and difficult, had not been so blind and so impenetrable as that through which "Pamforce" was at present engaged in making its way. Now, too, there was no British force closely co-operating with "Rosecol" and "Kartucol" to threaten the enemy's flank and rear, though some of General Northey's troops had made their way in a south-easterly direction from Mahenge, and were known to have crossed the Rovuma, and Colonel Rose, while still in command in Portuguese East Africa, had succeeded in getting the 3rd Battalion of the 2nd King's African Rifles dispatched to Mozambique, where, under Colonel Phillips, they were brigaded with a Portuguese force under Major Leal. There was, however, no immediate prospect of bringing von Lettow-Vorbeck to a definite action, for there no longer existed German posts, such as Ruponda, Massassi and Newala, the defence of which was important to him because their capture would work him a measure of moral and even of material injury. Instead von Lettow-Vorbeck, at this time, seemed to have the whole of the vast continent of Africa into which to retreat, and the prospect of surrounding or cutting off any large body of his forces was felt by all to be more remote than ever.

None the less, "Pamforce" continued to move forward down the road from Medo to Mwalia and from Mwalia to Koronje, with ever-lengthening lines of communication stringing out behind it, and with daily ambushes delaying its progress. These, often enough, were laid for it by small enemy posts consisting of one native non-commissioned officer and half a dozen *Askari*, but in such blind country it was on each occasion necessary to clear up the situation before the advance could be continued, lest the column should find themselves caught in some more elaborate trap with results that might well prove to be disastrous.

ADVANCE OF "ROSECOL"

Moreover, the character of the country, which greatly favoured the tactics that the enemy was now adopting, practically confined the British to a series of frontal attacks, as it did not admit of flanking movements being successfully carried out.

On the 15th April "Rosecol" left the camp at Medo, and began to advance down the road in the direction of Mwalia. The 4th Battalion of the 4th King's African rifles formed the advanced guard, the Gold Coast Regiment being in reserve. The former's advanced points were attacked, as usual, and the Battalion engaged a small enemy rear-guard, the progress made during the day amounting to only four and a half miles. From this time onward, the Gold Coast Regiment and the 4th Battalion of the 4th King's African Rifles took it in turns to lead the advance, and each was preceded at a short distance by an advanced detachment consisting of 300 rifles with the usual complement of machine and Lewis guns, and two Stokes guns of the Gold Coast Regiment. This leading detachment had points thrown out ahead on each side of the road and a line of skirmishers deployed behind them, the remainder of the detachment advancing in open order on both sides of the road, with connecting files between them and the main body in their rear.

On the 16th April the advanced detachment was supplied by A Company and two sections of I Company, under the command of Major Shaw. During the day small engagements were fought with an enemy rear-guard, consisting of one company, but the Stokes guns proved very useful and effective, the enemy being shelled out of successive positions from which, but for these guns, it would have cost much delay and probably many casualties to eject him. As it was, only two men of the Regiment and one Sierra Leone carrier were wounded. The column camped at 2 p.m., Major Shaw's detatchment digging itself in about a mile further down the road.

On the 17th April the 4th Battalion of the 4th King's African Rifles furnished the advanced detachment, that regiment being at the head of the column, with the Gold Coast Regiment following in reserve. During the afternoon the King's African Rifles became heavily engaged with the enemy, who had been reinforced and was now opposing the advance with three companies and six machine-guns. The road here ran through elephant grass nine feet in height, and it was found impossible to locate the enemy's positions. On the other hand, the King's African Rifles had dug themselves in across the road, the lie of which was accurately known to the Germans, and the former consequently sustained many casualties. The 4th Battalion of the 4th King's African Rifles was a newly raised force, largely composed of recruits, and the ordeal of being fired upon by an invisible enemy, against whom no effective retaliation was possible, was very severe. However, they held on, and in the afternoon A Company was sent forward to reinforce them. This company and the two Stokes gun-teams, which had been with the 4th Battalion of the 4th King's African Rifles all day, sustained 28 casualties before dark, losing 3 men and 1 battery gun-carrier killed, and 13 men, 6 battery gun-carriers and 5 Sierra Leone carriers wounded.

Next morning the Gold Coast Regiment took over from the King's African Rifles the position which the latter had occupied during the night, and was directed to hold the enemy in front while a strong detachment from " Kartucol " attempted a wide flanking movement on the right. Captain Duck with thirty rifles was sent forward from the position held by the Regiment to get in touch with the enemy in order to give the flanking detachment an objective. He speedily found and engaged the enemy, whereupon the rest of " Kartucol " advanced through the Gold Coast Regiment and joined in the fight. The enemy, however, had once again reduced his rear-guard to a single company, and on the 19th April " Kartucol " continued the advance, " Rosecol " following in the rear. On the following day the two columns were to have exchanged places, but the rations expected from the rear arrived so late on the night of the 19th April that this arrangement could not be carried out. The delay had been caused by the convoy being attacked by the enemy near Rock Camp. The officer commanding this convoy was killed, and much confusion was wrought by the ambush, though the carriers and their escort contrived to get through with the loss of a few bags of mails. There were many Europeans in camp who would far more willingly have foregone their dinners. In a captured diary Kohl was subsequently found complaining with disgust that the mails taken on this occasion contained no information concerning the progress of the war in Europe, and mainly consisted of " love to dear Jack."

"Kartucol," therefore, continued the advance and occupied Mwalia, while "Rosecol" camped for the night at Kalima, about four miles short of that place. The distance from Medo to Mwalia is not quite five-and-twenty miles. The column had left Medo on the 15th April and "Kartucol" had reached Mwalia on the 20th April, the average daily progress being therefore little more than four miles.

On the 21st April "Rosecol" remained in camp at Kalima, where it was joined by General Edwards and his staff. "Kartucol" during the day was shelled by the enemy, and on the 22nd April it moved forward and occupied an enemy position two miles in front of the camp at Mwalia. Both columns remained in these positions until the 26th April, when "Rosecol" moved forward and occupied Makuku, about twelve miles down the road, "Kartucol," which had preceded it, having advanced three miles further to a place called Mbalama. At Makuku the main road, hitherto followed, which leads from Mtuge to Lusinje, is crossed by another which runs south-west to Koronje; and Mbalama is situated some three miles down this latter track.

On the 27th April "Rosecol" advanced through "Kartucol," and marched down the road towards Koronje, with Nanungu, some forty miles further to the west and slightly south of the former place, as its ultimate objective. The advanced detachment, under Major Shaw, consisted of the Pioneer Company and A Company of the Gold Coast Regiment with two Stokes guns. A small party of the enemy was engaged and driven back; "Rosecol" camped for the night about four miles west of Mbalama.

Next day, 28th April, the advance was continued, being led this time by the 4th Battalion of the 4th King's African Rifles, two Stokes guns of the Gold Coast Regiment, as usual, accompanying the advanced detachment. About six miles were covered during the day, and as "Rosecol" was forming camp at about 3.30 p.m., patrols from the advanced detachment came into touch with the enemy, and Lieutenant McEvoy was wounded in the hand by a stray bullet, and a trumpeter belonging to the Stokes Gun Battery was killed.

On the 29th April the enemy was found to have abandoned the positions which he had occupied the night before; and at 7 a.m. the advanced detachment, consisting of half I and B Companies with two of the Gold Coast Stokes guns, advanced, the rest of "Rosecol" following half an hour later. Major Shaw, who was, as usual, in command of the advanced detachment, came into contact with the enemy at about 10.30 a.m., and thereafter the latter fought an intermittent rear-guard action—a series of harassing ambushes—until 4.30 p.m., when camps were formed for the night, Major Shaw's men occupying a position about a mile in advance of the rest of the column. In the course of the day only two men of the Gold Coast Regiment were wounded, the Stokes guns once more proving very useful in dislodging the enemy from successive positions.

On the 30th April, "Kartucol" passed through

"Rosecol" with the intention of attacking an enemy position, which was known to be held by four companies and one gun. The Headquarters of the Gold Coast Regiment, with half the Stokes Battery, the Pioneers and I Company, marched in the rear of "Kartucol" as reserve troops. Touch was not gained with the enemy until the afternoon, but owing to the country traversed being very difficult and blind, the progress made was so slow that no attack could be delivered upon the German position owing to the lateness of the hour. The two columns, therefore, formed a perimeter camp at about 4.30 p.m. at a place on the Koronje road about four hundred yards west of the Montepuez River. One Battalion from "Kartucol" occupied an advanced camp about one thousand yards further down the road leading to Koronje.

On the 1st May, the 1st Battalion of the 2nd King's African Rifles advanced along the road toward Koronje, while the 2nd Battalion of the same Regiment went out on the right to attempt to outflank the enemy's left. The country was still very difficult and extremely blind, and progress was again very slow. It was subsequently discovered, moreover, that from an observation post on the summit of Koronje Hill, to the left of the road, the enemy could follow every movement of the British troops. While, therefore, the 2nd Battalion of the 2nd King's African Rifles was laboriously working its way round to the right, its attempt to surprise and outflank the enemy was foredoomed to failure from the outset. Meanwhile, of course, this movement greatly delayed the advance of the rest of the force.

D.M.B. ENGAGED

The detachment of the Gold Coast Regiment which, under the command of Major Shaw, was with "Kartucol," was employed to escort the 22nd D.M.B. and the ammunition column of that force.

At about 5 p.m. the 1st Battalion of the 2nd King's African Rifles became heavily engaged, and simultaneously an enemy party of about forty rifles, which had worked its way through the bush to the rear, attacked the D.M.B. which was being escorted by fifty rifles of I Company. The latter, under Lieutenant Kay, acted with great steadiness and promptitude. At the moment when the attack was delivered, the Mountain Battery, which had just come out of action, was limbered up. For a moment the guns were in peril, but Lieutenant Kay held the enemy and beat off the attack while the mules and their loads were got away in safety.

The sound of the firing misled the 2nd Battalion of the 2nd King's African Rifles, which was out on the right, with the result that it rejoined the column in the rear of the enemy.

A perimeter camp was formed for the night, the 1st Battalion of the 2nd King's African Rifles digging themselves in at a point about eight hundred yards in advance of the main body.

On the 2nd May, the 1st Battalion of the 2nd King's African Rifles pushed out patrols which quickly came into touch with the enemy, who was soon after engaged by "Kartucol," which drove him back. No progress, however, was made during the day, and on the morrow it was found that, while the enemy's rear-guard was fighting "Kartucol," the position at Koronje had been evacuated.

"Kartucol" then advanced and camped near Koronje, the detachment of the Gold Coast Regiment under Major Shaw rejoining "Rosecol" in the afternoon.

On the 4th May "Kartucol" again advanced and located a strong enemy position near the Milinch hills, about six and a half miles west of Koronje, through which the road passes. On this day three officers and ten British non-commissioned officers belonging to the Gold Coast Regiment arrived from Port Amelia.

On the 5th May, "Rosecol" advanced and took over from "Kartucol," which then fell back to the camp which the former had hitherto occupied. The 4th Battalion of the 4th King's African Rifles encamped at a point down the road about a mile in advance of the main body of "Rosecol"; and patrols were sent out to the right and left to try to find a way round the enemy's position on the Milinch Hills. Both these patrols were furnished by A Company of the Gold Coast Regiment, that on the right being commanded by Captain Harris and that on the left by Lieutenant Withers.

On the 6th May Captain Harris returned and reported that the country to the north was much more open than that through which the columns had recently been advancing, and that it would be almost impossible to make a flanking movement from the right side of the road. On the 7th May Lieutenant Withers came in from the south bringing a similar report; and meanwhile patrols sent out by the 4th Battalion of the 4th King's African Rifles had on both days come into touch with the enemy just east of the Milinch Hills, and reported that the position which he was occupying was a very strong one. This was indeed the case, for the enemy was posted on the crests and slopes of two hills, both of which commanded the gut between them through which the road runs; yet on the 8th May it was discovered that the Germans had retired, and two companies of the 4th Battalion of the 4th King's African Rifles went forward and occupied the position which he had evacuated.

Meanwhile the lines of communication were lengthening behind the columns, and now measured approximately one hundred and forty miles from Mtuge, which in its turn is twenty-eight miles by road from Port Amelia. Also the heavy and increasing traffic over the road had not tended to improve it; and though road corps, recruited from South Africa and East Africa, toiled ceaselessly at its repair, the difficulties of transport and supply were becoming daily more and more acute. At this time, the columns at the front had been on very short commons for a considerable period, and the company officers of the Gold Coast Regiment reported that their men were not getting enough food to keep them fit to take part in active operations of so trying and arduous a character as those at present in progress.

On the 9th May the Gold Coast Regiment took over the Milinch Hills from the 4th Battalion of the 4th King's African Rifles; and on this day local natives reported to Colonel Rose that von Lettow-Vorbeck, with a large enemy force, was moving in a north-easterly direction toward Lusinje. This place lies about thirty-seven miles almost due north of Nanungu, on the main road from which the columns had branched off in a south-westerly direction at Makuku, as already noted. Accordingly the 4th Battalion of the 4th King's African Rifles was dispatched across country to Msalu Boma, which is situated on that road at a point, as the crow flies, about twenty-three miles north-west of Koronje, and twenty-seven miles east by south of Lusinje. The orders issued to this battalion of the King's African Rifles were that they should deal with any enemy parties weak enough to enable action to be taken with effect, but to avoid any serious engagement with his numerically superior forces.

It was believed that a fairly strong party of the enemy were occupying a hill on the right side of the road at a place called Jirimita, about five or six miles down the road from the pass through the Milinch Hills, and at dawn on this day two patrols were sent out, one under the command of Captain Leslie-Smith and the other under Lieutenant Bisshopp. Each patrol consisted of seventy-five rifles, drawn respectively from A and I Companies; and Captain Leslie-Smith, who went out on the right of the road, had orders to make a flanking movement and to come back to the highway at a point about four miles beyond Jirimita. Lieutenant Bisshopp, on the left, was instructed to make a wider and longer sweep, and to strike the road about three miles further on. It was hoped thus to outflank the enemy and to cut off his retreat. It was a difficult task in the broken country through which these two patrols had to work, at once to maintain a correct sense of direction, and accurately to estimate the distance traversed. However, both these small parties started off, expecting to be a night or two in the bush, and each in the end succeeded in exactly carrying out the orders issued to it.

Meanwhile, during the morning of the same day Lieutenant Wilson, with a patrol of twenty rifles drawn from the Pioneer Company, got touch with an enemy outpost of about the same strength at a point some two miles west of the Milinch Hills; and at 4.45 p.m. a second officer's patrol, under Lieutenant Beech, was sent out down the road in the same direction for a distance of two and a half miles without coming into contact with the enemy, whose outpost had retired since the morning.

At 6 a.m. on the 10th May, Lieutenant Withers, with fifty rifles and one Lewis gun of A Company, was sent down the road with orders to brush aside any small party of the enemy that he might encounter, and thereafter to try and ascertain the real strength of the force which was opposing the advance of the column.

Three and a half miles from the Milinch Hill Lieutenant Withers met a small party of the enemy, which he drove back; and about five miles out he found an enemy camp, strongly entrenched, which had evidently been designed to accommodate some four companies, but which had been recently burned. As far as it was possible to judge, this camp had been destroyed and abandoned two days earlier; and though the tracks leading from it were at once confused and confusing, conveying at first the impression that the enemy had retired in a northerly direction, it was subsequently ascertained that he had retreated down the main road. Just beyond the burned camp this road was found to bifurcate, one fork leading west-north-west and the other west-south-west. It was the latter route which the enemy had taken.

The main patrol camped at a point where the road bifurcated, and sent out small parties to reconnoitre along each of the forks, but neither of them came into touch with the enemy.

On the 11th May the patrols under Captain Leslie-Smith and Lieutenant Bisshopp, which had been sent out on the 9th May, rejoined the Regiment. As has already been noted, they had achieved the difficult feat of striking the road at the points aimed at, but for the rest, though Lieutenant Bisshopp's patrol had surprised and killed one enemy *Askari*, who had probably been left behind to watch the movements of the British, nothing more had been seen of the enemy, who must have passed down the road while these patrols were still making their way through the bush.

On the 12th May one of the battalions of the 2nd King's African Rifles from "Kartucol" took over from the Gold Coast Regiment, which returned to the main camp occupied by "Rosecol." On the following day the latter marched across country, in the wake of the 4th Battalion of the 4th King's African Rifles, which had preceded them on the 9th May, in the direction of Msalu Boma. The way led along a native footpath which only admitted of men marching in single file, but in order to beat out a track for the transport through the high grass and standing crops of maize

CAMP AT MSALU

and millet, the column advanced four abreast—a hard task for troops who had been insufficiently fed for many days, and who were now required to cover between daybreak and dusk a distance of eighteen miles. The column camped in the bush, and on the following day it joined up with the 4th Battalion of the 4th King's African Rifles at the *boma* at Msalu. This place, too, had once been a stronghold of a Portuguese revenue-farmer, and had been fortified against attack by the natives, but it had now been completely destroyed by fire.

At Msalu news was received that von Lettow-Vorbeck and the whole of his main force were at Nanungu, and that so far they had given no signs of any intention to move to the north toward the Rovuma River, or south to the Lurio, which divides the territory of the Nyassa Company from the Province of Mozambique. It was also learned that the King's African Rifles Mounted Infantry were at Lusinje, some six-and-twenty miles along the main road west by north of Msalu, and about thirty-two miles almost due north of Nanungu.

"Rosecol" remained at Msalu on the 14th and 15th May, the neighbourhood being clear of the enemy, but much infested by lions. The proximity of these brutes got upon the nerves of some of the inmates of the camp, and on the night of the 13th—14th May a carrier, who had had a nightmare in which they played a prominent part, awoke in a panic, shattering the silence with his yells and outcry. Instantly an indescribable scene resulted. Tumbling over one another to get at the camp-fires, the porters fought and scrambled for fire-brands which they waved wildly, and impeded by which they made desperate efforts to climb into neighbouring trees. The country here is orchard-bush, and the only trees available are small and stunted—altogether inadequate as places of refuge from the onslaught of a lion. The terrified carriers, however, were long past reason, and appeared to consider that their one chance of salvation lay in getting even a foot or two above the ground. The lions on this occasion existed only in their imagination, and order and confidence were presently restored. During the same night, however, the 4th King's African Rifles lost two sentries, one killed and one badly mauled by these brutes, so the terror of the carriers had at any rate some measure of justification.

With the arrival of "Rosecol" at Msalu the second phase of the advance, which had its beginning with the fight at Medo, may be regarded as concluded. The enemy had offered a persistent and fairly effective resistance to the progress of the columns along the main road through the difficult country which lies between Medo and the Milinch Hills. His main force, which was believed to be at Nanungu, was really encamped at Wanakoti, about three and a half miles to the north of that place; and against him were advancing "Kartucol" from the east, "Rosecol" from the north-east, and a weak column of perhaps 800 rifles, which General Northey had dispatched across the Rovuma in a south-easterly direction, under the command of Colonel Griffiths. Von Lettow-Vorbeck still had the choice of several lines of retreat, for at Wanakoti many tracks cross one another, and though the road to Koronje on the east and to Chisona on the north-west were closed to him by the British advance, the track leading south-west to Mahu was still open, and while retreating along it he would have opportunities of breaking off, should it suit his convenience to do so, in almost any direction.

CHAPTER XVIII

THE EXPULSION OF VON LETTOW-VORBECK FROM THE NYASSA COMPANY'S TERRITORY AND THE RETURN OF THE GOLD COAST REGIMENT

ON the 16th May "Rosecol" left Msalu, and marching along bush paths in a westerly direction, leaving the road to Lusinje on the north and having the Msalu River on its right, began a movement which was designed to cut the main road between Lusinje and Nanungu. Camping for two nights in the bush—orchard country which, though the soil was of a rocky character, was broken by frequent patches of cultivated land—the column crossed this road on the 18th May, and pushed on toward Chisona. On reaching the Lusinje—Nanungu road, a patrol was dispatched to examine the ford across the Msalu River, and on approaching it was fired upon by a party which proved to be composed of scouts belonging to the Rhodesian Native Regiment—part of the weak column which General Northey had sent out across the Rovuma River. Connection was thus established for the first time with this force.

On the 19th May "Rosecol" continued its march to Chisona, where it camped on the banks of the Msalu River at a place about two miles from the column from "Norforce" above mentioned, which was under the command of Colonel Griffiths.

The river was unfordable at this season of the year, but the battery-carriers quickly constructed a bridge under the personal supervision of Colonel Goodwin, who, as a former commander of the Pioneer Company, had proved himself, both in the Kameruns and in East Africa, to possess a special gift for such improvizations.

On the 20th May the column crossed the Msalu, and marched due south to within five miles of Chilonga, I Company leading the advance and doing what it could to widen and improve the existing paths so as to facilitate the passage of the column. On the 21st May the latter pushed on twelve miles in a westerly direction and camped at a spot some three miles to the north of the road to Mahua. Five companies of the enemy, under Kohl, were reported to be on this road; and it was here learned that "Kartucol" had entered and occupied Nanungu without opposition, and was advancing along the Mahua road. This advance had been opposed by Kohl during the day, one company of the enemy with one gun having been in action, while the rest of his force was held in reserve. Meanwhile Colonel Griffiths' column was marching parallel to "Rosecol," on a line a few miles to the north of it.

At this juncture General Edwards hoped to surround Kohl from the west, east, and north; and with this object in view "Kartucol" was ordered to advance along the Mahua road, Colonel Griffiths' column to march in a south-westerly direction, so as to get astride that road in the rear of the enemy, while "Rosecol" was instructed to march on a line about three miles to the north of the Mahua road and roughly parallel to it with the object of turning the enemy's left.

During the afternoon of the 22nd May Colonel Griffiths' force was heard to be heavily engaged, and "Rosecol" continued its march until 10 p.m., when it camped, Major Shaw in command of the Pioneers and B Company of the Gold Coast Regiment, and two Gold Coast Stokes guns, forming an advanced detachment encamped on high ground a few miles forward, overlooking the place where Colonel Griffiths was entrenched. During all these operations "Rosecol" was separated from "Kartucol" by the Mwambia Ridge—a high barrier of grey, granite hills, with unscalable, cliff-like sides, rising abruptly from the grass and bush and orchard forest at their base—which flanks the main road on the north for a matter of more than a dozen miles.

Colonel Griffiths' column, it appeared, had struck the Mahua road, and had entered and occupied Kohl's camp at Mwariba, meeting with very little resistance. Here he had possessed himself of practically all Kohl's heavy baggage—a really severe loss to the enemy at this juncture; but almost immediately afterwards he had been vigorously attacked, his small column being completely surrounded and suffering many casualties. Failing to push home his attack, however, the enemy had drawn off during the night and had then retired in a southerly direction.

Yet another attempt to envelop him had definitely failed.

The Gold Coast Regiment this day came into contact with the enemy for the first time since it had quitted the main road near Koronje on the

13th April. Its only casualty, however, was one man wounded.

On the 23rd May " Rosecol " advanced through Colonel Griffiths' camp, with Major Shaw's detachment about one mile ahead of it; and very shortly afterwards the latter became engaged with the enemy, who, with one company and two machine-guns, was covering the retirement of Kohl's main force. Major Shaw drove this enemy party back a matter of two miles, when he was relieved by the 4th Battalion of the 4th King's African Rifles, who now formed the advanced detachment of " Rosecol," supported as usual, however, by two guns of the Gold Coast Regiment's Stokes Battery.

On this morning the Regiment lost one British non-commissioned officer, Sergeant Kent, and one soldier killed, and three men wounded.

On the 24th May the 4th King's African Rifles advanced at 6 a.m., and forthwith became engaged with the enemy, whose strength had now been increased to at least two companies with four machine-guns. All day long the Germans fought a series of very stubborn rear-guard actions, and the progress made by dusk was only two miles. In the course of the day Lieutenant Percy and two battery gun-carriers, attached to the Gold Coast Stokes guns, were wounded.

On the 25th May " Rosecol " advanced along the Mahua road in the direction of Korewa, with " Kartucol " following in its rear; Colonel Griffiths' column having marched west on the preceding day with the object of once again getting astride the road behind the enemy, this time on the other side of Korewa. The enemy was not met with, however, Major Shaw occupying Korewa in the afternoon without opposition, and during the night news was received that Colonel Griffiths had struck the road at the point aimed at, and that he, too, had seen nothing of the enemy.

From Korewa patrols were sent out in several directions, and by the 27th May, it having by then become pretty evident that von Lettow-Vorbeck with the main body, followed at a short distance by Major Kohl and his redoubtable rear-guard, had crossed the Lurio River into the province of Mozambique, Colonel Griffiths' column marched that evening in pursuit.

On the 28th May B Company, less one machine-gun and one Lewis gun, left the camp at 6 a.m. for Wanakoti, thirty miles to the east, acting as escort to the 22nd D.M.B. The rest of the Regiment remained in camp at Korewa, where it was rejoined by B Company in due course.

With the retreat of von Lettow-Vorbeck southward across the Lurio River, the expedition into the Nyassa Company's territory, which had been begun five months earlier by the landing of Major Shaw's advanced detachment at Port Amelia, reached its natural termination. Yet another campaign, based so far as the British were concerned upon the port of Mozambique, was about to begin, though as yet no very extensive preparations had been made for its effectual initiation.

The Gold Coast Regiment, as it has been seen, had been transferred straight from the pursuit of von Lettow-Vorbeck through the Kilwa and Lindi areas and on to the banks of the Rovuma, to the very trying inland march from Port Amelia. Other units subsequently engaged in that enterprise had in the interval been afforded a period of rest, the 2nd Battalion of the 2nd Regiment of the King's African Rifles, for example, having been allowed to return for a space to their cantonments and to their womenkind at Nairobi. The men of this corps and those of the Gold Coast Regiment, who had done so much hard fighting in company, had learned greatly to trust and value one another, and though they were drawn from such widely different parts of the African continent and though the Gold Coast soldiers' knowledge of Swahili was still rather elementary, a species of blood-brotherhood had come to be recognized as existing between them. When the "Second Second," as this battalion of the King's African Rifles was familiarly called, had made its appearance in Portuguese East Africa, it had been warmly welcomed by the men of the Gold Coast Regiment, and the latter, it may be surmised, had listened not without envy to the accounts which their friends had to give them of the good time the former had enjoyed during their stay at Nairobi. Were the war-worn veterans of the Gold Coast Regiment never to enjoy a similar respite from patrols, attacks, counter-attacks and endless toils and fatigues? The men put the question to their officers. They would fight on if they must, embarking forthwith upon this new campaign which was clearly about to begin; but they would fight better, they felt, if in the interval they might have a taste of the delights of rest and home in their cantonments at Kumasi. Colonel Goodwin, who was now commanding the Regiment, and Colonel Rose, who was commanding the column to which the battalion was attached, shared the men's opinion, and General Edwards agreed that the Regiment had fairly earned a rest.

Accordingly, at 7 a.m. on the 1st June, the Gold Coast Regiment left the camp at Korewa, and began its march back to Port Amelia. From Medo to Ankuabe—a distance of five-and-twenty miles—it was conveyed by motor-cars, but the rest of that weary journey was accomplished on foot over a road which had been knocked to pieces by the traffic passing over it. A standing camp was established at Gara, between Mtuge and Bandari, which was reached on the 13th June, Colonel Rose having, on the preceding day, relinquished the command of "Rosecol" and resumed that of the Regiment.

The rest of June, July and the first twelve days of August were spent in refitting, and men of the Regiment who were doing duty at various points along the lines of communication were gradually recalled and collected. On the 29th July Colonel Rose and Major Read sailed for South Africa from Port Amelia on board H.M. Transport *Hymettus;* and on the 13th August Major Hornby with 37 officers, 17 British non-commissioned officers, 862 rank and file, and 135 stretcher-bearers, gun-carriers, etc., embarked on board H.M.T. *Magdalena* and on the 14th August set sail for West Africa.

At Durban, reached on the 18th August, Colonel Rose and Major Read rejoined the Regiment, and both here and at Capetown, where the transport arrived on the 27th August, several officers were landed who were taking leave in South Africa, Australia or Tasmania.

Accra, the capital of the Gold Coast, was reached without incident late on the 5th September, and on the following day the Governor, who had seen the Regiment off from Sekondi exactly two years and two months earlier, came on board the *Magdalena* to welcome and inspect the troops, and to thank them on behalf of the Colony whose name they bear, for the splendid fashion in which, through all the trials and dangers of the East African campaign, they had upheld its reputation.

Colonel Rose and Major Read disembarked at Accra, but the Regiment sailed on the evening of the 6th September for Sekondi, where it arrived early next morning.

From this port to Kumasi, whither the Regiment at once proceeded in special trains, its journey was a triumphal progress. At Sekondi itself a feast of native foods, such as these soldier-exiles had not tasted for two years, had been prepared for their consumption; and at every halting-place crowds had assembled to greet and cclaim the Regiment and to load the men with gifts. All along the line little knots of natives shouted and danced their welcome, and even after darkness had fallen every station at which the trains stopped was crammed by eager crowds of Europeans and natives alike, bent upon showing the men what pride the colony felt at the reputation which they had won for themselves, and how deep was the popular sympathy for all they had suffered and endured.

It was a royal home-coming, and when at dawn the men, worn out with excitement and fatigue at last arrived at Kumasi, their women met them at the station in a clamorous mob, and accompanied them in triumph to their cantonments, with the songs and dances wherewith the warriors of West Africa have always been greeted on their return from a victorious campaign.

But, alas! there were wailings and keenings too, mingling with the joyful tumult, for many a woman there was lamenting some poor fellow who lies buried far away on the other side of Africa, and would not be comforted because he was not.

The casualties sustained by the Gold Coast Regiment during the campaign in East Africa were as follows:—

	Killed in action.	Wounded.	Missing.	Died of diseases.	Invalided.
British officers . . .	9	21	—	3	30
British non-commissioned officers . .	6	9	—	4	15
Rank and file . . .	181	603	13	206	469
Gun-carriers . . .	9	56	—	16	28
Stretcher-bearers . .	—	3	—	—	—
Clerks	—	—	—	1	1
Carriers	10	33	—	40	24
Total	215	725	13	270	567

The strength of the Gold Coast Regiment actually in the field never much exceeded 900 rifles. The total of effectives belonging to the Regiment at any one time in East Africa never numbered much more than 3000, and from first to last the total number of officers and men of all ranks dispatched did not amount to much more than 8800. When these facts are remembered, the

EXPANSION TO A BRIGADE

above table will be found strikingly to illustrate the severity of the fighting in which the Regiment took so active a part, and to indicate the ravages caused by disease to which prolonged strain and hardship exposed it.

Meanwhile the recruiting efforts made by the Government of the Gold Coast, to which during 1917–18 Captain Armitage, C.M.G., D.S.O., the Chief Commissioner of the Northern Territories, had devoted special energy and enthusiasm, had resulted in the collection of a very large number of recruits at the various training-depôts throughout the Colony, Ashanti, and the Northern Territories; and the Regiment had proved itself to possess such fine qualities that, as the early end of the war was not at that time anticipated, the War Office decided to convert it from a battalion to a brigade. This consisted of four full battalions with a battery of four 2·75 guns, and a battery of eight Stokes guns, and it was constituted a brigade as from the 1st November, 1918, under the command of Brigadier-General Rose. It was an open secret that, as soon as its organization was complete, the Second West African Brigade, as it was now called, was to be dispatched on active service to Palestine.

Then, during the closing days of October and the first half of November, came the dramatic collapse of the Central Powers and of their Allies— the *débacle* in the Balkans, the surrender of Turkey, the rout of the Austro-Hungarian armies on the Italian front, the succession of hammer-blows delivered on the western front from the Swiss frontier to the sea, and finally the Armstice granted to a defeated, crime-stained enemy, the terms of which exactly reflected the magnitude of the Allies' victory, and the extent to which Germany and Germans had forfeited the trust and the respect of all mankind.

The reading of those terms from the balcony of the Public Offices at Accra to a large concourse of people, almost beside themselves with enthusiasm and delight, was recognized as closing the short career of the Gold Coast Service Brigade; and by the end of the following December its disbandment was completed. It had existed long enough, however, to enable the Gold Coast to boast that it, no less than its neighbour the huge territory of Nigeria, had been able to raise by voluntary enlistment a full brigade of soldiers for the service of the Empire in the Great War.

APPENDIX I

THE MOUNTED INFANTRY OF THE GOLD COAST REGIMENT

THERE is another Gold Coast unit, which never served with the rest of the Regiment, and which remained behind in Portuguese East Africa when the remainder of the battalion returned to the West Coast, and of its short but adventuresome career some brief account must here be given.

At the end of February, 1918, nearly two months after the arrival of Colonel Goodwin with the main body of the Gold Coast Regiment at Port Amelia, Lieutenant G. H. Parker, who has been mentioned in an earlier chapter as having been in temporary command of the Battery, was chosen by Colonel Rose to raise and train a small body of Mounted Infantry. He was told to pick out for this purpose, from a newly arrived draft of recruits from the Gold Coast, 170 men; and to him were attached Lieutenants Drummond and Saunders, and five British non-commissioned officers.

The men chosen were natives of the Hinterland of the Gold Coast, to whom, since they for the most part live beyond the range of the tsetse fly and the *Trypanosoma*, horses are more or less familiar animals. About 10 per cent. of them could ride in the hunched-up, Tod Sloan-like fashion peculiar to folk to whom saddles are unusual luxuries; but not a man among them had the vaguest ideas concerning horse-mastership and management.

Four riding-schools were constructed near the camp, upon the top of the hill which slopes on the one side to the waters of the Indian Ocean, and on the other falls in a sheer cliff to the beach at Port Amelia; and daily for hours at a time the European officers and non-commissioned officers

APPENDIX I

shouted themselves hoarse, while the men bumped round the *manèges*. A certain number were incurably horse-shy, and had to be "returned to store," but the majority were quite fearless and enjoyed their daily ride, and though horses had not been received at Port Amelia until the end of March, by the 30th May No. 1 Troop of the Mounted Infantry of the Gold Coast Regiment was declared to be fit to take the field.

This troop, under the command of Lieutenant Drummond, consisting of 1 British non-commissioned officer, 41 rank and file, 51 horses, 2 mules, and 2 camp-followers, left Port Amelia on the above-mentioned date, and rode up the well-worn track from Mtuge to Medo, and thence to Wanakoti, General Edwards' Headquarters. The troop arrived at this place just as the Gold Coast Regiment was about to begin its march back to the coast from Korewa.

It is not possible to follow the history of this troop in detail without embarking upon a full account of the campaign in the Province of Mozambique, to which the British were committed after the Germans had retreated across the Lurio River, and this forms no part of the plan of the present work. It must, therefore, suffice to note that "Kartucol" from this time onward followed hard upon the heels of the enemy forces, pursuing them without intermission nearly as far south as Kilimane. A little north of this place one and a half companies of the 2nd Battalion of the 3rd King's African Rifles, with a much larger force of Portuguese encamped at Nhamaccura, were attacked by the enemy, who, having possessed himself of the guns belonging to the Portuguese, nearly annihilated the small British detachment, Colonel Gore Brown, who was in command, being himself killed with a large number of his men.

After this the enemy went north once more, still pursued by "Kartucol," which had now cut loose from its transport and was living on the country; and the Germans shortly afterwards attacked and invested Namirrue, a place near the centre of the province, which was being held by a company of the 2nd Battalion of the 3rd King's African Rifles, under Captain Bustard.

Drummond's Troop of Gold Coast Mounted Infantry had

APPENDIX 1

worked its way down in a southerly direction from Wanakoti to Namirrue, scouting for the columns, and doing some excellent work; and it had joined up with Captain Bustard's little force just before the latter was surrounded.

Finding that the position which he occupied at the moment of the enemy attack was commanded by the German guns, Captain Bustard occupied a higher hill near at hand; and, though hopelessly outnumbered, cut off from water, and bombarded by a Stokes gun which had been captured by the Germans, he made a gallant fight of it, and held out for three days.

Meanwhile the three remaining troops of the Gold Coast Mounted Infantry, under Captain Parker, had sailed from Port Amelia on the 1st July, arriving on the following day at Mussuril Bay, in the entrance to which lies the island of Mozambique. The force consisted of 8 British officers, 10 British non-commissioned officers, 137 rank and file, 84 East Africans, 2 Indians, 11 other details, with 133 horses, 50 mules, and 141 donkeys.

The Mounted Infantry were disembarked at Lumbo, on the northern shores of the bay, and on the 5th July marched twenty miles to Monapo, where their depôt was established. On the 8th July the Squadron began its march to Nampula, eighty miles further inland, where at this time General Edwards had his Headquarters; and travelling an average of about twenty miles a day, it reached its destination on the afternoon of the 11th July. Here Captain Parker learned that No. 1 Troop was with Captain Bustard at Namirrue, and that it was thought that the small post established there would embarrass the retreat of the enemy, who was known to be advancing from the south.

On the following days the Squadron pushed on in the direction of Chinga, which lies five-and-forty miles to the west of Nampula, walking and leading most of the time, for sore backs among the horses were already giving occasion for anxiety. From Chinga on the 15th July the Squadron marched sixteen miles to Marrupula; and here on the following day Captain Parker received orders to press forward as rapidly as possible to Metil, and thence to take up certain

APPENDIX I

positions on the Ligonha River. Three days' rations were drawn, and though the nights were very cold, the capes and spare clothing were all left behind, the men being cut down to their body-clothes and one blanket each, in order to ease the horses of as much weight as possible.

On the 17th July the Squadron covered a distance of thirty-three miles to Calipo, and on the morrow reached Pequerra, and pushed on thence to the banks of the Lighona River, travelling on that day thirty-six miles between dawn and dusk.

The geography of the country was very imperfectly known, and the only available maps were grossly inaccurate. Moreover, whereas it had been anticipated that the Ligonha River would only be fordable in a few places, which the Squadron had been ordered to hold, it was found that the stream was quite shallow for a distance of at least twenty miles. This was discovered on the 19th July, on which day Metil was reached, the Squadron having marched one hundred and two miles to that place from Murrupula in fifty-seven hours—a very good performance for a newly raised body of Mounted Infantry.

From Metil one troop, under Lieutenant Poole, was sent eastward to Napue; a second, under Lieutenant Viney, went toward Muligudge, five miles south-east of Metil; and a third, under Lieutenant Saunders, back along the track towards Pequerra, twenty men and Lieutenant Broomfield remaining at Metil with Captain Parker. All these mounted patrols had orders to try to locate the enemy and to keep touch as far as possible with one another and with Captain Parker.

On the 23rd July news was received that Namirrue was invested by the enemy, and that though it was still holding out, Colonel Fitzgerald's column, consisting of the 4th Battalion of the 4th and the 3rd Battalion of the 3rd King's African Rifles, had had to retire when attempting to move to Captain Bustard's relief. As Captain Parker was instructed to get as many of his men together as possible in order to scout in the direction of Namirrue, the troops under Lieutenants Poole and Viney were recalled, and on the 24th July, Captain Parker moved back to Pequerra, and

APPENDIX I

thence proceeded through dense bush to the banks of the Ligonha. From here Lieutenant Viney with twelve troopers crossed the stream and went scouting in what was believed to be the direction of Namirrue. On the 26th July Lieutenant Broomfield with twenty men were sent to Lulete, Captain Parker and Lieutenant Saunders with twenty-eight men—all that remained at their disposal—moving up the left bank of the Ligonha. At 4 p.m. they came upon a track, surprised an enemy baggage-train, and captured nine porters, the baggage-guard making off. Lieutenant Saunders with a few rifles was left to watch the trail, and late that afternoon he had a brush with the enemy, and captured a German, an *Askari*, and about a dozen more porters, also killing one or two enemy soldiers.

On the 27th July Captain Parker set off for Pequerra with the prisoners, leaving Lieutenant Saunders with a few men to watch the track and to snipe and harass the enemy. Captain Parker fell in with a superior force of the enemy, lost all his prisoners and a good many of his men and horses, and was himself reported missing for three days. At the end of that time, however, he and the surviving remnant of his troop contrived to rejoin. Meanwhile Lieutenant Saunders also came into touch with the enemy, was wounded and had several of his men and nearly all his horses shot; while Lieutenant Viney, who was surprised and attacked just as he had off-saddled, was killed, his men, acting on his orders, dispersing into the bush. Immediately afterwards word was received that Captain Bustard at Namirrue had been compelled to surrender, and with him Lieutenant Drummond and what was left of No. 1 Troop of the Gold Coast Mounted Infantry.

This meant that the Gold Coast Mounted Infantry, which on the 5th July had numbered, including Lieutenant Drummond's troop, about one hundred and sixty-five rank and file, was now reduced to sixty-five men; and Captain Parker returned to the depôt at Mnapo to train and equip further drafts, while Lieutenant Broomfield remained in the field in command of the handful of mounted men still effective as a fighting force.

APPENDIX I

Though the enemy had won successes at Nhamaccura and at Namirrue, in both of which places he had succeeded in cutting off small British forces, he was now being hunted by "Kartucol" from the south into the grip of six converging columns; and for the first time in the history of the whole campaign he was so completely cornered that in the neighbourhood of Chalana—a place some five-and-forty miles inland from the coast of Antonio Annes—he was compelled to concentrate all his troops, combining them into a single force.

It was while the meshes of the net appeared at last to be securely drawn around von Lettow-Vorbeck, that Lieutenant Broomfield and his little body of sixty men of the Gold Coast Mounted Infantry specially distinguished themselves. It was of great moment to General Edwards that he should be kept fully and frequently informed of the exact position and movements of the enemy, and this service was rendered to him by Lieutenant Broomfield. For a week the Gold Coast Mounted Infantry maintained close touch with the enemy's main body. The country is here very thickly populated. The Germans, who were paying for all their supplies with cloth which they had looted from the Portuguese stores, had made themselves very popular with the local natives, who witnessed the wholesale destruction of the Portuguese *bomas* with ecstatic delight. The British, who they were assured were hired bravos engaged by the Portuguese to capture their deliverers, were proportionately unpopular, and the movements of Broomfield's two troops were again and again betrayed by the natives to the enemy. Often he had to change his resting-place three and four times a day; he was engaged with the enemy almost as frequently; yet his active patrolling continued without interruption, and General Edwards was kept regularly informed as to every move which the enemy was making. It was, in its way, an outstanding little bit of work, carried out with great coolness, persistency and skill, and it by itself would abundantly have justified all the labour which had been expended in raising and training the Gold Coast Mounted Infantry.

At Numarroe—which lies much further to the west and

APPENDIX I

must not be confused with Namirrue—von Lettow-Vorbeck surprised and captured at the end of August a small British detachment from what had formerly been one of General Northey's columns; but at Liome on the 31st August and on the 1st September he came in for the worst hammering he had experienced in the whole course of the campaign, losing some fifty of his Europeans and several hundreds of his *Askari* killed, wounded and captured. On this occasion Lieutenant Drummond and a number of other captives were able to make their escape.

Thereafter, as is now well known, von Lettow-Vorbeck broke away north, succeeded in crossing the Lurio River, and thence treked through the Nyassa Company's territory to Ngomano on the Rovuma, where at the end of November in the preceding year he had re-equipped and refitted at the expense of the Portuguese garrison. Crossing the Rovuma, he once more entered German East Africa, still hotly pursued by battalions of the indefatigable King's African Rifles; but when after the signing of the Armistice he finally surrendered, he made his submission to a small police post in Northern Rhodesia.

The Gold Coast Mounted Infantry, once more reinforced and under the command of Major Parker, joined in the pursuit as far north as Ngomano, but on this occasion saw no fighting. On the 3rd October, however, orders were received for them to return to the Gold Coast in order to rejoin the 2nd West African Brigade; and as soon as the necessary arrangements could be completed, the men of the Gold Coast Mounted Infantry were embarked at Port Amelia, and on their arrival at Accra were disbanded, and reabsorbed into the Gold Coast Regiment.

APPENDIX II

LIST OF HONOURS AND DECORATIONS AWARDED TO EUROPEAN STAFF AND NATIVE RANK AND FILE OF THE GOLD COAST REGIMENT DURING THE EAST AFRICAN CAMPAIGN.

(1) EUROPEAN OFFICERS.

		Date.
Brevet Lieut.-Colonel	Temporary Lieut.-Colonel R. A. de B. Rose, D.S.O.	7/2/17
	Major G. Shaw, M.C. ...	5/8/18
Brevet Major on promotion to Captain	Lieut. (Temporary Captain) T. B. C. Piggott, M.C. ...	5/8/18
D.S.O.	Major H. Goodwin	10/6/17
	Captain H. A. Harman ...	10/6/17
Bar to D.S.O.	Lieut.-Colonel R. A. de B. Rose, D.S.O.	5/8/18
M.C.	Captain (now Lieut.-Colonel) G. Shaw	24/11/16
	Captain A. J. R. O'Brien ...	24/11/16
	Captain R. H. Poyntz ...	24/1/17
	Captain J. Leslie-Smith ...	13/8/17
	Captain J. G. Foley ...	29/10/17
	Captain H. B. Dawes ...	5/8/18
	Lieutenant T. B. C. Piggott	10/6/17
	Lieutenant G. H. Parker ...	11/3/18
	Lieutenant R. F. Beech ...	11/3/18
	Lieutenant G. B. Kinley ...	30/4/18
	Lieutenant L. B. Cumming	27/7/18
Bar to M.C.	Captain (now Lieut.-Colonel) G. Shaw, M.C.	13/8/17

APPENDIX II

		Date.
Bar to M.C....	Captain A. J. R. O'Brien, M.C.	13/8/17
	Captain E. B. Methven, M.C.	5/11/17
	Captain J. G. Foley	17/10/18
Legion d'Honneur Croix d'Officier ...	Lieut.-Colonel R. A. de B. Rose, D.S.O.	22/10/17
Croix de Guerre	Major H. Goodwin, D.S.O.	4/1/17
Italian Silver Medal	Lieutenant. T. B. C. Piggott, M.C.	4/1/17
O.B.E.	Major H. Read	9/9/18

(2) BRITISH NON-COMMISSIONED OFFICERS AND MEN.

D.C.M.	7024 Corpl. J. Campbell ...	24/1/17
	9532 R.S.M. F. C. Medlock	10/6/17
	28399 Sergt. E. Thornton ...	19/7/17
	69845 Pte. S. G. Radford (R.A.M.C.)	19/7/17
	1847 Sergt. C. A. Thornett	17/6/18
Bar to D.C.M.	7024 Corpl. J. Campbell ...	19/7/17
(Russian) Cross St. George (3rd Class)	69845 Pte. S. G. Radford ...	12/11/16

(3) NATIVE RANK AND FILE.

D.C.M	3948 Corpl. Akanno Ibadan	19/7/17
	113 M.G.C. John Lagos ...	19/7/17
	3844 C.S.M. Mumuni Moshi	19/7/17
	6727 Corpl. Yessufu Kotokoli ...	19/7/17
	5827 Sergt. Moriambah Moshi	19/7/17
	5737 Corpl. Musa Fulani ...	6/7/17 and 19/7/17
	6557 Temporary Corpl. Seti Frafra	24/11/16
	8427 Pte. Yaw Kuma ...	19/7/17
	5493 Corpl. and Tem. Sergt. Chililah Grunshi ...	No date

APPENDIX II

			Date.
D.C.M.		8581 L/Corpl. Granda Dikale	19/7/17
		7339 Trptr. Nuaga Kusase	18/4/17
		5048 Corpl. Sandogo Moshi	No date
		5397 Dr. Musa Karaki	No date
		5655 Sergt. Alhaji Grunshi	19/7/17
		7817 Pte. Seidu Chokosi	20/9/17
		5860 L/Corpl. (Acting-Corpl.) Issaka Dagarti	18/10/17
		4188 Sergt. Yessufu Mamprusi	18/10/17
		7426 Bugler Nufu Moshi	1/10/17
		4157 C.S.M. Musa Wongara	11/4/17
		5225 Sergt. Mamadu Moshi	25/5/17
Bar to D.C.M.		4961 Sergt. Bukara Kukawa	24/11/16
		6557 Temporary Corpl. Seti Frafra	15/8/17
Military Medal		4188 Sergt. Yessufu Mamprusi	19/7/17
		6689 Pt. Akuluga Moshi	19/7/17
		6414 Sergt. Palpuku Grumah	19/7/17
		182 M.G.C. Kwenjeh Moshi	19/7/17
		109 M.G.C. Dogali	19/7/17
		7842 Pte. Adama Bazaberimi	19/9/17
		7248 Pte. Allassan Grumah	15/12/16
		4765 Sergt. Braima Dagarti	15/12/16
		6690 L/Corpl. Kuka Moshi	15/12/16
		6756 Corpl. Timbala Busanga	15/12/16
		6675 Corpl. Yero Fulani	15/12/16
		13 H.G.C. Imoru Dodo	6/2/17
		5593 Corpl. Nuaga Moshi	11/4/17
		6688 Pte. Nubela Busanga	11/4/17
		6833 Pte. Sebidu Moshi	11/4/17
		4388 B.S.M. Bukare Moshi	23/5/17
		137 Hdm. G. C. Kwesi John	23/5/17
		94 G. C. Lawani Ibadan	23/5/17
		959 Sergt. Member	23/5/17

SERGT. SANDOGO MOSHI, D.C.M.

APPENDIX II

		Date.
Military Medal ...	8481 L/Corpl. Ntonge Etun	24/11/16
	3851 Sergt. Ali Wongara...	24/11/16
	170 S. B. Bawa Hausa ...	24/11/16
	200 S. B. Musa Kano ...	24/11/16
	5658 L/Corpl. Sulley Ibadan	24/1/17
Meritorious Service Medal	V. 103 Corpl. J. W. H. Amartey	17/6/18
	O.R.S. G. M. Fraser ...	17/6/18
	31 Qr.Mr.-Sergt. S. Amonoo Aidoo	17/6/18

APPENDIX III

STRENGTH OF THE GOLD COAST REGIMENT ON JULY 31ST, 1916.

Officers	55
British non-commissioned officers	13
Rank and file	1702

STRENGTH OF THE EXPEDITIONARY FORCE ON JULY 6TH, 1916.

Officers	36
British non-commissioned officers	15
Clerks	11
Rank and File	980
Carriers (battery)	177
Carriers (other)	204
Storemen	1
Officers (R.A.M.C.)	4

STRENGTH OF THE DRAFTS SENT FROM THE GOLD COAST TO REINFORCE THE EXPEDITIONARY FORCE.

First draft—25th November, 1916 :—

Officers	4
Clerks	1
Rank and file	402

Second draft—21st April, 1917 :—

Officers	2
British non-commissioned officers	1
Rank and file	500

APPENDIX III

Third draft—5th July, 1917 :—
    Officers 3
    British non-commissioned officers 2
    Rank and file 799
Fourth draft—6th October, 1917 :—
    Rank and file 401
Fifth draft—10th December, 1917 :—
    Rank and file 500

N.B.—Date shown in each case is that of departure from the Gold Coast.

APPENDIX IV

Letter from the General Officer Commanding "Pamforce" to the Officer Commanding the Gold Coast Regiment.

FAREWELL MESSAGE TO THE GOLD COAST REGIMENT BY THE GENERAL OFFICER COMMANDING PAMFORCE.

THE departure of the Gold Coast Regiment from my Command furnishes me with a fitting opportunity to place on record my high appreciation of the distinguished and gallant services which the Gold Coast Regiment has never failed to render me within the period that I have had the honour to command Pamforce.

The greatest testimony to the excellence of the services rendered by the Gold Coast Regiment is to be found in the fact that during the period which the Regiment has formed an integral part of Pamforce, it has assisted in reducing the enemy forces by at least one-half of his former strength, and the measure of the achievement of the Regiment is the contrast between the strength of the enemy force when Pamforce was formed and his strength to-day.

I would desire at this juncture to pay a high tribute of my regard to the Officer Commanding, Officers, British Non-Commissioned Officers, and the Native Ranks, for the initiative, resource, and daring which has characterized the service of all during this particularly difficult phase of the campaign, while I would wish expressly to place on record my high appreciation and gratitude for the able and efficient support that has been so loyally extended to me by Colonel R. A. De B. Rose, D.S.O., to whose soldierly qualities I feel I owe much.

I bid good-bye to the Regiment with deep regret, but

nevertheless with confidence that, no matter in what other theatre of war the Regiment may be called on to serve, the Gold Coast Regiment will ever prove itself worthy both of the confidence of King and Country by upholding the highest traditions of British arms, and the sacred heritage of the Flag of Saint George.

I wish you all God-speed, good luck, and a safe return, and so farewell.

      (Sgd.) W. F. S. EDWARDS,
            Brigadier-General,
    General Officer Commanding Pamforce.

Wanakote,
3rd June, 1918.

Letter addressed to the Officer Commanding the Gold Coast Regiment by the Acting Colonial Secretary.

No. 5276/M.P.11393/18.

      Colonial Secretary's Office, Accra, Gold Coast,
            6th September, 1918.

SIR,

  On the occasion of your return to the Colony with the first portion of the Gold Coast Regiment which is now on its way back from active service in East Africa, I am directed by the Governor to convey to you and to ask you to transmit to the Officers, European and Native Non-Commissioned Officers and the men of the Gold Coast Expeditionary Force under your command, the thanks of the Government of the Gold Coast for the brilliant and gallant services which they have rendered, and His Excellency's warm congratulations to them on their safe return.

2. The fine reputation which the Regiment won for itself in Togoland and subsequently in the Kameruns has, I am to add, been confirmed and enhanced by its behaviour during the campaign in East Africa; and the whole Colony is proud of the record of the Regiment which bears its name and is recruited from its inhabitants.

3. The heavy losses in Officers, Non-Commissioned

Officers, and men which the Regiment has sustained since it left the Colony on the 6th July, 1916, though they are the inevitable result of its prowess, are deeply mourned in the Gold Coast and its Dependencies, and I am to take this opportunity of expressing His Excellency's heartfelt sympathy with you and with the Officers, Non-Commissioned Officers, and men of the Expeditionary Force, which you have commanded with such conspicuous success.

4. His Excellency hopes that the Regiment will now, for a period, be able to enjoy the rest which it has so nobly earned, but that, if the war continues, a further opportunity may be afforded to it, at no very distant date, once more to render active and valuable assistance to the Empire,

I have, etc.,
(Sgd.)   C. H. HARPER,
Acting Colonial Secretary.

Lieutenant-Colonel R. A. De B. Rose, D.S.O.,
 Officer Commanding Gold Coast Regiment,
  Coomassie.

Resolution passed by the Legislative Council on the 28th October, 1918.

That this Council do record its proud appreciation of the reputation as a fighting force won by the Gold Coast Regiment in East Africa ; and that this Council do request His Excellency to convey to Lieutenant-Colonel Rose, D.S.O., and to the Officers, Non-Commissioned Officers, and men of the Regiment its congratulations on the distinguished record of service in the field, which the Regiment has maintained throughout the Great War, and its deep sympathy with all ranks in the heavy casualties which the Regiment has sustained.

INDEX

A COMPANY of the Gold Coast Regiment, 4, 31, 35, 37, 38, 50, 53, 61, 82, 84, 119, 131, 135, 215, 222, 236, 244, 253, 260
Accra, 4, 275, 278; volunteers from, 56; school at, 64
Æneas, the transport, 5
Aeroplane, British, shot down, 155
Aeroplanes, use of, 111
Africa, East, climate in August, 18; bush fires, 18; commencement of the dry season, 71; the carrier, 151
African, an ancient, acts as guide, 114
Aidoo, Quarter-Master Sergt. S. Amonoo, awarded the Meritorious Service Medal, 289
Airship, German, 188
Aleppo, 189
Amartey, Corpl. J. W. H., awarded the Meritorious Service Medal, 289
Ankuabe, 227; capture of, 228
Ant-bears, 111; size of holes, 112
Antonio Annes, 284
Arab house, 208, 215
Armistice, terms, 277
Armitage, Capt., Chief Commissioner of the Northern Territories, 277
Armoured Car Battery, the 7th Light, 167, 174
Arnold, Captain, 206
——, Lieut., death, 39
Ashanti, 4
Askari, the German native soldier, 22; reasons for the fidelity, 74, 77; result of the military system, 75-77, 203; reputation, 77; desertion, 166
Austro-Hungarian armies, rout, 277

Avenell, Colour-Sergt., 112
Awudu Arigungu, Sergt., killed, 96
—— Bakano, Sergt.-Major, killed, 105

B COLUMN, march to Naurus, 204
B Company of the Gold Coast Regiment, 4, 20, 29, 35, 37, 50, 54, 61, 78, 79, 82, 93, 95, 101, 121, 131, 138, 153, 156, 167-169, 172, 175, 201, 228, 242, 270, 272
Bagamoyo, 10, 39
Baillie, Lieut., 112, 124, 167, 172; wounded, 174, 178; brought to safety, 177
Baldwin, Lieut., 146
Baluchis, the 129th, 47, 58, 142, 144, 154, 155, 156, 164; at Makangaga, 94; casualties, 145; engagement at Mwiti, 200
Baluchis, the 130th, 40
Banda, or bush-huts, 234
Banda Hill, 49, 51, 53
Bandari, 219
Bangalla, 207; river, 199
Barrett, Lieut., 226; advance on Chirimba Hill, 241; wounded, 246, 248
Baverstock, Colour - Sergt., wounded, 105
Bazaberimi, Pte. Adama, awarded the Military Medal, 288
Beattie, Colour - Sergt., 56; wounded, 82
Beaumont's Post, 86, 87, 89, 90, 94
Beech, Lieut. R. F., 82, 235, 263; awarded the Military Cross, 286
Beka, 131, 132
Belgian troops, advance on Mahenge, 108
Benham, Captain, illness, 131
Berry, Lieut., 40

295

INDEX

Beves, General, in command of the Division, 91; plan of attack, 93; at Narungombe, 107; at Lindi, 133
Biddulph, Capt., 51; wounded, 51; death, 56
Biltcliffe, Lieut., 90; at Port Amelia, 208
Bisshopp, Lieut., 226, 235, 237; at Muapa, 230; advance on Chirimba Hill, 241; patrol-work, 262-264
Bliss Hill, 44
Bogoberi, gun-carrier, 84
Bomas, or entrenched forts, 217
Bompkin, Major von, taken prisoner, 59
Brady, Capt., 112
Bray, Lieut., 80; killed at the battle of Nkessa, 39
——, Lieut., 89; at Lingaula Ridge, 91; wounded, 105
Briscoe, Capt., 112, 191
British columns in East Africa, disadvantages in fighting, 148-152; transport, attack on, 87
Brits, Brig.-General, in command of South African mounted troops, 11
Broomfield, Lieut., 282, 283, 284
Brown, Colonel Gore, killed, 280
Buckby, Capt., 135, 136
Buffalo, charges through No. 1 Column, 199
Bukari, Acting-Sergeant, awarded the D.C.M., 80; death, 80
Bulu, 225
Busanga, Corpl. Bila, 139
——, Pte. Nubela, awarded the Military Medal, 288
——, Corpl. Timballa, wounded, 69; awarded the Military Medal, 288
Bush fighting, 3, 151, 158; fires, 18, 110; huts, 234
Bussell, Lieut., 131
Bustard, Capt., 280, 281; surrender, 283
Butler, Capt. Jack, at the battle of Kikirunga, 26-29; killed, 29, 32; characteristics, 29
Bweho Chini, engagement at, 180

Calipo, 282
Campbell, Corpl. J., 112, 131; awarded the D.C.M. and Bar, 59, 287; bravery, 103
Capetown, 274
Cavalry, the 25th, destruction of the camp, 183; at Lulindi, 195
Chaimite, the, 221
Chalana, 284
Chaqual, canvas bag of water, 117
Chasi, 16
Chaundler, Lieut., 235
Chemera, 44, 46, 71
Chigugu, 182, 186, 208
Chikukwe, 180
Chilonga, 269
Chinga, 281
Chingwea, 166, 185
"Chini," meaning of the word, 47
Chirimba Hill, 239; advance on, 240-244; action at, 244-247
Chisona, 266, 268
Chiure, 222
Chiwata, 191, 195
Chokosi, Pte. Seidu, awarded the D.C.M., 288
Chuplies, meaning of the word, 9
Clarke, Lieut., 224, 234, 237
Clifford, Sir Hugh, Governor of the Gold Coast Colony, 4; banquet to the officers, 4
Column, No. 1: 98, 101, 117, 126, 132, 134, 142, 143, 153, 157, 159, 163, 164, 166; at Ukuli, 94; march to Ruponda, 184; at Ndanda, 187; occupy Mwiti, 187; Luchemi, 194; at Luatalla, 198; charged by a bull buffalo, 199; at Bangalla, 201; broken up, 204
——, No. 2: 94, 96-98, 102, 103, 104, 118, 127, 166, 195
——, No. 3: 94, 99, 102, 195
Cumming, Lieut. L. B., 288; awarded the Military Cross, 286
Cuneen, Colour-Sergt., 167, 172; killed, 173, 178
Cunliffe, General, 108

D Company, 56
"D. M. B.," the Indian Mountain Battery, 94, 96, 233, 242, 247, 259, 272

INDEX

Dadoma, 11, 12, 109
Dagarti, Sergt. Braima, awarded the Military Medal, 288
——, Corpl. Issaka, awarded the D.C.M., 288
Dakawa, 16
D'Amico, Capt., 55
Dar-es-Salaam, 10, 12, 20, 40, 41
Dar-es-Salaam-Lake Tanganyika Railway, 72, 109
Dawes, Capt. H. B., 144, 224, 225; wounded, 194; captures Pumone, 227; at Ankuabe, 228; awarded the Military Cross, 286
Depôt Company, 78; mobilized, 87; at Port Amelia, 227
Derajat, 94
Dhow, or sailing-boats, 220
Dikale, Corpl. Granda, awarded the D.C.M., 288
Dobell, Major-General, in command of the British and French troops, 1; at Liome, 1
Dodo, Imoru, awarded the Military Medal, 288
Dogali, M. G. C., awarded the Military Medal, 288
Donho, 34
Downer, Lieut., 56, 112; at Gold Coast Hill, 58
Drummond, Lieut., 279, 280, 285
Duck, Capt., 214, 216, 255
Duncan, Lieut., killed, 51
Durban, 5, 274

East African Brigades: the 1st, 10; the 2nd, 10, 35; the 3rd, 60; Mounted Rifles, 21; capture Germans, 22
Edwards, Brig.-General W. F. S., Inspector-General of Communications, 8; inspects the Gold Coast Regiment, 8, 12; at Port Amelia, 233; Rock Camp, 238; Kalima, 256; plans to surround Kohl, 269; at Nampula, 281; farewell message, 292
Eglon, Lieut., 93; at Lingaula Ridge, 95; killed, 101, 105
Enslin, General, 17
Etun, Corpl. Ntonge, 229; awarded the Military Medal, 289

Fitzgerald, Colonel, 282
Flatman, Capt., killed, 240, 248
Foley, Capt. J. G., 56, 82, 224, 243, 248; at the battle of Rumbo, 83–86; awarded the Military Cross and Bar, 89, 286, 287; at the battle of Mitoneno, 145
Foster, Lieut., exploit at Ruangwa Chini, 155; act of heroism, 176; awarded the Military Cross, 177; the D.C.M. and Bar, 287
Fra Fra, Temp. Corpl. Seti, awarded the D.C.M. and Bar 287, 288
Fraser, G. M., awarded the Meritorious Service Medal, 289
Fulani, Corpl. Amandu, killed, 69
——, Corpl. Musa, awarded the D.C.M., 287
——, Corpl. Yero, awarded the Military Medal, 288
Fulanis, 56

G Company of the Gold Coast Regiment, 4, 31, 35, 36, 38; broken up, 44, 46
Gara, 274
German East Africa, mission stations, 22
Germans, surrender at Kamina, 1; retreat, 24, 121, 124, 139, 146; casualties, 32, 81; evacuate Nkessa, 39; bombard Kibata, 48; attack on Gold Coast Hill, 53; accuracy of firing, 56; evacuate it, 58; treachery, 63; attack on Njimbwe, 67; headquarters at Massassi, 72, 162, 194; expelled from the Rufiji, 72, 74; reasons for the fidelity of the native soldiers, 74, 77; result of the military system, 75–77, 203; ambush against, 79–81; flag of truce, 81, 86; fire on a British transport, 87; attack on Narungombe, 98–104; retire to Mihambia, 109, 120, 124; at Ndessa, 116; defeated at Bweho Chini, 130; rear-guard actions, 131, 271; engagements at Nahungen, 134–139; Mitoneno, 144–146; advantages of their position, 148–152; at Ruangwa

Chini, 156; stores captured, 159, 164; defeated at Ruponda, 164; capture of their correspondence, 165; fear of their Commander-in-Chief, 165, 166; attacked at Lukuledi, 172-178; at Nangus, 185; taken prisoners, 195; surrender, 196, 202; evacuate Medo, 249; campaign in Mozambique, 280-285
Germany, declaration of war, 1; armistice terms, 278
Gifford, Colonel, in command of Pamforce column, 233
Gold Coast Colony, 4; recruiting campaign, 277
Gold Coast Hill, 49; attack on, 53-55; evacuated, 58
Gold Coast Mounted Infantry, campaign in Mozambique, 279-285; at Accra, 285
Gold Coast Regiment, mobilized, 1; invasion of Togoland, 1; the Kameruns, 2; courage and endurance, 2, 105; at Sekondi, 4, 275; appearance, 4, 9; on board the *Æneas*, 5; inspection at Durban, 5; at Kilindini, 6; journey to Ngombezi, 6-8; service kit, 8; characteristics, 9, 15; join up with the Royal Fusiliers, 11; march to Msiha, 12-15; at Dakawa, 16; march to the Ngere-Ngere, 17-20; transport burnt, 19; at Metomba, 22-24; the battle of Kikirunga, 25-32; casualties, 32, 39, 55, 67, 104, 132, 139, 146, 178, 181, 194, 248, 276; at Kiringezi, 34; occupy Nkessa, 39; march to Dar-es-Salaam, 40; on board the *Ingoma*, 41; at Kilwa Kisiwana, 44; march to Chemera, 44-46; reduction in the *personnel*, 46; march to Mtumbei Chini, 47; attack on Gold Coast Hill, 50-55; reinforcements, 56, 112; total strength, 57, 88, 89, 92, 113, 205, 276, 290; at Ngarambi Chini, 61; Njimbwe, 65, 69; shortage of food, 68, 261; discipline, 68, 129; march to Mitole, 70, 78; at Mnasi, 79;

Migeri-geri, 82; Rumbo, 86, 89; Ngomania, 95; Makangaga, 95; join up with No. 2 Column, 95; retransferred to No. 1 Column, 98; attack on Narungombe, 101-104; at Mikikole, 110; Liwinda Ravine, 117; sufferings from thirst, 125-129; at Mbombomya, 127; Ndessa Juu 129; Kitandi, 130; march on Nahungen, 131; attack on, 134-139; meeting with the Nigerian Brigade, 140; attack on Mitoneno, 144-146; bathing and washing, 147; in reserve, 153; advance on Ruponda, 163, 185; march to Lukuledi, 167, 168; at Lulindi, 198; Bangalla River, 199, 207; selected for service in Portuguese East Africa, 209; at Mingoya, 214; transferred from H.M. *Salamis* to H.M.S. *Lunkwa*, 215; at Port Amelia, 222, 274, 279; Meza, 230, 234; at the battle of Chirimba Hill, 244-247; advance on Mwalia, 253; at Milinch Hills, 261; respite from fighting, 273; reception at Kumasi, 276; list of honours and decorations awarded to, 286-289; farewell message from Brig.-Gen. Edwards, 292.
Gold Coast Service Brigade, 277; disbanded, 278
Goodwin, Lieut.-Colonel H., 31, 35, 37, 58, 207; wounded, 58; in command of the Gold Coast Regiment, 60; appointed Acting Lieut.-Colonel, 89; awarded the *Croix de Guerre*, 89, 287; the D.S.O., 90, 286; invalided to the base, 91; in command of Companies, 141; advance on Mihomo, 141; at the battle of Mitoneno, 144, 146; attack on Lukuledi, 174; voyage to Port Amelia, 215, 279; on board H.M. *Hongbee*, 216; advance on Chirimba Hill, 244
Grant, Colonel, 94
Greene, Capt., 82
Greene, Capt., killed at the battle of Nkessa, 39

INDEX

Green's Post, 61
Gregg's Post, 110, 113, 119
Griffiths, Colonel, 266; in command of "Norforce," 268; captures Mwariba, 270
Grumah, Pte. Allassan, awarded the Military Medal, 288
Grumah, Sergt. Palpuku, awarded the D.C.M., 57; the Military Medal, 288
Grunshi, Sergt. Alhaji, awarded the D.C.M., 288
Grunshi, Corpl. Chililah, awarded the D.C.M., 287
Gush, Capt., 167; wounded, 177, 178

HANDENI, base at, 11, 15
"Hanforce," 118, 153
Hannyngton, Brig.-General, in command of the 2nd East African Brigade, 10; telegram of congratulation, 33; military operations at Kilwa, 43; plan of attack, 49, 113, 153; awards decorations, 57; resumes command, 107
Harman, Capt. H. A., 47, 50; wounded, 53; awarded the D.S.O., 90, 286; at Minoya, 214, 215; Mahiba, 225; Namaaka, 235; advance on Chirimba Hill, 244, 245
Harman's Kopje, 50, 51, 55
Harper, C. H., letter from, 294
Harris, Capt., 260; at Port Amelia, 208; Mkufi, 222; advance on Chirimba Hill, 240
Hart, Colour-Sergt., at Mkufi, 225
Hartland, Capt., 112
Hassan Bazaberimi, Company Sergeant-Major, killed, 87
Hausa, S. B. Bawa, awarded the Military Medal, 289
Hellis, Capt., 56
Hill, Major, 104
Hongbee, H.M., 216
Hornby, Major, 112, 274
Hoskyns, Major-General, in command of the First Division, 10
Hymettus, H.M., 274

I COMPANY of the Gold Coast Regiment, 4, 31, 35, 36, 38, 40, 46, 89, 90, 135, 144, 164, 177, 222, 225, 228, 236, 242-247, 253, 269
Ibadan, Corpl. Akanno, awarded the D.C.M., 287
Ibadan, G. C. Lawani, awarded the Military Medal, 288
Ibadan, Corpl. Sulley, awarded the Military Medal, 59, 289
Igumi, 186
Indian Cavalry, the 25th, 153
Indian Mountain Battery, or the "D.M.B.," 94, 96, 233, 242, 247, 259, 272
Indian Ocean, 219, 279
Ingoma, the transport, 41
Isaacs, Lieut., taken prisoner, 39; released, 196
Issaka, Kipalsi, Corpl., bravery, 125

JAUNDIS, 56
Jerimita, 262
John, Hdm. G. C. Kwesi, awarded the Military Medal, 288
Jumbe Nambude, 200
Jumbe Nwinama, mission station, 187
"Juu," meaning of the word, 47

KALIMA, 256
Kameruns, 1; fighting in, 2
Kamina, wireless installation at, 1
Kano, S. B. Musa, awarded the Military Medal, 289
Karaki, Dr., Musa, awarded the D.C.M., 288
"Kartucol," 233; advance on Chirimba Hill, 242, 244; Mwalia, 255; Koronje, 258-260; pursuit of the Germans, 280
Kassanga, 34
Kay, Lieut., 259
Kelton, Capt., 50, 55
Kent, Sergt., killed, 271
Kerr, Hauptmann, 116
Kibata, mission station, 43, 47, 57; shelled by the Germans, 48
Kibega river, 65
Kidugato, 41
Kigome, 11
Kihendye, 97

Kihindi Hill, 142, 143
Kihindo Juu, 127
Kihumburu, 98, 99, 100
Kikirunga Hill, 25, 26 ; battle of, 28-32
Kilageli, 96
Kilimane, 280
Kilima-njaro, 7
Kilindini, 6, 11, 209
Kilney, Lieut., 53
Kilossa, 11, 12, 109
Kilwa Kisiwani, 42, 44, 78, 87
Kilwa Kivinje, 73, 78, 79
Kimamba, 17
Kingani River, 10
King's African Rifles, 48, 50, 58, 65, 94, 97, 142, 143, 157, 166, 168, 177 ; at the battle of Kikirunga, 30; advance, 33; at the battle of Nkessa, 37; Rumbo, 87; Narungombe, 101-104; Mihambia, 117, 119; Nahungen, 134; occupy Lukuledi, 180 ; advance on Massassi, 182 ; at Ndanda, 186 ; Mahiba, 227 ; dispatched to Mozambique, 252; advance on Mwalia, 254 ; Koronje, 258; Jerimita, 262; Nairobi, 273
Kinley, Lieut. G. B., 95 ; encounter with Germans, 79-81 ; awarded the D.S.O., 82 ; the Military Cross, 89, 286
Kiperele Chini, 158
Kipondira, 98
Kiringezi, 84
Kirongo, 78, 79, 96
Kirongo-Ware, 96
Kissalu, 84 ; mines on the road, 40
Kisserawe, 41
Kitambi, 47, 55, 71, 78, 235
Kitandi, 128, 130
Kitiia, 109, 113, 116, 119
Kiwambi, 63
Kiyombo, 61, 65
Koenigsberg, 48
Kohl, Major, at Chirimba Hill, 239; plans to surround, 269; loss of his baggage, 270 ; retreat to Mozambique, 272
Koloi, 226
Kondoa-Irangi, 11
Korewa, 271, 272

Korogwe, 11, 44
Koronje, 252, 256 ; advance on, 258 ; evacuated, 259
Kotokoli, Corpl. Yessufu, awarded the D.C.M., 287
Kukawa, Sergt. Bukara, Bar to D.C.M., 288
Kuma, Yaw, awarded the D.C.M., 287
Kumasi, 2, 4, 276
Kusase, Nuaga, awarded the D.C.M., 288
Kwevi Lombo, 16

Lagos, John, awarded the D.C.M., 287
Lamont, Lieut., 112, 243, 248
Leal, Major, 252
Legislative Council, resolution, 294
Leslie-Smith, Capt. J., wounded, 105; at Namarika, 235; patrol work, 262-264; awarded the Military Cross, 286
Lettow-Vorbeck, von, Commander-in-Chief, 59; at Massassi, 72, 133, 148, 162; attack on a British transport, 87; defeat at Bweho Chini, 130; pluck and resource, 151, 166, 198; forces, 152; at Ruwanga, 163; refuses to surrender, 166; actions, 181; concerted movements, 182; at Newala, 194; expelled from German East Africa, 196, 198; captures ammunition at Ngomano, 207; march on Port Amelia, 208 ; character of his military operations, 212, 251; at Nanguari, 218 ; raiding parties, 213, 221; at Nanungu, 265 ; Wanakoti, 266 ; retreat to Mozambique, 272; surrender, 285
Ligonha River, 282
Lihonja, 159
Likawage, 79
Lindi, 73, 108, 118, 133, 148, 207
"Linforce" Column, 148, 161, 251 ; joined by the Nigerian Brigade, 162; advance to Mtama, 167 ; actions, 181, 185
Lingaula Ridge, 91, 93, 95
Liome, 285
Lions, at Msalu, 265

INDEX 301

Liwale, 73, 78, 118
Liwinda Ravine, 109, 110, 111; water depôt at, 113, 117
Lome, 1, 76
Lorenço Marquez, 216
Loyal North Lancashire Regiment, 10, 35, 87
Luatalla, 198
Luchemi, 190, 194
Lugomya River, 61
Lujendi River, 213
Lukigura River, 10
Lukuledi, mission station at, 167, 169–171; attack on, 168–178; destruction of the church, 183
—— River, 169, 186
Lulete, 283
Lulindi, 195, 198
Lumbo, 281
Lunkwa, H.M.S., 215
Lurio, 213, 222, 265; River, 214, 272, 285
Lusinje, 256, 261
Lustalla, 201

MACPHERSON, Capt., 86, 87; at the battle of Nkessa, 36; Rumbo, 90
Mafisa, 17, 41
Magaruna River, 222
Magaura River, 86, 91
Magdalene, H.M.T., 274
Magogoni, 41
Maguida River, 228
Mahazi, 15
Mahenge, 109
Mahiba, 225
Mahiwa, 208; action at, 181, 198
Mahu, 267
Makangaga, 79, 94, 95
Makindu River, 16
Makochera, 207
Makonde Plateau, 188, 190
Makotschera, 73
Makuku, 256, 262
Mama Juma, Sergt.-Major, 173
Mambir River, 190
Mamprusi, Sergt. Yessufu, 173; wounded, 175; awarded the D.C.M. and the Military Medal, 288
Manambiri, 235
Manasara Kanjaga, Sergt.-Major, awarded the D.C.M., 57

Mangano, 159
Manyambas, 190, 195
Marenjende, 127
Marrupula, 281
Maruchiras, 190
Massambassi, 20
Massassi, mission station at, 72, 133, 148, 182, 208; headquarters of the Germans, 72, 162, 194
Matandu River, 43
Matombo Mission Station, 22, 24, 25
Mawerenye, 127
Maxwell, Lieut., 112
May, Colour-Sergt., killed at the battle of Nkessa, 39
Mbalama, 256
Mbalawala hills, 201
Mbemba, 158
Mbemkuru River, 118, 131, 132, 133, 135, 141, 144, 147, 153, 157, 159, 160; valley of, 132
Mbombomya, 110; water-holes at, 115, 117, 127
Mborio, or fortified posts, 217
McElligott, Capt., 112, 123, 124, 135, 138, 144; patrol work, 191–193, 201
McEvoy, Lieut., wounded, 257
Mecklenburg, Duke Adolf Fredrich of, Governor of Togoland, 76
Medlock, Sergt.-Major F. C., awarded the D.C.M., 90, 287
Medo, 223, 235, 238, 250; engagement at, 236; evacuated, 249
Member, Sergt., awarded the Military Medal, 288
Methven, Capt. E. B., 112; at Liwinda Ravine, 113; scouting expedition, 114; advance on Mihambia, 122, 123; attack on, Nahungu, 136; gallant deed, 139; at the battle of Mitoneno, 145; attack on Ruangwa Chini, 156; march to Lukuledi, 167; attack on, 171–173; wounded, 173, 178; awarded a bar to the Military Cross, 179, 287
Metil, 281, 287
Meza, 224, 230
Mgeta River, 39, 40
Miesi River, 199, 201

INDEX

Migeri-geri, 82
Mihambia, 109, 115, 119; attack on, 117, 120; evacuated, 124
Mihomo, 141
Mikesse, 78
Mikikama, 99
Mikikole, 110, 113, 117
Milinch Hills, 260
Mingoya, 208, 214
Minokwe, 97
Mission stations in German East Africa, 22
Mitole, 45, 46, 71, 78
Mitoneno, 142; advance on, 143; engagement at, 144-146
Miwale Hill, 190; River, 190
Mkufi, 222
Mkundi, 194, 195; River, 17
Mnapo, 281, 283
Mnasi, 78, 79, 89
Mnero, mission station at, 159
Mnindi, 95
Mnitshi, 110, 114, 115, 117, 127
Mombassa, 6
Montepuez River, 238, 258
Moon, eclipse, 93
Morogoro Mission Station, 11, 12, 24
Moschi, 10
Moshi, Pte. Akuluga, awarded the Military Medal, 288
——, Sergt.-Major Bukare, 85; awarded the D.C.M., 57; the Military Medal, 288
——, Corpl. Kuka, awarded the Military Medal, 288
——, Kwenjeh, awarded the Military Medal, 288
——, Sergt. Mamadu, 84; awarded the D.C.M., 288
——, Sergt. Moriambah, awarded the D.C.M., 287
——, Mumuni, awarded the D.C.M., 287
——, Corpl. Nuaga, awarded the Military Medal, 288
——, Bugler Nufu, awarded the D.C.M., 288
——, Corpl. Sandogo, awarded the D.C.M., 288
——, Pte. Sebidu, awarded the Military Medal, 288
Mountain Battery, the 24th, 58

Mountain Battery, the 27th, 94, 117, 119, 134, 142, 157, 177
Mozambique, 216, 272; campaign in, 280
Mpara, 44, 78
Mpepo, 109
Mpingo, 110, 114, 121, 122, 126
Mpoto, 195
Msalu Boma, 262, 264; River, 268; bridge across, 269
Msiha, 12
Mtama, 167, 181, 208
Mtandula, 97
Mtua, 208
Mtuge, 219, 221, 223, 225
Mtumbei Chini, 47, 71
—— Juu, Mission Station, 43, 47, 48, 55
Muapa, 229
Mudge, Sergt., killed, 246, 248
Mule, the transport, character, 151
Muligudge, 282
Murray, Capt., in command of H.M.S. *Lunkwa*, 215
Murray, Lieut., 86
Murrupula, 282
Musa Fra-Fra, Corpl., instinct for discovering water, 70
Mussuril Bay, 281
Mwalia, 251; advance on, 253-256
Mwambia Ridge, 270
Mwariba, 270
Mwengei, 57, 58
Mwiti Mission Station, 187, 190, 200; River, 195

Nahungu, 181; attack on, 184-189, 206
Naiku River, 182
Nairobi, 7, 273
Nairombo, 195
Nakalala, 196
Namaaka, 235; fight at, 236-238
Namarala, 227, 228
Namaranje, 46
Namarika, 234
Namatwe, 61, 70
Nambingo, 201
Nambunjo Hill, 121, 126; perimeter camp at, 122
Namburage, 61
Namehi, 153
Nampula, 281

INDEX

Namirrue, 280, 281, 282, 284
Nanguari, 213
Nangus, 185
Nanungu, 256, 265, 269
Nanunya, 223, 226, 228
Napue, 282
Narungombe, 98, 107, 109; attack on, 99-104
Nash, Lieut., 201
Natovi, 284
Naurus, 205
Naylor, Colour-Sergt., 136
Ndanda, mission station, 186, 207
Ndessa, 110, 116; attack on, 118
Ndessa Juu, 129; water-holes at, 130
Ndomondo, 186
Nelson, Colour-Sergt., 61, 63; shot, 64; discovery of his body, 67; burial, 68
Nerungombe, engagement at, 94
Newala, 73, 188, 194; Germans surrender, 196; abandoned, 211
Ngarambi Chini, 60, 61, 70
Ngaura River, 83, 86
Ngere-Ngere, the, 17, 20
Ngomania, 95
Ngomano, 197, 207, 285
Ngombezi, 8, 12
Nhamaccura, 280, 284
Nicholl, Rev. Captain, 68
Nigerian Brigade, 74, 127; at Rufiji, 108; advance on Ruale, 118; engagement at Bweho Chini, 130; meeting with the Gold Coast Regiment, 140; march to join up with "Linforce," 161; actions, 181; occupy Chiwata, 191; capture a German hospital, 195
Nigeri-geri, 78
Nivanga, 78
Njengao, action at, 181, 198
Njijo, 78
Njimbwe, 61, 63, 65, 66, 69, 70, 74
Nkessa, battle of, 85-89, 196
Nkufi, 213
"Norforce," 268
Norris, Lieut., at Pumone, 228
Northey, General, 252; advance on Mpepo, 109
Nuaga Kusasi, battery trumpeter, 88

Numarroe, 284
Nyassa Company territory, 216

O'BRIEN, Capt. A. J. R., 47; awarded the Military Cross and Bar, 56, 286, 287; wounded, 105
O'Brien, Capt. J. M., 249
O'Grady, General, 20, 50, 57, 181
One-Stick Hill, 58
Orr, Colonel, 202; in command of the 3rd East African Brigade, 91, 93; in command of No. I Column, 94; attack on Ruangwa Chini, 157

PAKHALS, or long tins, 114, 126
Palestine, 277
"Pamforce," 212, 221; at Meza, 280; division of, 233; advance to Koronje, 252
Parker, Capt. G. H., 123, 222; trains the Mounted Infantry, 279; at Mussuril Bay, 281; awarded the Military Cross, 286
Path, cutting a, 97
Pathans, the 40th, 54, 55, 56, 59, 65, 74, 82, 94, 102; casualties, 67; at the battle of Rumbo, 83-86
Payne, Sergt., 181
Pequerra, 282, 283
Percy, Lieut., 56; wounded, 132, 271
Phillips, Colonel, 252
Piggott, Capt. T. B. C., wounded, 53; awarded the Italian Silver Medal, 89, 287; the Military Cross, 90, 286
Pike, Lieut., at Port Amelia, 208
Pioneer Company of the Gold Coast Regiment, 4, 35, 36, 38, 51, 65, 70, 78, 94, 101, 119, 126, 135, 186, 164, 174, 190; at the battle of Kikirunga, 26-32; Migeri-geri, 89; ambush against, 90; at the battle of Mitoneno, 146; Wangoni, 206; Port Amelia, 223
Poer, Capt. H. C. C. de la, Special Service Officer to the Gold Coast Regiment, 8
Pomba Bay, 214, 217
Poole, Lieut., 282

Pori Hill, 135, 136, 139
Port Amelia, 207, 208, 217, 279; defence of, 214
Portal, Sir Gerald, on the East African carrier, 151
Portuguese East Africa, 72; ammunition at Ngomano captured, 207; division of, 216
Potter, Lieut.-Col., in command of the training depôts, 209
Poyntz, Capt. R. H., 31; at the battle of Nkessa, 36-38; advance on Gold Coast Hill, 51; wounded, 53; awarded the Military Cross, 59, 286
Pretorius, Major, 17; acts as guide to the Nigerian Brigade, 161
Pumone, 224, 225, 227
Punjabis, the 29th, 37
Punjabis, the 33rd, 90, 94, 102
Pye, Capt., 51; killed, 53

RADFORD, Pte. S. G., awarded the D.C.M. and Cross of St. George, 287
Read, Major H., 44, 87; voyage to Accra, 274; awarded the O.B.E., 287
Reid, Lieut., 238
Ridgeway, Colonel, in command of No. 2 Column, 96
Rifles, the 55th, occupy Newala, 196
Road-mine, explosion, 247
Robertson, Lieut., 224
Rock Camp, 238; convoy attacked, 255
Roofs, corrugated iron, result, 218
Rose, Lieut.-Col. R. A. De B., in command of the Gold Coast Expeditionary Force, 4, 274; telegram of congratulation, 33; knocked over by a shell, 53; reconnaissance, 58; in temporary command of the 3rd East African Brigade, 60; Brevet Lieut.-Colonel, 71; attack of dysentery, 91; rejoins the Regiment, 112; attack on Mihambia, 117; occupies Nambunjo Hill, 121; in command of B Column, 204, 207; on board H.M. *Salamis*, 215;
at Port Amelia, 221; at Ankuabe, 228; in command of "Pamforce" division, 233; escape from an explosion, 247; at Accra, 275; in command of the Second West African Brigade, 277; awarded the Bar to D.S.O., 286; Legion d'Honneur Croix d'Officier, 287; letter from C. H. Harper, 294
"Rosecol," 233; advance on Chirimba Hill, 240, 242; Mwalia, 253-256; at Kalima, 256; advance on Milinch Hills, 260; at Msalu, 265, 266, 269; advance on Korewa, 271
Rovuma River, 72, 73, 130, 187, 188, 197, 199, 207, 265, 285
Royal Fusiliers, join up with the Gold Coast Regiment, 11
Ruale, 118
Ruangwa Chini, 154; attack on, 156-158
Rufiji River, 12, 24, 43, 61, 71, 72, 108, 109, 197
Rumbo, engagement at, 82-86
Rungo, 97
Ruponda, 160, 163, 164; 185; food depôts at, 181
Ruwanga, 163, 181
Ruwu, the, 17, 39, 40

SALAMIS, H.M., stranded, 215
Sanananga, 224
Sandani, 10
Sassaware, 73
Saunders, Lieut., 279, 282; wounded, 283
Saunderson, Lieut. R. de Bedick, killed, 175, 178; career, 175
Schnee, Herr, Governor of German East Africa, 195, 196
Schutzen Company, the 8th, 163
Scott, Lieut., wounded, 96
Sekondi, Port of, 4, 275
Shaw, Colonel G., 50, 54; at the battle of Kikirunga, 29, 30; awarded the Military Cross and Bar, 56, 106, 286; at Rumbo, 85; appointed Acting Major and Second in Command of the Gold Coast Regiment, 91; in com-

INDEX

mand of No. 2 Column, 96; attack on Narumgombe, 101
Shaw, Lieut., 181
Shaw, Major, advance on Mihambia, 119; at Kitiia, 119; march on Nahungu, 131; attack on, 137; march to Chingwea, 167; attack on Lukuledi, 177; at Port Amelia, 208, 214, 219; advance on Chirimba Hill, 241, 242, 244; occupies Korewa, 272
Shepperd, Brig.-General, in command of the 1st East African Brigade, 10; Chief of Staff, 208
Shields, Lieut. George Hilliard, 61; attack on Gold Coast Hill, 53; treachery of the Germans, 63; killed, 64; head-master of the Government Boy's School at Accra, 64; discovery of his body, 67; burial, 68
Sierra Leone Carrier Corps, 91, 236
Smith, Lieut. S. B., 112, 167, 172, 174; attempt to surprise the signal-station at Mpingo, 121; failure, 122; surrounded, 123; Staff-Officer, 204; at Port Amelia, 208
Smuts, General, Commander-in-Chief, Headquarters at Lukigura, 10; plan of attack, 11; at Dakawa, 16
Soeiro, Signor Abilio de Lobao, Governor of the Nyassa Company, 221
Songea, 73, 109
South African Infantry, the 7th, 94, 97, 102; the 8th, 94, 102
Sovar River, 225, 226
Stokes Battery, 104, 117, 185, 243, 248, 254

Tabora, gold coin, 204
Tafel, Major von, 109, 194, 198; surrender, 202
Tanga, fall of, 10
Tanga-Moschi Railway, 7, 10, 11, 44, 72
Tanganyika, Lake, 11, 78
Taylor, Colonel, in command of No. 3 Column, 94

Taylor, Lieut., 53; wounded, 54
Thornett, Colour-Sergt. C. A., killed, 246, 248; awarded the D.C.M., 287
Thornton, Colour-Sergt. E., at Port Amelia, 208; awarded the D.C.M., 287
Thirst, sufferings from, 13, 45, 107, 125-129
Togoland, invasion of, 1
Transport of the army, need for protection, 149
Tulo, 84, 86, 40
Turiani, 16
Turkey, surrender of, 277
Tyndall, Colonel, 83, 85

Ujiji, 11
Ukuli, 91, 94
Ulanga, 109
Uluguru Mountains, 23, 24, 25, 26, 84, 48, 196
Unguara, 65
Utete, 61, 63, 66

Venter, Major-General Van der, in command of the Second Division, 11; Commander-in-Chief, 207, 208
Viney, Lieut., 282; killed, 283
Voi, 7

Wami River, 10
Wanakoti, 266, 272, 280
Wangoni, 206
Watercourses, tropical, eccentricities, 47
Water depôt, attempt to establish at Liwinda Ravine, 114; shortage of, 13, 45, 107, 123, 125-129
Watt, Capt., 228
Watts, Capt., at Port Amelia, 208
Webber, Capt., advance on Medo, 236; Chirimba Hill, 241, 242
Wet, General de, 212
Wheeler, Capt., 31, 37, 50; wounded, 53; at Mkufi, 222; Mtuge, 225; advance on Chirimba Hill, 244

Wiedhafen, 73
Willoughby, Lieut., 112
Wilson, Lieut., 263; at Namarala, 228
Withers, Lieut., 260, 263; at Port Amelia, 208
Wongara, Sergt. Ali, awarded the Military Medal, 289
Wongara, Musa, awarded the D.C.M., 288
Woods, Lieut., reconnaissances, 114, 115; patrol on the Mbombomya road, 121; attack on, 123; at the battle of Mitoneno, 145; advance on Lukuledi, 167, 171; killed, 173, 178
Wray, Captain, 56, 124; attack on, 125; wounded, 125, 132

ZANZIBAR, island of, 39
Zeppelin, recalled, 189

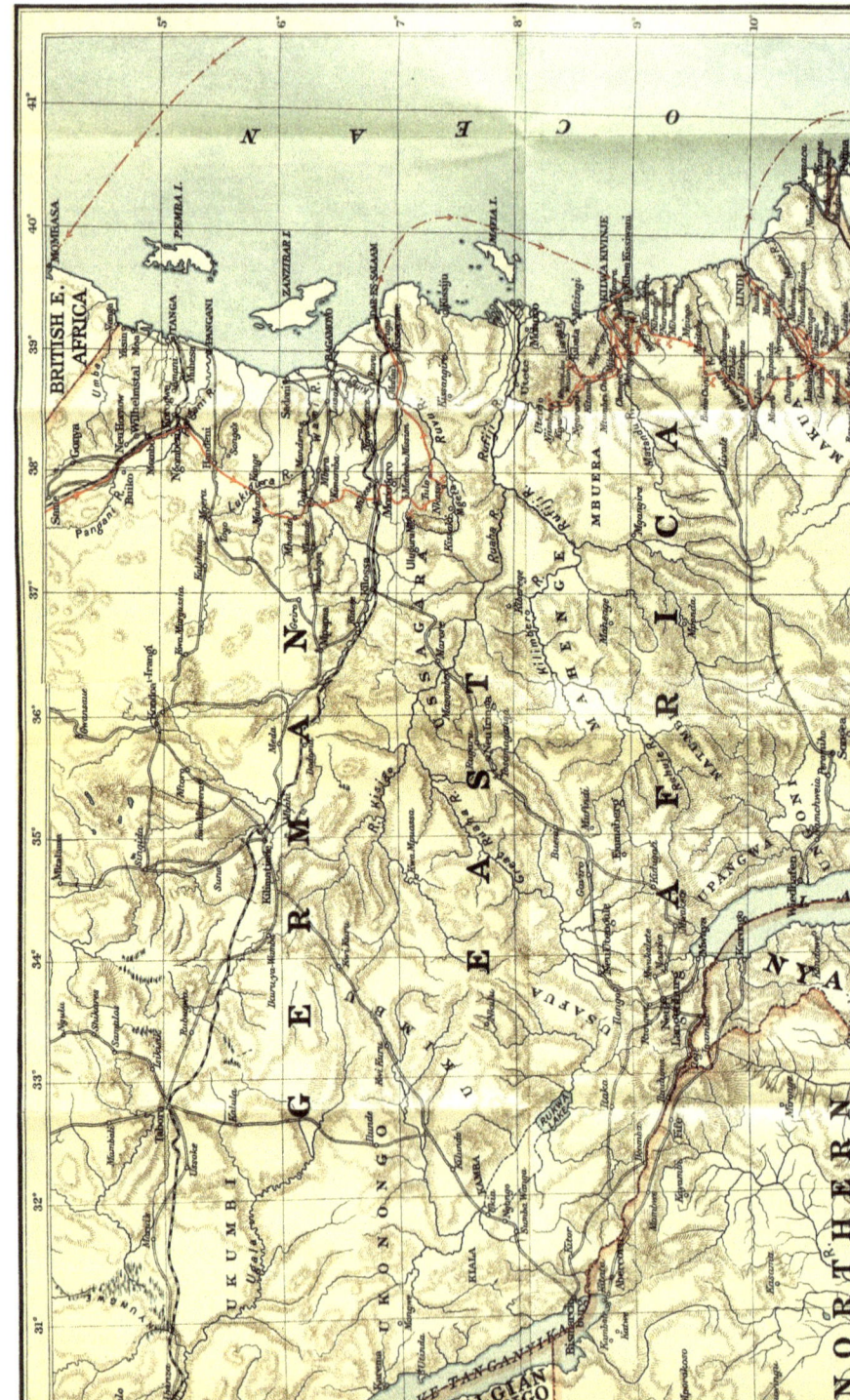

www.ingramcontent.com/pod-product-compliance
Lightning Source LLC
Chambersburg PA
CBHW052045220426
43663CB00012B/2443